The Toughest Job

*The Crossroads of
One Man's Peace Corps*

SCOTT HENRICKSON

Copyright © 2016 Scott Henrickson

All rights reserved.

ISBN-10: 1518799361
ISBN-13: 978-1518799365

In memory of my mom Ann
(October 26, 1947–July 4, 2014)

Everything can be taken from a man but one thing: the last of the human freedoms—to choose one's attitude in any given set of circumstances, to choose one's own way.
–Viktor E. Frankl

CONTENTS

1	Diversion	1
2	Privilege	3
3	Immersion	9
4	Training	27
5	Adjustment	45
6	History	65
7	Inauguration	69
8	Faith	89
9	Sanctuary	111
10	Fraternity	131
11	Vocation	147
12	Vacation	161
13	Transition	189
14	Doubt	203
15	Return	215
16	Monument	229
17	Departure	251
18	Mission	255

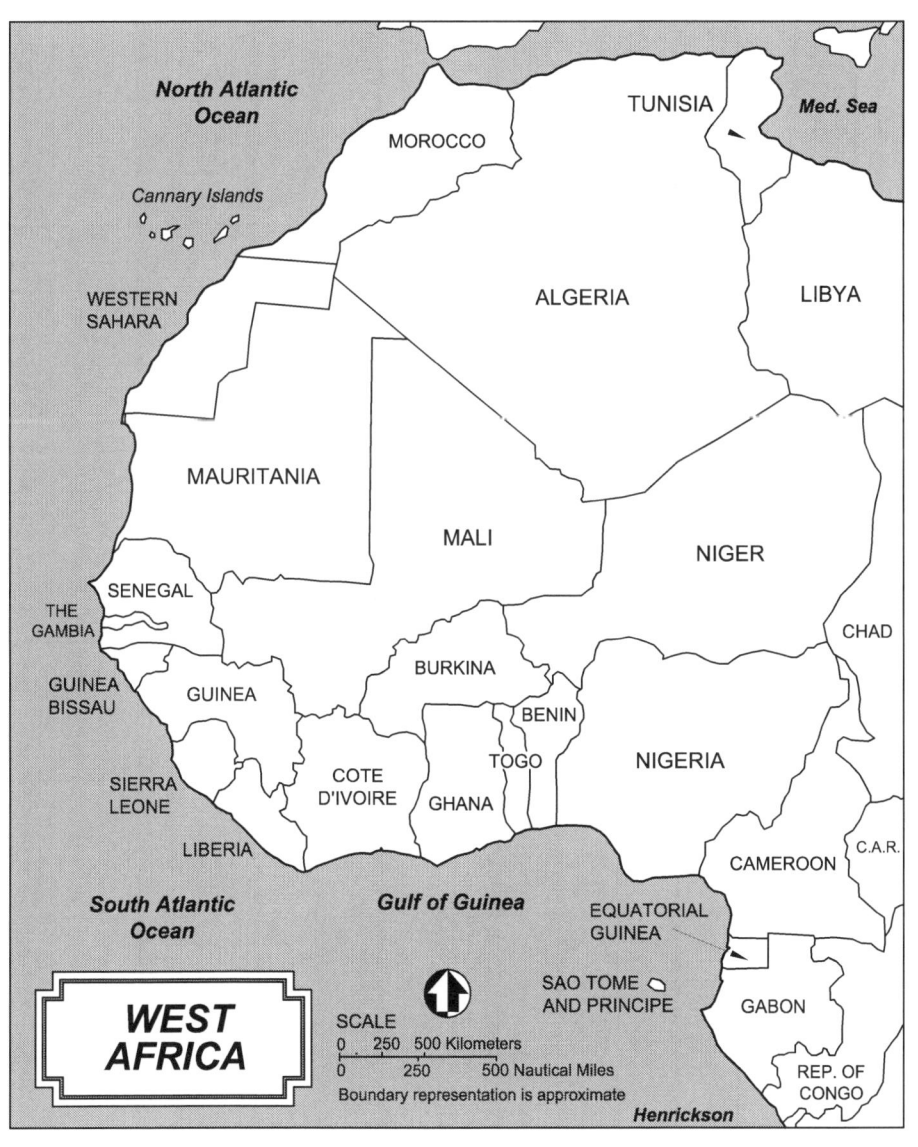

CHAPTER ONE

DIVERSION

Air Afrique flight attendants, fitted with green and white aprons and cheaply made paper hats, moved their arms in unison to a voice amplified in French. This was not the French I had heard over the last twelve weeks. This was European French, a frenchy-French, with an emphasis on accent and style. I could barely understand. So what language did I learn? Did I attend the wrong training? Was I on the wrong plane? Did it matter?

As heat waves shimmered off the pavement, we barreled down the runway and into the air, bound for the Ivory Coast. Once clear of Dakar's city limits, Senegal appeared barren and desolate. Small patches of green against a sea of gold were the only indications of life below in an unforgiving desert.

Our flight seemed to take longer than was advertised, so I routed through the seat back pocket, reading the airline magazine, the emergency briefing card, even the vomit bag of all things, trying to pick up new French words or expressions. In the restroom I lingered longer than was necessary until all instructions, labels, and placards were read and understood. After being immersed in the language for so long, it was more of an impulse than anything else.

The pilot made an announcement to prepare for landing, not in the Ivory Coast but in Lagos, Nigeria, one thousand kilometers further east and four countries beyond our destination. I did not expect this layover in Lagos, nor did I welcome it. Large metal placards affixed to prominent places in the New York and Dakar airports warned U.S. citizens against traveling to Lagos. In training we heard that Americans were not safe in urban Nigeria, murdered for their money and dumped on the outskirts of town by thieves masquerading as taxi drivers. Whether this was true or not, none of us cared to find out.

We landed on a poorly paved airstrip surrounded by lush tropical vegetation. From my vantage point, there were no terminal buildings or parking areas, no vehicles or pedestrians. All I could see were the rusted carcasses of old airplanes in the tall green grass at the jungle edge. We waited on the tarmac for what seemed like hours. The cabin of mostly African passengers sighed and groaned. As the complaints reached a crescendo, the airplane's main hatch door opened to a blast of hot humid air. An African official dressed in a blue military uniform made his way down the aisle—a black wooden club in one hand and a pistol in a holster around his oversized waist. The official was followed by more oversized men in similar regalia, moving slowly and deliberately, spacing themselves out evenly within the cabin. I kept my gaze forward and down, trying not to be too conspicuous. No such luck. One official asked to see my identification and inspected it with a keen eye. Other passengers were inspected as well. Then, without further incident, they were gone.

I don't know why we flew to Lagos, nearly doubling the distance we'd planned to travel. It was not to refuel or to unload passengers, and nobody boarded the plane except the Nigerian officials. As far as I could tell, there were no problems at the Abidjan airport that prevented us from landing. Perhaps this was a scheduled stop and I misunderstood the itinerary? Perhaps there was a fugitive in our midst? I asked around but nobody seemed to know, which made me all the more desperate for answers.

Over the next couple of years, I'd discover that the answers were not always available. Life did not proceed the same way in Africa as it did in the United States. Decisions were made differently, and I could no longer anticipate the outcome the way I once did. Over time I learned I could give in to Africa, on occasion, to buckle up and hold on for the ride, to trust myself and others despite the risks. While this diversion to Lagos was a bit unnerving, it was the diversions that defined the experience and made life remarkable.

CHAPTER TWO

PRIVILEGE

I first recall hearing about the Peace Corps through television commercials as a child. Their message was for Americans to volunteer two years of their lives to help meet the need for trained men and women in the developing world.

Two years! What kind of person willingly gives up two years to work for free in some foreign land? Who leaves their friends and family and everything that America has to offer? Not me. *The toughest job you'll ever love,* I determined at an early age, was for the desperate and confused.

Then in 1986, as a high school junior, I happened upon an agent of this Peace Corps hosting a slide presentation at the Worcester Public Library. She was an attractive young woman in her mid- to late- twenties dressed in a long colorful dress from a more spirited place. She also had an air of confidence not possessed by girls my age. I was immediately smitten. No way would I be able to focus on my Genghis Khan book report now, so I took a seat in the back of the room with the others.

Her first slide was a circular emblem with a wind-blown American flag in the center and the words *Peace Corps* in an arc along the top in blue letters. In place of the fifty stars representing the United States, this flag had only one white star evolving into a dove through a three-phase supernatural mutation. The emblem's association with Old Glory was unmistakable and clearly deliberate. However, in the dark room, bold against the bright white screen, the emergence of the dove seemed to almost defy the renowned symbol of American patriotism and distinguish the emblem as something unique.

The images that followed depicted life in a harsh desert environment in a forlorn corner of the world. Houses made of mud and straw and scrap aluminum were clustered beneath the meager shade of a solitary tree. Residents equipped with rudimentary hand-held tools were hard at work in fields and in dirt courtyards. And goats and chickens and scrawny dogs roamed unfettered through the dusty landscape.

The stories complementing the images were anything but harsh in the eyes of this young woman. She spoke of her membership in the Peace Corps with absolute veneration, particularly the friendships she had made living and working in a remote village in sub-Saharan Africa. She relayed tales of success and failure in trying to alleviate the effects of famine, disease, and poverty, and how those experiences forever altered her values and priorities. She celebrated a people, a culture, somehow maintaining an obligation to their community despite persistent hardship. Such an indelible mark had been made on this woman that I wondered why she left Africa in the first place. Her display of courage and goodwill had definitely made an impression, though I was not about to give up raucous adventures with my friends for a noble desert experience.

A year later I graduated from high school with no marked interests or life plan. I applied to a few colleges but did not have the grades or financial means to attend. I considered working more hours as a cook at a local restaurant but feared I'd become like the other cooks and never leave. And I looked into joining the military but wasn't certain I'd be a good soldier if I disagreed with the motive or the mission.

While I was trying to decide, I took courses close to home at the now defunct Worcester Industrial Technical Institute. I enjoyed the curriculum so I stayed until I completed their two-year program in architecture and construction. The faculty was mostly retired clerks and trades workers. But it was the energy of a twenty-seven-year-old instructor named Bryan, fresh out of graduate school, that got me interested in engineering. I continued my studies at the University of Massachusetts-Lowell, commuting back and forth from Worcester, working nights and weekends to pay the bills. And in May 1993, before I knew what I wanted to do with my life, I graduated with a bachelor's degree in civil engineering.

That summer I bought my first suit and tie and set off to find employment in my field. I targeted the Boston area where I met with numerous private sector firms ramping up for the city's famed Big

Dig project. After a four-month search, I received no offers. Nothing. Not even a second interview. The market was either flush with junior engineers or I was not yet qualified for the job I envisioned. It also crossed my mind that maybe I was not suited for private sector work. Each of my interviewers described their company's mission with such conviction, yet I shuddered at the prospect of working long hours as an entry-level underling, generating profit for these potentates while I groveled for my pittance. No doubt I was rationalizing my failure to obtain an engineering job. Nevertheless, there had to be a better way to spend my time on earth and a greater mark of achievement or enjoyment. I thought about the Peace Corps, but to me it was still something other people did when they'd reached the end of their rope.

I turned my attention towards short-term volunteer experiences, so as not to squander my education. In the fall semester, I tutored math and science three days a week for a special education program at Fitchburg High School. The kids I tutored were rebellious and lacked respect for authority figures; many had spent time in juvenile facilities and some lived with friends or relatives because their parents were unfit, deceased, or had abandoned them. But a couple of students responded well to my presence. Perhaps they knew I chose to be there, without pay, whether to discuss math or science or life outside of class. It was therapeutic for everyone, and the experience made me feel as if I was contributing something of value, something greater than any contribution I could make to the field of engineering in that short span of time.

I planned to return for the spring semester but instead accepted an offer to volunteer with the Student Conservation Association at Mammoth Cave National Park in Kentucky. The three-month commitment to the SCA came with free housing and a fifty-dollar per week stipend to cover food and miscellaneous expenses. Fifty dollars wasn't much to live on. If I were inclined to drive to town, eat out, see a movie, buy a few beers, or make a tangible purchase, I'd easily exceed my allotment. As a result, I learned to sacrifice, to combine meals and share provisions with my park neighbors, and to redefine what was necessary or fulfilling.

While I enjoyed working in a national park, the decision to move from Massachusetts to Kentucky cost me an eight-year relationship with a girl I had been dating since high school. Nearing the end of my term in Kentucky, I was still dealing with the heartache and fallout of the breakup, but I was also becoming aware of my newfound liberty. As it turns out, it was this precarious blend of anxiety and liberty that helped bring my fate into focus. Deep down, I knew I was on a course that would only be satisfied by the ultimate in government-sanctioned, quasi-volunteer assignments that did not involve killing or proselytizing. And I possessed all the attributes to apply, including a college degree, classroom credits in a foreign language, notable volunteer experience that painted me as a real humanitarian, prudent spending habits, and no girlfriend, kids, or lingering debts. Most of all, I had no other viable offers. *The toughest job you'll ever love*, I now deduced, was my best prospect for a livelihood.

When I returned to Massachusetts I began filling-out the twenty-some-odd page Peace Corps application with professional references, in-depth medical and dental examinations, and a criminal background investigation. I finished the application in only a few days, but it took most of the summer to assemble all the pieces, as my professors and physicians and local crime fighters did not share my sense of urgency.

Then, one crisp fall day in New England, I received a phone call from a recruiter in Boston inviting me to train in Senegal for eventual placement in the Ivory Coast. The Peace Corps did their best to break me of any delusions I had about joining their group, with their onerous application and lengthy delays, but to no avail; my delusion had become an ideal. I successfully navigated the hoops and hurdles and accepted the recruiter's offer without hesitation.

On New Year's Day, 1995, I bid my family and friends farewell and flew from Boston to Philadelphia for a three-day, pre-training orientation before departing for West Africa. It was my first time on an airplane, having grown up in a single-parent household that didn't allot for such things. At the hotel, I was met by an assemblage of men and women from my training group. For whatever reason, I'd envisioned a more diverse conglomeration of grubby, half-baked liberals and peace freaks—passive hippies born from the 60s who felt compelled to save the world and answer the call for service. Instead, we were four dozen middle-class Americans sporting our newest fleece jackets and travel backpacks from the Christmas holiday, as composed as freshmen at a fraternity party before the hazing begins.

We ran the gamut of role-play exercises until we had a good idea of who everyone was, where we were born and raised, and what inspired us to join. If we did not meet during the orientation, we met up afterwards in the city's bars and restaurants, where we spent our *per diem* allowance like it was our last three days on earth. Most of the group, including myself, was in their mid-twenties, fresh out of college, with the means to defer their American lives for two years. Some were inspired to join the Peace Corps by the romantic notion of altruism, to improve conditions for those less fortunate. Others acknowledged that the Peace Corps was their ticket to graduate school, or a better job, or a chance to travel the world—a final furlough to bolster the spirit and the resume before life's inevitable commitments. There were even those who revealed that the Peace Corps was their chance to meet an African spouse.

These motivations applied to me as well, less the search for a spouse. Ultimately, what separated me (and certainly others) from countless Americans who have never considered joining the Peace Corps was a kind of despair. Not the type of despair the world's destitute must face to survive, nothing of the sort. More of an idealistic, self-imposed, despair of the privileged; of not being able to find the most lucrative or captivating job, or maintain that idyllic story-book relationship, or fully acquiesce to a life as a consumer of products and popular culture. It was only when I failed to achieve my preconceived notion of success that I was compelled to employ my civic-minded aspirations. Sure, I bought into the Peace Corps mission, hoping I could make a difference, but the mission alone wasn't enough for me to abandon everything familiar for such a significant duration of my life. I could save the world, like so many before me, if I could first reform my restless unqualified soul.

CHAPTER THREE

IMMERSION

We checked out of the hotel before dawn to board the bus that would take us to New York's John F. Kennedy International Airport for our flight to Senegal. A fellow trainee, Forrest, and I walked a few blocks to a convenience store for something to eat. This early on a winter morning, the City of Brotherly Love was cold and dark. Many of the homeless were sleeping in storm drains for the warmth that emanated from below. A short black man asked us for spare change, but we refused. Too many souls to feed. Not enough change to go around. Too much fraud and abuse in the world for the love amongst brothers to be unguarded.

Instead, Forrest offered the man his winter coat. He reasoned he would not need it in Africa and it would only take up valuable space in his pack, as we were each limited to eighty pounds of total baggage. The man was elated. He modeled the coat to show us how well it fit, and rubbed his shoulders with crossed arms to illustrate the warmth it would provide. On our way back, he gave Forrest a high-five, completing the transaction.

The bus ride to New York was brief and uneventful. I mostly stared out the window, reflecting on the adjustments and sacrifices that lay ahead. I suspect others were doing the same as the mood was quiet and subdued the entire trip. In contrast, the flight across the Atlantic was long and turbulent. At times it felt like we were dropping out of the sky, which prompted the plane's faithful to make repeated pleas for salvation. But the storm eventually subsided, and some ten hours after takeoff we arrived without injury or intervention at the Yoff International Airport in Dakar, Senegal.

Our group was anxious to set foot on African soil so we hurried from the plane into the terminal, through the turnstiles, and outside to an early morning calm. A solitary light affixed to a wooden pole in an empty parking lot was all that illuminated our way down a long set of stairs to the street, as if the airport were closed or they had not fully expected our arrival. Brilliant stars glistened without the obscuring glow from an urban sprawl, making darkness feel profound and the airport more remote than it actually was. The cool, dry morning air was just as explicit. Breathing became an indulgent, conscious activity rather than some intrinsic function of the body. I could have stayed there all morning but we had further to go.

Two dilapidated school buses sat idling in the street; so much for that good clean air. The drivers welcomed us to Africa and assembled everyone for attendance, ensuring nobody got lost or fled between the plane and the curbside. We loaded our baggage in short order and drove down a solitary asphalt road. The bus strained and whined with mechanical difficulties, but nobody appeared too concerned. Everyone was too fixated on the nocturnal life that appeared abruptly in the fringe of the headlights, such as the children curled up on straw mats sleeping beneath makeshift wooden tables; or the men in long robes walking in haste to meet or flee the dawn of another day; or the goats impelled by the light into a unified, near-suicidal dash across the road.

About an hour in, we abandoned the asphalt and navigated along sandy terrain through a poorly lit residential neighborhood of concrete block houses. Surrounding each house was a security wall built to heights exceeding that of the modest one-story dwelling, restricting our view of the dormant compounds. The walls, similar in proportion to each adjoining property, transformed our route into an intricate maze of concrete, sand, and stars.

At the end of this maze was a brightly lit compound against the night sky. The artificial light revealed a large fortress with three-meter-high walls crowned with shards of broken glass. We exited the buses and dragged the baggage along the sandy ground through the large steel gates. Too tired to acknowledge our arrival with fanfare, we retired to our rooms for some much deserved rest. And just like that we were residents of West Africa, a world apart from America.

Later that morning we awoke to a wondrous glimpse of our new surroundings. Tall trees and exotic flowering plants stretched high above, deflecting the sun's rays, keeping the morning cool and comfortable. Birds and small insects sang their song in the thick canopy above, and lizards of orange and gray scattered about with each encroachment upon their space. It was an idyllic setting for just about anything.

After a meal of root vegetables over rice, we moved like a herd from the dining hall to a circular, open-aired, thatched-roof pavilion. A small thin African man named Kayego entered the pavilion and welcomed us, in both French and English, to the Peace Corps training facility in Thiés, Senegal. Kayego, originally from Kenya in East Africa, was the director of the facility and responsible for our training and care during the twelve-week stay. His face was fixed with a permanent smile, and he appeared poised to manage such a large group of volunteer hopefuls.

Kayego introduced us to the staff, who hailed predominately from the local area. Among them were a dozen language instructors and various support personnel such as cooks, launders, facility caretakers, and security guards. They looked as if they enjoyed their work—though earning significantly more than the prevailing wage may have had something to do with that.

Kayego then gave us an orientation to the compound that would constitute our home, school, and social milieu in preparation for Peace Corps service. Eight barrack-style buildings—remnants of a once-vested military presence—had been renovated into our sleeping quarters, classrooms, and dining hall. Half a dozen mud huts served as smaller classroom venues. Two large thatched-roof pavilions were used for meeting space. We even had a modern toilet and shower facility with working flushers and knobs. Though structures consumed most of the area, there was still space for a full-size volleyball court, a paved basketball court, and a vegetable garden.

Everywhere you looked the grounds were impeccably maintained and landscaped. Trees and flowers that might not normally survive the dry season flourished due to routine care and ample watering. The leaves and petals that fell from above, or trash that found its way to the ground, were raked and disposed of continuously; the fine sand groomed clean and smooth like an upscale tropical resort. Our new home was a virtual haven, a refuge, protecting us from the hardships of a different kind of Africa—the Africa beyond the gates of the compound.

* * *

 I knew very little about Senegal or my service country of the Ivory Coast before committing to the Peace Corps. I knew only what I retained from television, where Africa is generalized as one large impoverished continent fighting continuously for independence, food, and life, and where rare exotic animals populate the tropical jungles and endless savanna. Only when American interests were jeopardized did I hear more about a particular place or people on the Dark Continent. Warlords in Somalia. Apartheid in South Africa. Music celebrities singing *We Are the World* for famine relief. Sally Struthers filming cute, poverty-stricken children for donations. These were the events being channeled to my home and school. This was what I knew, or thought I knew, of Africa.
 What I learned was that Senegal was located in Western Africa on the Northern Atlantic Ocean at the southwest fringe of the Sahara Desert. If the outline of Africa were likened to an elephant's ear then Senegal would be located on its outer tip, its latitude on par with Bangkok or the Central American countries of Guatemala and Honduras. Senegal has approximately 192,000 square kilometers of total land area (about the size and shape of the state of South Dakota), and borders Mauritania to the north, Mali to the east, and Guinea and Guinea-Bissau to the south, with the Gambia carving out a thin corridor of existence around the Gambia River.
 Within Senegal's borders there are over twelve million people belonging to numerous ethnic and tribal groups such as the Serer, Toucouleur, Mandingo, Wolof, Fulani, and the Diola (pronounced Jewla); those of European and Lebanese heritage; and a number of Mauritanian refugees. However, more than ninety percent of the population is Muslim, unified in its belief and practice of the Islamic religion, frequently portrayed in America as a dogma that incites terrorism and maniacal behavior.
 I learned that many countries on the African continent have been dominated in recent centuries by colonialism, carved up by opportunistic and militaristic countries for the wealth of their resources. Senegal was no exception, existing primarily under French control from the 1700s—as the first French outpost in black Africa—until 1960 when it achieved full independence. Senegal has remained independent under four presidents, the last elected to office

in April 2012. Despite Senegal's sovereignty, the colonial legacy of French occupation still prevails, especially in the capital city of Dakar, in the form of its common language, mannerisms, services, architecture, and government structure.

* * *

On our first training day, we met individually with the instructors to demonstrate how well we could speak and comprehend the French language. I had taken only two years of French in high school, some eight years previous, so my interview was brief and despondent, and an embarrassing display. We were ranked based on these sessions and placed with other trainees with similar command. As it turned out, I was not the poorest francophone in the lot, but I would have to work hard at being intermediate.

Before dispersing for the day, Kayego announced the primary directive for our stay in Senegal: "From this moment on, you are required to speak only the French language while in the confines of the training facility. Conversing in English is permitted only outside after classes or during technical sessions to maintain the integrity of the subject matter. You will adhere to this strict policy of immersion."

That evening the group assembled in the dining hall, summoned by the strike of a wrought-iron gong that would signify each meal, group meeting, or wake-up call. The tables were preset with plastic plates, chrome utensils, cloth napkins, and long thin *baguettes* of freshly baked bread. The elder female cooks filed into the room, one by one, with a feast in large bowls balanced upon their heads. An attempt was made to provide us with a meal that resembled American cuisine to ease our transition from the fatty preservatives of America to the bland starchy foods of Africa. The results, however, were laden with palm oil, nullifying the flavor of the dish they tried to emulate. But it was dinner, and plenty of it, so only the most finicky complained or resorted to hidden food stores.

As we passed the bowls to one another, very few of us could muster the courage to converse in our new language. When instructors asked us questions, the room got quiet and everyone would just listen in. I wanted to speak French but it wasn't worth the risk of embarrassment. I was content just to point to the item I wanted and grunt like a cretin. I retired to my room in silence, anxious to be heard again.

The next day I made my way to the mud hut designated for my class level and took a seat facing the chalkboard with three other trainees. Our instructor entered the mud hut and flipped a switch that illuminated the single bulb dangling from a frayed electrical cord above, which was hardly necessary with the bright sunlight pouring through the door. The instructor's name was Yague. He was a thin Senegalese man with rich brown skin who wore a black denim jacket and struggled to keep his oversized matching pants cinched at the waist without tugging and pulling at them frequently. He spoke to us in clear, simple French. If we absolutely did not understand his directive, he would speak to us in English as a last resort. Yague was a likable character with a good sense of humor and enormous patience. As a result, we did not fear making blunders and progress was accelerated.

Throughout the first week, we focused on learning various nouns and verb conjugations, and formulating simple sentences. We mastered the basics through repetitive drills by following the instructor's lead on pronunciation and form. At one point Yague graduated to an exercise where we would read a question written in English on a piece of paper, then ask that question in French to the person on our right. That person would then respond in French.

I sat at the far right so I directed my question to the other male trainee on the far left. Yague handed me a piece of paper that read, "What time do you eat breakfast?"

I turned, still in a haze from all the traveling, and said to the guy, "*A quelle heure mangez-vous ton petit ami?*"

The woman next to me shrilled loudly, "Do you know what you just said to him?"

Yague burst out laughing, suspecting that I had made an honest mistake. The class could barely continue. For days, Yague tormented the guy by repeatedly asking, "Hey Matt, what time do you eat your boyfriend?" without a retort.

Formal class instruction continued each day from 0800 to 1800, with a two-hour midday *sieste,* five days a week, with a half-day session on Saturday. Breakfast was fruit and a baguette with butter, jam, or chocolate spread. Lunch was always root vegetables over rice, scooped by hand from large aluminum bowls, shared amongst four people sitting cross-legged on plastic mats. Most of the group followed lunch with a long nap until classes resumed. Others read or wrote letters in the shade. I'd attempt to stay awake and study, but the heat was too intense to stay focused. If I managed to stay awake, I was lethargic during class and useless the rest of the day. Eventually I gave in, accepting the premise of daily, two-hour, guilt-free naps long before their geriatric necessity.

After class let out, many of us would take to the grounds for a game of volleyball or basketball. Language instructors would participate; thus, courtside chatter had to be in French or reprimands would follow. Even cuss words had to be in French, which defeated the abrasive and offending purpose of the good ole American cuss word. Someone would yell, "Ah shit!" when a spiked volleyball went out of bounds, which was followed by a chorus of "*En français.*"

Trainees also ventured into the streets of Thiés for their exercise and a reprieve from the policy of French immersion. Some would advance just beyond the gates to kick around a soccer ball or a hacky sack or to hang out at the small beverage kiosk, while others would explore further reaches of town.

Despite the freedom to converse in English once beyond the gates, a reprieve was never guaranteed. The people of Thiés did not speak English, or even French in most cases, accustomed to functioning in their native language of Wolof. Those living or working near the compound were accustomed to seeing Americans, but due to the trainees' busy daytime regimen, few interactions had occurred. When the trainee had an opportunity to interact with the Senegalese people, there weren't many chances at clemency. The trainee was expected to know how to communicate in the local language and relate to the culture, just as Americans have those expectations of their foreign population. If we failed during class, we were scrutinized and exonerated, and maybe enjoyed a hearty laugh. But if we failed in public, we were useless and possibly offensive. Imagine addressing an African citizen, leader, or diplomat in elementary French and inquiring as to the time they eat their boyfriend! I'm sure it would not advance my standing or reputation no matter how inadvertent; and my reputation might be the least of my worries.

There were afternoons I, too, needed to escape the confines of the compound, so I would join the devout runners and try to keep pace. We'd run a block north to the railroad tracks and follow it west upon a well-worn, single-track footpath, past the busy schoolyard where young boys played *futbol* using crumbling bricks as goal posts. Children not in the game would spot our white skin and run alongside, clapping and chanting *toubab bou! toubab bou!* in unison until they tired or grew bored. Our instructors claimed *'toubab bou'* was the non-derogatory term for a white person given to the first white doctors and missionaries who traveled to Africa from Europe, derived from a Wolof verb meaning *to convert*. Derogatory or not, we could not avoid the stigma of being different.

We'd set our sights on the distant silhouettes against a blazing red sun. As we got closer, the silhouettes came into focus as women returning from the market or the field with large woven baskets upon their heads. We took care not to startle these women or the infant children cradled to their backs with cloth that matched the mother's garb. They would glance at us indifferently, one hand supporting the substantial weight of the basket and its contents, the other working a splintered piece of bamboo between teeth and gum, resulting in a remarkable gleam of white in contrast with their dark brown skin.

We'd break away from the tracks and run out to the sandy fields of the ominous *baobab* tree. The *baobab*, lacking fruits and foliage during the height of the dry season, loomed large with the fading sun. Its enormous girth and contorted, coral-like branches contributed to a haunted, unsettling feeling, and our increased pace. When we wore out our welcome amidst the hallowed fields, or just ran out of steam, we doubled back along the tracks to the training facility.

On occasion we braved a run through the neighborhoods, known as *quartiers*, which were always bustling with activity and wonder. The Senegalese people are accustomed to sports, especially *futbol*, so our tour was not out of the ordinary. Running was a decent way to wind down after class. In addition to beholding the unique desert landscape, running was a way of assimilating to our new culture at our own pace. Locals who requested that we stop to converse were usually curious about the United States, what we were doing there, and how we could be of service to them. The most popular requests came from twenty-something males who asked us to become their American correspondent or to serve as a character witness for their visa application to the western world. It was a relatively harmless request, but the frequency made it tedious and overwhelming at times, forcing the trainee to either relent or to devise a polite or abrupt way to refuse.

Though I felt safe running just about anywhere in Thiés, Kayego gathered the group one evening to inform us that two of our female trainees were physically attacked while jogging. From what I gathered, two African men had separated the two trainees by dragging them to opposite sides of a dirt road under the cover of darkness. One woman broke free and rushed to aid the other woman. In the commotion, the two men fled. While neither of the trainees were seriously injured, it could have been far worse had they not fought off their attackers. Though violent crime did not seem to be prevalent in Senegal, anything could still happen. Both women were promptly flown back to the U.S. to address any lingering issues, and both returned to Senegal to rejoin the group.

This incident was an early wake-up call. It forced us to reassess the dangers of our environment, and for some it was a chance to reconsider the perils of a two-year commitment in a foreign land. As creatures of habit, though, the lessons faded with time for all but those directly impacted, leaving the rest of us to re-immerse ourselves in that shroud of invincibility, where it is safe from harm and hassle.

Abiding by Kayego's policy of immersion was an excellent method of learning French in just twelve short weeks. However, within the gates of the compound, amongst our English-speaking peers, we were far from immersed. We spoke English in our rooms or when the staff was not listening, engaging each other in the only language that yielded results. Sure, we were robbing ourselves of the opportunity to enhance our language skills, but it was just as vital to socialize, make friends, and establish your standing within the group.

To ensure each trainee would be prepared for actual cross-cultural encounters, we were assigned a family in the community to visit and interact with. The Peace Corps paid these families an amount sufficient to cover our meals and transportation; otherwise, they volunteered to serve as hosts for the second and tenth weekends of our stint for what Kayego called *homestays*. Most families had participated in previous homestays and knew what to expect from the trainee, but the distressed trainee knew nothing of what to expect from these exotic strangers. We were, if only for two weekends, truly immersed.

Thiés is a small desert city, alive with commerce and commotion. City streets are paved with asphalt, but desert sands blowing in from the northeast, covering the asphalt under drifts of fine grains, have not relinquished their stronghold of the area. Horses pull carts filled with a desert's harvest amidst the erratic movement of taxi cars and pedestrians moving in droves.

The *quartier* where my family lived was a sprawl of newly constructed houses protected by the familiar gated wall of concrete block that delineated territory or land use. Every so often, you'd come across a house that never quite got finished, with the crumbling remnants of a family's dream left behind, now serving as a sanctuary for goats feasting on the tall wild grass within. When I arrived, my family was standing on the sandy road in front of their house, waiting to meet their adopted trainee. The father introduced himself first. He was a medium-built, neatly-groomed, bearded man named Soleil, dressed in trousers and a faded button-down oxford shirt. His family consisted of his wife, his younger brother Sylvean, his five-year-old daughter Rama, and his three-year-old son Lemon.

Soleil was a math teacher at a local high school. By impulse or by mandate, he corrected much of my archaic French grammar and pronunciation with patience and tact, helping me to understand fundamental aspects of the West African tongue. Soleil's wife spoke only the native language of Wolof and depended on Soleil to translate every word. For the most part, she remained in the periphery the entire time, attending to the chores that supported the family, so much so that I cannot recall her name.

Soleil and I spent the afternoon getting to know each other. He had hosted six other trainees at different times spanning a five-year period. He showed me an atlas of Africa on the wall indicating where they had served as volunteers, and he revealed what he knew of the history and culture of the Ivory Coast. He was definitely proud of his role as cultural mentor to the program, and by all accounts he was good at it.

As I relaxed on the living room sofa, Rama and Lemon sat with me, ignoring their father's halfhearted plea to play outside. They stared at me intently from both sides, entranced by the features of my face, tugging at my ears and nose, my hair and beard, touching my white skin with looks of astonishment. Both five-year-old Rama and I were learning the French words for the various parts of the body in our classes. We reviewed the words pertaining to the face and the digits of the hand, reciting the parts in unison as we pointed them out on each other: *"l'oeil, le nez, la bouche, les dents...,"* rapidly, then in random order until we were confident we had mastered the lesson. In the kitchen the mother laughed mildly at the disparity while maintaining the rhythmic pounding of a long wooden pestle to the mortar, transforming a manioc root into a form that would become dinner with the help of a spicy peanut sauce.

I spent the rest of the afternoon atop the flat roof, observing the dynamic city of Thiés and the magnificent earthen colors of dusk. Lemon joined me, struggling to get his small three-year-old body up the steep stairway without assistance. He did not attempt to talk. He just hung out in my vicinity, alternating between kicking a deflated soccer ball around and climbing on me to see what I found so captivating along the desert skyline.

Before dinner I descended from the roof and joined Sylvean in front of the blue-glow of evening television. Sylvean had come to live with his brother's family after fleeing his home in battle-torn northern Senegal. He enjoyed his elder brother's hospitality but held out that he would soon be able to return to the north. Sylvean was extremely inquisitive about the United States and all that it had to offer, but his inquiries only came during television breaks. Despite my unique presence in his home, his attention was transfixed on the actions and flashes of the screen.

The evening lineup featured *The Undersea World of Jacques Cousteau,* African wrestling, *futbol* matches, and various syndicated American shows from the 1980s like *Knight Rider* and *McGuyver* dubbed in French. During commercials plugging the latest imports, the children recited the lyrics of the catchy jingle in unison, whether or not they knew what the product was or how it was consumed. Soleil, a devout and proficient Muslim, would periodically retreat to a plastic woven mat behind the couch, praying in the direction of Mecca, Saudi Arabia. Upon standing from a kneeling position, he would discipline his rowdy children with one swipe of the finger, quieting them until the next commercial break.

I was amazed to witness the popularity of television in Soleil's home and throughout Thiés—a technological enhancement I naively thought might not exist for the majority of the people. But I was wrong. Television was alive and well, entertaining, informing, and persuading its audience. Like many Americans, the Senegalese people derived knowledge and formed opinions from the primetime broadcasts, to the point where they thought Americans had talking sports cars that could dispense practical advice through the front fender, or that we could make explosive devices out of tin foil and chewing gum. I was a guest in Soleil's home to be immersed in our cultures' differences, yet I was being soaked in the similarities.

I retired early to my room—an eight-foot by ten-foot space with a lone window barred on the outside as a deterrent to theft. A thin straw mat was placed in a corner for my bedding. All other furniture, objects, and decor had been removed for the weekend. The children were reprimanded for visiting the bearded white man who spoke French at a first grade level, now occupying their space. As I sat quietly and read, the children's curiosity waned and they wandered off to sleep. I turned off the overhead light and lay on the mat with my pack as my pillow and stared through the window at the light from ancient stars. I thought of my life and the events that brought me to this small cell in Africa, far from anywhere familiar. I thought of my irrelevance and mortality in a large, overpopulated, unforgiving world. Moreover, I thought of no other place I'd rather be at that moment than on that hard floor in that concrete hovel with the power of our celestial universe glimmering silently through the window.

Meanwhile, my fellow trainees were scattered throughout Thiés, impaired or enlightened by their own homestays. I hadn't known this group for more than three weeks, but there were a number I considered to be decent like-minded people. I often wondered what would become of them. Could we become meaningful friends and acquaintances? Would they become disillusioned and quit the Peace Corps before I got to know them? Would they endure the two years and become disillusioned all the same? Might I have to rescue any of them from isolation and madness, deep inside the jungles of our host country? Or worse, would any of them have to rescue me, holed-up in front of a television, watching reruns of *Knight Rider* and *McGuyver* in French?

We continued with French language training, moving from the mud hut to the more relevant classroom of our new environment. We toured the garden, the courtyard, and the kitchen, translating the word of an object from English to its French equivalent. During more ambitious days, the instructor sent us to town to complete small assignments such as purchasing stamps at the post office or navigating our way through the bustling open-air market to bargain for fruit or cloth.

As the weeks elapsed, the class structure changed dramatically. Trainees were rotated between instructors, exposing us to a variety of teaching styles and accents unique to each instructor's native region. We also learned salutations, slang, and colloquial expressions sure to enhance our social standing with the African people. Without these skills, we hampered our ability to connect with others by taking ourselves too seriously.

Armed with the rudiments of West African French and basic Wolof salutations, we were now ready to make excursions outside of Thiés. On weekends, after a half-day session on Saturday, we were given free rein of the country as long as we returned for dinner on Sunday evening. We took advantage of this time to explore the capital city of Dakar and Senegal's extensive coastline.

Midway through training, five trainees and I decided to head west to Dakar one weekend. We walked down to the bus station, known as *le gare routière,* or *le gare*, and reserved our place on a twelve-seat bush taxi decorated with colorful etchings. At first glance, our bus looked as if it were plastered with Loony-Tune cartoon characters. Upon closer inspection, I realized the décor depicted symbols and leaders of the Islamic religion with scripture from the Holy Qur'an, which is more sanctified than the wild zany antics of Bugs, Daffy, and Elmer Fudd (unless you were an American kid raised in the 70s).

After waiting for the bus to fill beyond capacity with baggage, passengers, and livestock, we headed west along the same asphalt road that had supported our first overland travels in Africa. In Dakar, urban entrepreneurs were anxious to sell us locally crafted merchandise such as masks, drums, and stringed instruments. Their aggressive, unrelenting approach did not yield any purchases within our group, disdainful about being generalized as gullible tourists. However, many of us took the chance to haggle for a better deal, to gauge the value of the items for future purchases.

We took a one-kilometer ferryboat ride to the small island of Ile de Gorée, with its beautiful white sandy beaches and pastel-colored houses—a place so inviting it conjures thoughts of abandoning the toils of labor in exchange for idle days in isolated beauty. Once on the island, we walked between crowded houses on intricate footpaths that led to hidden coves and architectural relics from earlier centuries. I broke from the group and followed one such path along the shore to a terraced wall of a dying fortress. With a bit of time and gumption, I managed to scale the wall to the top where large iron cannons set on crumbling concrete pillars deteriorated in the firing range of the hot African sun. And in the distance was a wonderful view of the endless ocean to the west with Dakar and mainland Africa to the east.

I abandoned my perch and wandered back into town, exploring houses that displayed the impressive work of local artisans, everything from paintings to sculptures to jewelry. I then happened upon a large rose-colored building with a line of tourists, both African and non-African. Without knowing the nature of this attraction, I paid the admission price of 500 West African francs and followed the others into the courtyard of the first floor. The tour guide gathered us together and proceeded to tell the remarkable history of the site.

Ile de Gorée—Island of Shame and Sorrow—was a transshipment point for tens of thousands of African men, women, and children who were torn from their homes and villages and sold into slavery. Discovered in 1444 by the Portuguese, the island became an integral part of slave history for more than three centuries. Slaves from Gorée were shipped to the French colonies in the Caribbean, the Portuguese colonies in Brazil, and the Spanish colonies in the Atlantic (Cuba). Some ended up in French Louisiana, ancestors of today's Creole people, or as African Americans who have since migrated elsewhere. The House of Slaves, or *Maison des Esclaves*, was constructed around 1784 and used as a holding cell for human cargo for many years. Slave trade on Gorée was officially abolished by Napoleon in 1815, but the lack of enforcement by the French government resulted in a clandestine slave trade until 1848.

I walked the hallways of the House of Slaves, then down into the dark basement where slaves were once shackled and detained, awaiting their fate, robbed of their freedom and liberty to serve wealth and indolence. As I stood there amongst the sobering crowd, I could not help but reflect on the physical and emotional sufferings of those affected by indentured slavery. I could not help but imagine the horror of being violently punished for being born a particular race.

In the House of Slaves, I felt as though compassion is no more inherent a quality in humans than is greed or hatred. And as a learned quality, compassion must compete with the more lucrative machinations of our times. It is difficult to visit a place like the House of Slaves and believe we are anything more than simple organisms wired for self-preservation with the tendency to justify our deeds and rationalize our importance. As the island's name had professed, I was overcome with shame and sorrow, not because I felt responsible for centuries of human and racial atrocities, but because I belonged to a civilization of sentient beings failing to obtain its lofty potential.

Back on the first floor, I came upon a portal in the wall that led down to the rocky cliffs and the Atlantic Ocean. The opening, as seen from my position in the darkened hallway, framed a beautiful, endless, bright blue ocean scene worthy of any picture postcard. Carved in a piece of wood above the opening were the words: *"La porte aller sans retour"*—The door to go without return.

When I wasn't busy studying in the evenings, or feigning to study to meet girls, I was off enjoying other pursuits such as reading books or writing letters back home replete with idealism and self-righteousness. Sometimes I'd go into town with friends to share liter-sized beers at an outdoor bar called a *maquis*. When I got tired, I'd make my way back to my room and crawl beneath my government-issue mosquito netting and into bed. The screen door slammed shut on tightly coiled springs to keep the buzz and bite from the mosquito at bay, but my roommate Austin and I left the solid interior door open to allow the heat trapped within the room a chance to escape into the cold desert night.

In the evening, new sounds in concert with the fragrance of nearby activity floated through the air on the drift of Harmattan winds out of the Sahara. The aroma of wood smoke emanating from the last of the neighborhood cooking fires climbed the compound wall and into our room, followed by the dull clamor of aluminum pots being cleaned and organized by young children in the nearby courtyards. Eventually, the sounds and smells dissipated, seeping into the fabric of my possessions and my memory.

Africa quickly emerged as a place of wonder, vivid and distinct, and my senses began to sharpen to my new surroundings. The daily ritual of people became my sole source of entertainment, delivered without monthly billing, commercial interruption, special effects, computer editing, scripted melodrama, or canned laughter. With no television, radio, or other forms of gadgetry, Africa's rituals were all that remained. I had no choice but to tune in.

In early February, I was roused from a deep sleep by an altogether new and unique sound from a distant Thiés. It was a harsh, piercing cry followed by a voice, loud and direct, broadcasting information in strange tongues by means of a handheld megaphone. It was the beginning of Ramadan, the Muslim period of fasting and abstinence, and the night voices were signifying its commencement with the sighting of the crescent moon and the beginning of the ninth month of the lunar calendar. The next morning our language instructors appeared more exuberant than usual, prepared for the sacrifices they would soon endure. Curious about their routine, and the religion that mandated such behavior, we all but deposed of the daily lesson plan to learn more about our hosts.

Muslims in Africa and elsewhere are followers of the Islamic religion, which believes in complete submission, surrender, and obedience to God Allah, creator of all, and Supreme Being for Muslims, Christians, Jews, Buddhists, Hindus, and Atheists. Muslims must adhere to the tenets of the holy book of Islam, the Qur'an, delivered unto the people of God by the prophet Muhammad in the year 569 A.D. Within the Qur'an there are five pillars of faith that every devout Muslim must abide by in order to establish piety in their lives and community. These five pillars consist of creed, prayers, fasting, purifying tax, and pilgrimage. Fasting (the third pillar of Islam) is an abstinence from food, liquids, and intercourse from sunrise until sunset during the entire month of Ramadan—the period in which the Qur'an was revealed as a guide for all mankind. Fasting is performed to practice self-restraint, to discipline the present life and be held accountable for the next, and to honor God Allah and the prophet Muhammad.

As February continued, so did the fast. Restaurants in the city remained vacant or closed during the daylight hours, and people in the streets or those working in the market or fields limited their physical efforts, taking refuge under the shade of a tree, a roof overhang, or an awning to avoid the hot sun and the threat of exhaustion or dehydration. Muslims no longer capable of fasting, such as elders or pregnant women, abandoned their sacrifices for sake of nourishment and health, as warranted by the Qur'an. Even the instructors, as young and seasoned as they were, appeared faint and lethargic as the days went on, the effects of their sacrifice taking hold.

As a gesture of solidarity, trainees attempted periods of fasting for a day or more, though we were told that Allah would not recognize our fast because we were not Muslim. Even so, we wanted to support our friends and gain insight into their sacrifice. Kayego proclaimed that we were learning a good lesson in cultural sensitivity by fasting with our Muslim instructors. And he was correct. We did practice what it meant to be culturally sensitive during the most celebrated and formidable period of the Muslim year. However, my one-day, half-assed attempt at fasting only resulted in short-lived hunger pains. I did not experience the long-term effects of fasting, or even begin to understand the sacrifices of Ramadan. Expecting anything more than a craving for food from a one-day fast would be like expecting the promise of a modern Christian heaven by refraining from laughing or farting in church during a sermon. It's not likely to happen. Cultural sensitivity is requisite, but it's too small a gesture. If I were to learn more about the Muslim people, I would need to immerse myself even further, and in twelve busy weeks that didn't seem possible.

As February came to a close, I heard the crier, the messenger, somewhere in the desert city of Thiés, amplifying his evening message for the last time that year. It was the end of the lunar month and the period of Ramadan was complete, and by the guidance and grace of the man on the megaphone, we could now rest peacefully.

CHAPTER FOUR

TRAINING

To acquaint the Peace Corps trainee with the personal health issues of living and traveling in Africa, a medical staff of two doctors (one male, one female) was employed at the training facility on a part-time basis. They were from the developed countries of the U.S. and Ireland, respectively—a necessary measure due to the language and cultural differences, and our uneasiness with African doctors and facilities. They appeared twice per week to conduct classroom lectures, and every Friday to perform the slew of inoculations against the unfamiliar pestilences of the developing world.

Classroom lectures were conducted on such topics as diet and nutrition, sexually transmitted diseases, and the prevention of malaria. If we didn't eat meat or didn't trust the source, we were advised to identify the animal being served as our totem or ancestral emblem so as not to offend the host. We were also told that many of the continent's afflictions were contingent on our choices, behavior, and hygiene practices, though we were still susceptible to the unpredictable nature of the African environment, which includes the Ebola virus, the guinea worm, the tsetse fly, and others.

The Ebola virus was unequivocally the most intimidating of medical misfortunes. Ebola is transmitted through contact with bodily fluids such as mucus, saliva, vomit, and blood. A few days after transmission, the victim can expect flu-like symptoms, bloody diarrhea, and vomiting. About two weeks later, there's a chance the victim bleeds out through the eye sockets, ears, nose, and other orifices as the major organs fail, killing the human host in a most violent fashion.

Such fatalities have become all too possible in Africa, with recent cases in the Republic of South Sudan, the Democratic Republic of the Congo (formally Zaire), Guinea, Sierra Leone, Liberia, and

Nigeria. To date, there is no licensed treatment or vaccine for Ebola, and it has a mortality rate of 50-90%, depending on the strain that is contracted. What makes matters worse is that there is no definitive proof as to where the Ebola virus lurks, or what plant, animal, or organism serves as its vector, although chimpanzees, gorillas, fruit bats, monkeys, forest antelope, and porcupine have been implicated. It is believed that a person can only contract Ebola through direct contact with blood, secretions, organs, or other bodily fluids from a carrier (which includes embalming of an infected dead person) or by contact with contaminated medical equipment, particularly needles and syringes, placing Ebola at the top of the food chain.

Then there is the guinea worm (aka dracunculiasis), a parasitic infection living as worms ingested by water fleas then ingested by humans. Many Africans obtain their drinking water from streams and other open bodies of water. If a person swallows the water from an infected stream, chances are they will be infected with the guinea worm parasite. Once ingested, a person's stomach acid will digest the water flea but it will not digest the worm itself, which can grow the width of an average earthworm, up to three feet in length. After one year in the system, a blister will develop, usually on the infected person's leg or foot as the worm emerges through the skin like a creature from a science fiction movie. If that person enters a body of water to bathe or to alleviate the blister's painful burning sensation, the temperature change may cause the blister to erupt, exposing the ulceration. Adult female worms that are exposed can release a milky white substance containing millions of immature worms, thus contaminating the water and perpetuating the cycle.

A guinea worm can be removed through surgery, but in West Africa where medical facilities are scarce, understaffed, and too expensive for the average citizen, surgery is not an option (especially for those with no choice but to drink water from polluted streams). Therefore, the only remedy is to patiently extract the worm from the body when it emerges, coiling it around a small stick like a winch, day-by-day, centimeter-by-centimeter, careful not to pull too hard and break the worm. With some skill, the worm will stay intact during this process and be removed within a few weeks to a month.

Stomach viruses and mysterious gut-wrenching disorders were the most common afflictions for trainees and volunteers, with the major culprits being giardia, salmonella, shigellosis (or shigella), and amoebic dysentery. Each of us could expect greater than normal gastric activity from mite-sized parasites taking refuge in our warm cozy bellies. The distress and pain of Friday's inoculations were negligible compared with the anguish of retching in some exotic fashion. Unfortunately, I did not always heed the warning signs and I learned this lesson the hard way.

A medication that most of us took on a weekly basis was an anti-malaria prophylaxis pill called Mefloquine. Mefloquine, also know as Larium, allegedly kills or prevents the growth of malaria parasites delivered through a bite from an Anopheles mosquito. Mefloquine has also been implicated for such adverse physical and physiological effects as anxiety, sleep disturbance, depression, heart palpitations, hallucinations, even psychosis. Most notable of these effects were the strange Technicolor dreams everyone seemed to be having. It was as if the drug could summon our most suppressed memories and display them in vivid detail with sexual overtones and bizarre correlations. Despite the abnormality of these nocturnal productions, the medical team was hard-pressed at convincing me these dreams were an *adverse* effect of taking Mefloquine, especially early on when they added a certain essence to my evenings.

About midway through the twelve-week training program, French classes were limited to the first half of the day while the second half was devoted to our occupational discipline. The instructors for the technical sessions were recently returned volunteers from the Ivory Coast or other African countries. They were Americans, slightly older than the average trainee, with a wealth of experience in applied development work and a firsthand knowledge of what we could expect during our tenure.

Along with fifteen others, I prepared for my role as an Urban Environmental Management (UEM) volunteer. The UEM group was composed of engineering and community development backgrounds to provide both technical and social resources at the same urban site. UEM was the only Peace Corps assignment in the Ivory Coast, and one of only a handful throughout the world, which paired volunteers at the same location. Instructors for the UEM group lectured us each afternoon on the sanitation and environmental health issues of West Africa. We spent brilliant sunny afternoons tooling around with our trowels and shovels, experimenting with different composting and concrete mixtures, or constructing trash receptacles and drainage systems from old automobile tires or recycled materials. We also spent time in Dakar on field trips to the water treatment plant, solid waste landfill, and city planner's office.

In the meantime, the other trainees were busy practicing their own vocations. Eighteen women and two men, with backgrounds in health and medicine, were anticipating assignments in village clinics as Health Agents. The remaining eight awaited their fate in a pilot program to bring clean water to the more rural villages as Rural Water & Sanitation volunteers. "Water-San" volunteers had a similar objective as UEM, but since they'd be working in small isolated villages they would not have the same material resources as the UEM group. Consequently, the Water-San program recruited a different breed of person—an individual, we surmised, with the resolve to produce water from sand.

One of the more practical exercises we completed was the building of mud stoves for the cooking of daily meals. We traveled by pickup truck to a *quartier* in suburban Thiés where the familiar maze of concrete block wall tapered away. With tools and a lunch packed in coolers, we were greeted at the road by a group of a dozen African women. These women were heavy from their starchy diets, but healthy and active in appearance, tone and taut from years of physical labor. Each wore cloth of a color and pattern that represented their family or tribal history. For some, that meant only what they could afford at the market. The first piece wrapped around their waist as a long skirt; the second piece wrapped around their upper body over a T-shirt to secure the child nearest to infancy against their back.

A trainee named Steve thought he'd try out his Wolof greetings starting with *"Na nga def"* which means, "How are you?" The women responded, *"Mangi fi rekk"* as expected. Steve then uttered the phrase, *"Naka sa doogoo da?"* There was a pause; the women looked at each other and started clapping their hands in a fit of laughter. Steve apparently asked them, "How's it hanging?" Come to find out, it's a double entendre that alludes to a literal inquiry, with a response being *"Mungee dalla"* which means, "It's hanging." It was a big hit, and it definitely broke the ice.

We split into groups of four and followed the women on foot to their respective courtyards. Each family's cooking shelter was blackened with soot from the inside out due to the smoke of numerous fires. As the family grew in size and the operation grew larger, the cooking area spilled outside to the courtyard so that the shelter was just used for storage. Plastic bowls and aluminum pots of various shapes marked the cooking area. Traces of rice, *atcheké*, and fish bones could be found on the dirt, scoured and scraped from pots and left for the dogs and chickens in a moist pile of refuse.

The women had gathered materials for our mud stoves beforehand, so we went right to work. The base of our improved stove was the earth, compacted naturally by foot traffic over the years. We arranged three coconut-sized rocks as a crude tripod and placed the family's most reliable aluminum pot upon the rocks, balanced between three points of contact. A large empty #10 tin can was placed in between two of the rocks as a form for the opening where the firewood would be placed. We then went to work, mixing cow dung, earth, and water to the consistency of a thick mud and piled it around the rocks in a dome-like formation. The mud was stacked to leave a small gap between the pot and the stove so that smoke from the fire could escape without being suppressed.

While the mixture was drying, the African women gathered in one of the courtyards and sang songs in a high-pitched but soothing tone in Wolof with French interspersed—a modern language all its own. The songs, from what we could gather, spoke of a woman's role in the community and the struggles they faced. They sang about our female trainees, adding their names within verses as a tribute to their strength and commitment for leaving their homes and families to help the African people.

We removed the tin can from the mud stove and cleared the inside of its debris. We then troweled on a shellac made from the leaves of the *baobab* tree that would protect the stove against cracking. Now complete and ready for use, the mud stove would reduce the quantity of fuel by about two-thirds, as the heat is retained longer within the stove. As a result, the family would save on the cost and effort of obtaining wood, additionally reducing the harvesting of trees in a desert area meager in timber resources.

From what I gathered, most of the women used the improved stoves consistently. Women who owned the cheaper, thinner aluminum pots abandoned the idea because the higher temperatures would scorch their food. But if only a percentage of the women converted to the improved stove, the project was a worthy endeavor. It required little investment of time, effort, and material resources to produce something of tangible worth. It required no additional knowledge or revenue to operate. And for us, it revealed a voice of strength and unification in the community, a resource for development and change—the voice of the African women. If only it could be heard more in a male-dominated Africa.

In addition to the lectures and field trips, the UEM group was required to complete two major projects before we'd be considered worthy for the fraternal fiefdom of Peace Corps volunteers. The first project was for UEM and Water-San groups to combine forces and construct a latrine at a local school. Latrines, also called pit privies or out-houses, are facilities used throughout the developing world or in remote locations as a means of disposing of human excrement. In Senegal, latrines are commonly found in residential compounds where piped sewer systems are not feasible. The components of a typical latrine consist of a deep pit covered with a platform or slab with a squatter hole and an enclosure for privacy. It was rare to find a latrine at a primary school in Thiés, as it's an accepted practice for children to relieve themselves on the school grounds, even unload on their own playground when nature called.

The school to receive the latrine was like most others in Thiés—a one-story concrete structure trowel-finished with a mortar layer to hide the seams and cracks of each block course. The roof was framed with inexpensive lumber to a slight pitch and covered with long sheets of corrugated metal, which offered adequate protection against heavy rains and the hot sun but lacked the properties to quiet and quell extreme weather conditions. Doors were fashioned out of wood with a simple lockset to keep trespassing to a minimum and furnishings secure. Specially formed blocks with gapped patterns were situated to allow airflow into the classrooms in lieu of windows and casing, and it was all painted a bright shade of yellow, rose, blue, or green. Over time, sun, sand, and neglect worked these bright colors to an earthen hue of brown or gray.

The school was located a few kilometers beyond the city's commercial district, where the expanse of public land was more dispensable for services such as education. Out front, a large dirt courtyard had been created from the trodden play and business of children. Out back, numerous *baobab* trees shared the landscape with heaping piles of trash embers and unburned blue plastic bags that had been lifted by the wind and caught in the low brush.

To maintain the schedule, instructors had to plan, design, finance, and purchase tools and materials for the latrine while we were busy fumbling through language class. Two Senegalese masons were hired to dig the three-meter-deep hole and make the concrete blocks. All we had to do was dress in suitable construction wear, pile into pickup trucks, and labor for the day.

We split into small groups and worked on aspects of the latrine not yet completed by the masons. One group did nothing but cut steel rebar and tie them together with wire as the reinforcement for the floor slabs. Others nailed wooden forms together for the slabs and kept the forms wet to slow the absorption of water from the concrete mixture. Others mixed cement with water and gravel to the proper ratio, resulting in the phenomenon called concrete. Though our hands were callused and our clothes were dirty, most of us enjoyed the work, unleashing pent-up blue-collar aggression suppressed by years of sheltered white-collar academia.

The children took recess outside in their white and blue- or brown-check school uniforms, and formed a circular procession for the daily calisthenics. A few stray children made use of the curing blocks, using them to designate the goal boundaries for their *futbol* games. Others gathered around us in clusters, staring intently, curious about our ways. We'd put them to work doing small chores, like weighing down the end of a board to be cut or picking up scrap materials to the envy of their more dubious classmates. Overall, they were helpful and a source of great humor.

Two children stood out in the hierarchy of the schoolyard. A small, popular ten-year-old named Yakouba was the ringleader of gang activity for the elementary grades. His head was shaven to the scalp and he was constantly smiling beneath a pair of oversized woman's sunglasses. To our favor, Yakouba followed us around, mimicking our English to near perfection. We took advantage of this influence and taught him the phrases, "Right on, brother" and

"Peace, man." His henchman was a tall thin kid of about twelve years old with cold, deep-set eyes named Sae, who employed his own style of law and diplomacy on the younger, weaker kids. These two, along with their procession of devoted cronies, ruled the school grounds, bellowing "Peace, brother!" as they brutally pushed their classmates face-first to the ground in heaps of Senegalese frailty.

The work moved quickly. We completed the latrine, two handwash cisterns, and improvements to the drainage area below the cistern in just a few weeks. We even had time to paint the latrine doors a bright rose color. Project number one was complete. We met our objective and passed with satisfactory results. But to what capacity was it best served? To provide the trainees with the knowledge applicable to their assignments? To provide a bathroom facility for a countless number of students? We thought we had achieved both.

In appreciation for our effort, the school district organized a *fête*, or celebration, to commemorate the grand opening of the latrine. Hoards of children, their siblings, their parents, and local citizens had gathered around the two-cabin structure. All told, there may have been two hundred people or more. As planners and engineers, we worried over whether the pit was large enough to handle the volume of feces that it might receive at this event. There was no telling what they had in store. Fortunately, for everyone's sake, there were no food vendors anywhere near the school, and the latrine only had to support the occasional bowel urge.

The ceremony began with an introduction of the key players. Members of the community were given the opportunity to say a few words, and they all praised the Peace Corps for our contribution to the school and our concern for the welfare of the children. With the crowd growing restless from the vain recognition of others, selected trainees discussed the oral-fecal cycle using posters animated with cartoon Africans defecating, wiping, washing, and eating in a hygienic manner. Others discussed the importance of hand washing and regular latrine maintenance through songs we hoped would linger in the children's psyche long after we were gone.

Slowly the crowd moved in, reducing the area within the open middle, jostling their way to a better view. Sensing the deterioration of the crowd's patience, the administrators dubbed the latrine open for business and introduced the long-awaited troupe of *tam tam* drummers. People were soon dancing freestyle to the rhythmic percussion of African drums and soul-penetrating voices in the name of the modest offering from the Americans. Trainees brave enough to experience cross-cultural humiliation joined in, dancing to their own beat and uproar from the crowd.

A cloud of dust appeared over the chaos, obscuring the latrine, and it lingered as the festivities approached their end. We packed up our soiled posters and the last of the tools and piled back into the pickup trucks. As we drove away, I took one last glance and waved to the young children running behind us. The latrine was the only tool left behind—the bright rose color of its doors now tinted an earthen brown from the settling dust.

Project number two was called the Sub Sector Project, or SSP, by the instructors. Despite its ominous, bureaucratic-sounding title, it was no more than an effort to venture into the community to address a particular sanitation deficiency, and then coordinate with the benefactors on a sustainable solution. Due to time constraints, we were to check-in on previous years' SSPs rather than starting something new. Topics included hygiene education in the schools, the impacts of pigs and goats defecating in high-traffic areas like the market, and the defiled sanitary condition at the bus station. I chose a topic I thought would add variety to my training and offer a reprieve from building shit repositories. I hastily selected gray water disposal systems.

For much of Senegal, gray water from bucket-baths and dishwater is discarded into a hole in the ground. This hole is known as a *puit perdu,* meaning "lost pit"—an accepted necessity in the village courtyard. Our concern was that people thought disposing gray water in an abandoned well or an infrequently used corner of the compound was an adequate solution to their gray water problem. If they could no longer see the gray water, it was conveniently and thoroughly disposed. Out of sight, out of mind. Aquifers and groundwater were not topics of dinner conversation, and bacteria were generally not visible impurities in their drinking water. As long as the sun and soil absorbed the liquid from their discarded waste, they could live with a small pile of debris to be swept into oblivion over time.

I was paired with trainee named Megan, and we were to visit a compound that had received three different *puit perdu* design types the previous year. Megan was short with long curly red-hair, and fluent in French, having spent time in Paris during college. After graduating and working a stint with the World Bank, Megan joined the Peace Corps as a community development trainee with the UEM program. She was one of eight people I could be paired with for two long years. As a result, I frequently appraised our relationship in anticipation of the merger.

Our first visit to the host compound was cordial. We greeted everyone with traditional Senegalese handshakes and repetitive sayings that expressed a mutual interest in family, health, and welfare. And we explained what we wished to accomplish on the heels of our predecessors. We then toured the compound and the three pits.

Pit number one, their primary system, was a large circular hole, one meter deep by one meter in diameter located in the middle of the courtyard. According to the old plans, the pit would be lined with concrete blocks to keep soil from caving in, but with gaps for gray water to infiltrate into the earth. On top was a circular concrete cover with a hole in the center where the gray water was poured. Upon removal of the heavy cover, we found the hole full of a dark putrid slime, bubbling and emitting an awful stench—the cause and effect of their problematic system.

We moved on to pit number two in a far corner of the compound by the side of the house. Research indicated the pit would contain a metal barrel much like the 55-gallon variety used to contain oil or fuel reserves, with holes punctured in the sides for drainage. When we removed the cover, there was only a dry shallow pit. Where the barrel ended up was anyone's guess, and nobody claimed to know its whereabouts.

Pit number three was simply a hole filled with large rocks as a crude trickling filter, but nobody knew where it was constructed. After an unsuccessful search for the ruins, we presumed the system was buried and gone. Sand had filled the pores in the system; time had created pores in their memory.

We suggested maintaining two systems: the one they used most with the block liner and a secondary system with a perforated barrel. We scheduled a time the following week to clean their primary system of its mire, after which we would complete the digging of the secondary system. All that was needed was a barrel, which the family agreed to supply. Things were looking up.

One week later, we returned toting implements of construction, ready to help purge the compound of its sanitary woes. However, it appeared that no one was prepared to wage our war on sludge. The elder men were sitting under fruit trees drinking palm wine, the children were busy playing *futbol*, and the women were making dinner. There was no sign of the young men—the workforce.

A man named Amadou and four teenage boys arrived an hour later. Amadou was average height for a Senegalese man. He had short, clean-cut hair and an athletic build, with an air of confidence that suggested that he might be the head of household. Turns out, Amadou was the official contact for past SSPs so he was familiar with the scope of our work. He stated that his family was adamant against furnishing materials for the training exercise, and he was aggravated that we would suggest such a thing. He stated it was the responsibility of the Peace Corps to finance a replacement barrel for the pit, just as they had financed materials for the initial three systems, and that no work would proceed until that point. Suddenly, things had gone south.

Further inquiries revealed that the Peace Corps had indeed allowed previous groups to spend funds on the SSP. Our group would've been allowed to spend funds this year, but unanticipated expenditures from the latrine project forced the agency to distribute monies more prudently, warranted by absolute necessity.

Megan and I returned to the family compound a few days later, equipped with more than just shovels and a wheelbarrow, this time we arrived with a development strategy. Neither of us thought that the Peace Corps was responsible for replacing the barrel since relocated under their charge; nor did we wish to succumb to demands for monetary contributions, sensing it was a possible ploy by Amadou to take advantage of the trainees' giving nature and access to funding. We confronted Amadou with our stance and told him there was no money for follow-up endeavors. If his family wanted our assistance, it would be without financial support. We did not want his family to demand a new barrel each year, and we did not want trainees in future years to have to sustain the donations of their predecessors.

Realizing that a shiny new barrel may be too valuable an asset to bury in the ground, we softened our stance and offered a compromise. If the family could generate a used barrel that maintained its shape and strength, we would generate the materials needed for removable pit screens that would filter the discarded wastewater of its larger solids and reduce the obstructions to the system. No mention was given as to how one generated their contributions, just so long as it was produced within one week.

Megan and I assembled the wood-framed screens with scrap materials found or pilfered from more ambitious training projects. When our instructors asked us how we were progressing, we responded with optimism but offered limited details. We knew the stalemate over the barrel could result in an inability to accomplish anything. We also knew that our final presentation could be marred by our refusal to purchase an eight-dollar barrel. Nevertheless, we were committed to our stance no matter what the outcome, believing it was the most sustainable approach.

Again we made the familiar trek to the compound across town. With each step we became more and more anxious, worried we had alienated the family by challenging them beyond their means. As we closed in on the gate, we could hear the sharpening of metal, the pounding of steel—preparation for a bloody insurrection against Peace Corps trainees. They would have our heads mounted on wooden sticks before the day's end, our bodies simmering in a large kettle (or a new metal barrel) for a great feast.

We entered with paltry screens in hand, ready to accept our fate for the mismanagement of the project. To our surprise, we were not ambushed by men with freshly-honed metal objects. Instead, we observed the diligence of young workers perforating a metal barrel with hammers and spikes. The barrel was far from new. The bottom was missing and the sides were slivered with rust and decay, but it held its tubular shape as specified. It would suffice. Amadou and his family, for whatever reason, ended our stalemate and produced a barrel. All was right with the world.

We dug the hole for the new pit behind the house and placed the barrel on a thin bed of gravel. Around the rim, we placed flat stones and mortared them together as a base to support the concrete cover and keep rainwater from flowing in. The work moved quickly. In a couple of hours we had their secondary system online, ready for use.

We then moved to the primary system in dire need of cleansing. The workers and I put on shin-high rubber boots borrowed from the training facility, gasped for one last breath of fresh air, and started shoveling the muck into wheelbarrows. Each thrust conjured the nastiest, most wretched liquid-solids ever produced, making our labors seem like punishment for a crime of humanitarianism. From there the waste was hauled off to another hole and mixed with dry soils to dissipate into the subterranean world.

Normally I would revel in an opportunity to perform physical labor for a cause that I believed in, sweating and blistering until its satisfying completion. But this chore was different. Instead of enjoying the rewards of a hard day's work, we endured a rotten, festering mélange of food refuse, bathwater, and indiscriminate effluent stewing over time. Our tools and clothing were ruined forever. Our respiratory systems defiled by hazardous emissions. Our patience and disposition taxed to their limits, burdened by self-inflicted idealism. This was not your ordinary, fulfilling, labor-intensive work. This was the *toughest job* I was supposed to love.

As the tenth week of our training approached, so did my second homestay visit with my Senegalese family in rural Thiés. The majority of the trainees had visited their families during the time between mandatory stays, but I had not. My family was a good distance away, discouraging impromptu visits, and I did not feel like I had made a great impression during my first stay. I felt more like a burden than a family member. Some might say these are one and the same, but to me it was all the excuse I needed to avoid visiting more often.

Instead of taking a taxi, I walked through *quartiers* I had yet to explore, and I purchased a bag of oranges as a small token of my gratitude. The entire family was there by the sandy road to greet me like before. The children accepted the oranges with pleasure, devouring them within minutes, dropping the peels where they stood.

Later in the day, I was on the stairs with Sylvean and his friends talking about Michael Jordan or a slice of American popular culture that young African boys heard about in the local media. The conversation turned into requests for merchandise through my contacts back in the United States. Most notable were requests for new Air Jordan sneakers if it wasn't too much trouble, to wear while they were playing *futbol*.

Every one of these boys could have used better footwear for athletics, as they usually wore cheap plastic sandals called Jellies and could easily turn an ankle (though they hardly ever did), but I was frustrated with their demands, discouraged that I'd failed to relate to them in a more significant way. It became apparent that I was viewed merely as a resource, a conduit through which to obtain commodities from the most excessive nation in the world. No matter how much I assimilated to their African culture, I could not eliminate the disparity that existed between us. To them, I would always be a white American—their sneaker pimp.

I convinced Sylvean to take a walk with me down the street to the elementary school where we had built the latrine. It had only been a few weeks since the ribbon-cutting festival, so I did not expect a major decline of its condition. More than anything, I needed the walk to evade the demands of Sylvean's friends, and to contemplate a new approach the next time I was requisitioned for the bounty of American goods and services.

Dusk had settled on the school grounds and the colors that gave character to objects faded in the shadows, then into night. I walked around the latrine, observed its simplicity and inspected its workmanship now that the site was not crowded with people. I was content with the results, proud that my efforts had seemingly contributed to the welfare of the human populous. I then attempted to enter the facility and validate the structure I'd helped construct. I tried the door handles but they were both locked. How could this be? Why would anyone lock the doors to a latrine? Our latrine! There was nothing to steal inside: no light fixtures, no toilet paper, no plunger or cleaning products. Perhaps the custodians did not wish to clean the random defecate of passers-bye with poor aim.

Sylvean hypothesized that the latrine was the school's possession, theirs to lock if they so chose, and the less waste that dropped down its hole, the better off the school. Not understanding the gist of his statement, I asked him why the school would be better off if they did not allow the use of the latrine. He responded simply, "Less shit, less smell." Without rebut, I walked across the schoolyard, dropped my pants and crapped behind the bushes, abating my load and his argument into one big smelly pile.

That night I stayed at my family's house, sleeping on the same mat on the same concrete floor as I had during the previous homestay, again displacing my small adoptive siblings to their parent's room. When I awoke I packed my things and prepared for the walk back to the training facility. With only two weeks left, I needed as much time to prepare for the SSP presentation and to study for the final French exam. My homestay family understood. I said my goodbyes knowing this was likely the last time I would see these generous strangers who'd accepted and tolerated my presence in their home.

Before I plodded down the sandy road, Soleil brought everyone out to the front of the house and presented me with a parting gift. Near the front door was a lone five-foot-high tree encircled by a few courses of concrete block, planted in remembrance of our chance encounter—a tree his children named Scott. The tree appeared weak and feeble, without a trace of foliage or budding. It looked more like a severed branch stuck vertically in the ground. Without care and watering, it would not last through the first dry season, but that didn't matter. The gesture alone was one of the best gifts I've ever received, supplied out of pure goodness. I am glad to have known Soleil—a man of character, whose actions prompt one to consider the strength of one's own character.

At long last, the day of our SSP presentation had arrived. For weeks I was troubled over the prospect of speaking French in front of a crowd and embarrassing myself with nervous drivel. I was also concerned about promoting a strategy that seemed rather aberrant, alienating all those involved. Moreover, I did not feel that Amadou and his family were satisfied customers due to a lack of capital expended; I even felt that our presentation could turn contemptuous if Amadou, listening to the other groups summarize their projects, thought his household was slighted in any way.

We gathered in the courtyard dressed in the most formal attire from our limited wardrobes and awaited the arrival of our Senegalese guests. The first group arrived late but relatively punctual. Then, one by one, the others arrived without mention of their tardiness, following a timetable measured by sunlight and sentiment and not by the mechanical markings of a clock; a timetable referred to as "African time" because of its disparity in pace with the developed world.

To maintain a semblance of order, each of the seven or eight UEM groups were allowed to invite two representatives from the community, preferably those who'd played a substantial role in the project. Most complied with this request; ours did not. Arriving with Amadou were five or six teenage boys dressed in collared shirts and trousers.

We assembled to the foldout chairs in the large classroom building. Each presentation was intended to last thirty minutes, with contributions from the trainees and the recipient business or family, but this modest timetable was never achieved. Presentations lasted over an hour, on average, supplemented with a colorful, sometimes outrageous barrage of local politics from the more outspoken Africans in the crowd. At times the atmosphere seemed out of control and beyond the realm of sanitation, but the instructors eventually reined them in.

Megan and I sat patiently, listening to each group present their findings. Then we took to the podium and delivered our spiel. I recited prepared fragments of events outlined on a cue card; Megan finished up with a qualified fluency that carried the presentation, clarifying my introduction and carefully summarizing the project. Then Amadou took to the podium, exalted by a rousing applause from the devout teenage lackeys sitting in the back. Amadou praised our steadfast commitment to the health and welfare of his family and our devotion to the agency's mission without mentioning the incidents that had caused us so much grief and anxiety. After a few routine questions, Amadou took his seat to another rousing ovation, consummating the SSP presentations on an optimistic note.

I talked with Amadou while his posse polished off the donuts and fruit punch and posed for photographs. Amadou had done this sort of thing before, and he knew the drill: remain positive, put on a good show, and reap the rewards of sugary snacks and successive training projects. He did not need to be informed about hygiene, sanitation, or the mission of the Peace Corps. He was proficient in the subjects, probably knew more than we did. Amadou was successful because he'd already learned a valuable lesson as a young African man—that of his own sustainability.

As a consequence of our concerted efforts, the Peace Corps arranged for Megan and I to serve as volunteers in the small town of Bangolo in the western highlands, where the Ivory Coast borders

Liberia. For the next two years, we would work together toward fulfilling the mission of the Corps. We would also rely on each other for immediate social and logistical needs while isolated from our compatriots. If the relationship faltered, we could not easily separate. If there were irreconcilable differences, we could not part ways and split up our friends and colleagues without creating a bitter, hostile living environment. We had no choice but to endure this unique marriage or retreat to the States.

During the final week, each volunteer candidate met with a panel of instructors to be tested in French speaking and comprehension. It would be our final test before receiving consent to board the plane for the Ivory Coast. Each candidate, waiting outside in the hot sun, was called into a dark cavernous room by a commanding voice. The individual took a seat in a lone chair facing the instructors for what felt like an interrogation. Failing this test meant failing to volunteer.

With the same enthusiasm they'd maintained through twelve weeks of training, the language instructors rattled off questions about the candidate's daily routine, their family and friends, and Africa in general. At first the questions were elementary, without much attention to accent or tense. As the trial continued, however, the questions became more complex. The candidate labored on, inspecting the instructor's body language for clues, asking additional questions to join the discourse with fluency. Surprisingly, French flowed between instructor and trainee, like water through a pipe for some, like sludge through a pipe for others, but it still managed to flow. We'd progressed so quickly we had difficulty convincing ourselves how much we'd learned. When the day was done, every volunteer candidate was granted permission to make the flight to the Ivory Coast.

On our last evening, we packed our bags and stacked them in the courtyard for loading onto buses. Sleeping that night was difficult, restless, like reliving Christmas Eve as a child. At 0400 we were roused by the final strike of the wrought-iron gong. We returned our bed sheets, mosquito netting, and other borrowed items, then bid our caretakers' farewell, glanced at the enclosed paradise one last time, and boarded the bus for Dakar.

Light from the morning sun arrived just ahead of our two-bus caravan, illuminating a cast of characters who found livelihood at the airport. The first to approach were the market women. They sprang from the roadside prep table and jockeyed for position. Swiftly and aggressively, they moved to the passengers who displayed the most interest, thrusting their large aluminum bowls into the air at the open windows, clamoring for their wares to be chosen. There were cakes and breads, fruits and fish, and small *sachets* of water, all similar in presentation and apparent quality. The only distinction between items was fabricated from one's own prejudices. If I liked the swirl pattern of chocolate within a particular vanilla cake, I might choose from that bowl. If the bowls were chock-full, I could've assumed it was a fresh batch and jumped at the chance or assumed it was a slow day and bargained more. Or, if I thought that a fair and valiant battle was waged, I might have rewarded the victor by procuring from the contents of her bowl.

On this day, I quietly rebelled against the more forceful and dominant market women with their collusion of size and strength, and I selected my breakfast from a small girl of about ten years old in the back of the crowd. As I called her over to the window, she approached without a word, balancing the large bowl full of cakes on her head while she calmly worked the knot in her skirt where she kept coins to make change. It was possible that she completed the only sale of her career based solely on her meek appearance, or maybe that's how she gained advantage over the market giants, with a subtle appeal to the traits of a left-leaning American, proud of his liberty to choose, deliberate in his attempt to help the weak amongst the disadvantaged from time to time.

A gauntlet of men was lurking in the shadows. Some were traveling, as indicated by the formality of their attire, while others were employed by the airline in some fashion. The majority of those welcoming us that morning were self-employed opportunists, contemplating the best technique to capitalize on the affluence of travelers. They came at us from every direction. There was the common beggar, the entrepreneur selling junk from the cover of a gym bag, and the thief creating diversions to pilfer what he could. They were convinced that if one could afford a flight to and from distant lands in luxurious comfort, then one could certainly contribute a portion of one's wealth, voluntarily or otherwise. To my knowledge, none of these characters succeeded. Instead, it was our group who made out like bandits, capitalizing on the richness of a culture and the unique opportunity of Peace Corps training.

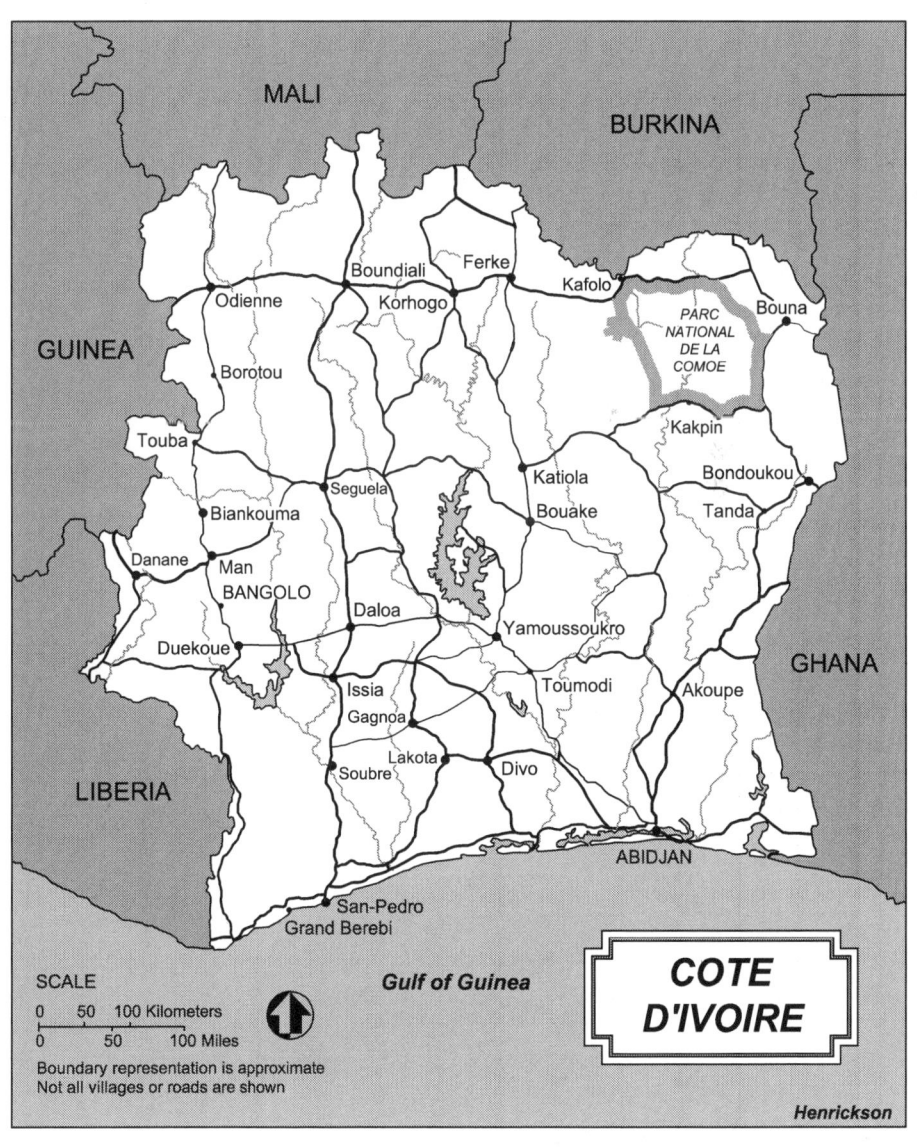

CHAPTER FIVE

ADJUSTMENT

After the diversion to Lagos, Nigeria, we landed at the Felix Houphouët-Boigny Airport in Abidjan. As the doors opened, a blast of hot humid air replaced the controlled temperature of the cabin. I immediately started perspiring through my clothes and gasping for relief. We made our way down the stairs, across the tarmac, and into the terminal where large murals of Papa Boigny—the country's beloved president and champion of independence from 1960 until his death in 1993—hung on the walls with praise and acclaim.

We were then bused to the rural *quartier* of Yopogone for three weeks of "in-country" training, which included an orientation to health and safety, bicycle repair, and how to stay out of trouble, much like the sessions performed in Senegal but specific now to the Ivoirian culture. In-country training also involved a series of excursions. The first was to travel up-country to villages and towns to observe veteran Peace Corps volunteers at their sites for a few days. From there, we were to travel to the urban hub closest to our assigned sites to meet our host country counterparts for a regional seminar on teambuilding. Finally, before our training was complete, we were to report to our sites and stay there for a few days, introduce ourselves to the community, arrange for housing and other logistics, and think about our commitment. If we survived all of that, and made it back to Abidjan without getting lost, killed, or disenchanted, we could swear in as Peace Corps volunteers.

On the first evening, we were invited to the Peace Corps hostel in the Deux-Plateau *quartier* to attend a party in our honor. So at dusk, after we were showered and presentable, four dozen Americans began wandering around the streets of suburban Yopogone with the hopes of hailing a taxicab. With no taxi dispatch center, walking aimlessly was our only strategy. Surprisingly, word got out that there was money to be made in Yopogone, and within a half-hour we were all loaded into taxicabs and on our way to the festivities.

The Peace Corps hostel was in a rather affluent section of town, located amongst the international and diplomatic community as a safety measure against crime or crisis. The houses were as large as any middle-class dwelling in Middle America, protected by the same concrete security walls they had in Senegal. The streets of Deux-Plateau were mostly paved, with grassy islands between driveways that flourished with tall prospering coconut, papaya, and mango trees. Parked along the street were Mercedes-Benz and Volkswagen luxury cars imported from Europe to complement the neighborhood's European lifestyle. At each gate there was a security guard dressed in a dark blue uniform, waiting for trespassers, perpetrators, or someone to talk with to relieve the boredom of sitting in a chair for a twelve-hour shift. Most of the time, day or night, these guards were sound asleep.

We entered the compound to a driveway that led to a carport attached to a two-story building. The building had a ground-level porch of marble tile with three columns that held the second-story overhang in place, and there was a manicured lawn in front. And sitting on the porch, in rickety wooden chairs, were real live Peace Corps volunteers. I had spent so much of the previous three months getting to know my own group that I never gave much thought to the volunteers already in-country, our future comrades and cohorts. Twenty-six American men and women had lived and worked in the I.C. for a year before our arrival, each with their own unique experiences. And it suddenly dawned on me that we weren't the only Americans with a fresh perspective on life in Africa, just the latest ones.

Our arrival appeared to be a welcome change, not because of any lingering dysfunction or disdain within their group, but for the sake of variety. Our arrival represented a new era, a transition to a new pecking order. Above all, our arrival was the advent of new faces, fresh meat on display, and the evening's event was our introduction to the desperate, horny crowd. We spent the evening outside drinking local beer, listening to stories of hardship and sickness, prodding the volunteers for information to help allay our fears of the unknown. At times the stories seemed outlandish and extreme, fabricated for a reaction, but if the guinea worm was capable of crawling out of a person's leg, creating its own egress through the skin, then anything was possible, even their bullshit.

We toured the hostel that would become a home away from home. The first floor had a kitchen, a bathroom, and a medical office with examination room to care for medical evacuees from countries all over West Africa. There was also a large living room with a wall full of books brought or discarded by the previous volunteers, a television with a video cassette recorder for ailing medical patients, and four old grimy couches facing the television screen in various tiers.

Upstairs there were six rooms of varying sizes, with beds or mattresses in every conceivable space. A person's possessions were kept on top or at the foot of the mattress due to a lack of storage space. The rooms were ventilated with louvered windows and a ceiling fan, but that still wasn't enough to relieve the stifling heat and humidity, or to remove a peculiar stench from an area beset by Americans with differing hygiene practices. "The hostel smells of ass!" uttered one volunteer, almost proud of the achievement out of a futility to control it.

When everything was done to gain an endorsement from the group, we headed back to the streets and found taxicabs to bring us back to Yopogone. I was one of the last to leave, around midnight. I got into a cab with two other trainees. We gave the driver directions but we still got lost. While on the highway, driving well below the speed limit, we were pulled over by a police car that was hiding behind an overpass. The officer made us exit the vehicle and wait near the trunk. He took the cab driver aside and started shouting at him. The cab driver was not intimidated. For ten minutes they argued, then the officer returned and began interrogating us too. But his French was too quick and emotionally charged to be understood by us neophytes. Over and over we asked the officer to repeat his question, as if we were in language class, until finally the cab driver turned to us, rubbed his thumb to the tips of his fingers, and said, "*L'argent! Il veux de l'argent! Dollar!*"

Our first night in the Ivory Coast, our first bribe, and all I had on me was 1000 CFA (U.S. $2) tucked away in my back pocket. My fellow trainees had about the same, if not less, as the Peace Corps had yet to dole out our per diem allowance for the next pay period. Between the three of us, we barely had enough for cab fare, and none of us had our passports as they'd been gathered up by officials to obtain our *carte de séjour,* or in-country identification.

When the cab driver repeated the request, we asked him why, as if we had no idea what a bribe was. "Why does a police officer want our money?" we said in poor French that lent conviction to our ignorance. So the officer made us wait by the side of the road until we were ready to understand. He was not about to say he was bribing us. Bribes should be relinquished naturally, without argument, like a toll at an interstate tollbooth. If he went so far as to say the money was a bribe instead of a preordained fee for passage, he might feel defeated. And though we feared the consequences of challenging the officer, we also felt that shroud of invincibility again, with an added duty to resist the bribe and fight corruption.

The officer's supervisor drove by and pulled over beneath the overpass. He got out in a hurry and walked toward the taxicab as if he were going to beat the bribe out of us, shaking us upside-down by the ankles as the money we'd lied about fell from our pockets. After a short discussion with the bribing officer, the supervisor stood before us as we cowered in fear, sweaty and disheveled from the heat, front pockets turned inside out like rabbit ears to accentuate our depleted financial condition. The police had no choice but to throw us in jail or let us go. We were obviously unprepared to partake in this new ritual, and too pathetic to take up any more of his time.

By sunup we were allowed to leave with the driver and return to Yopogone. The next day we heard stories on the radio about Abidjan police officers rounding up individuals without identification and detaining them indefinitely until they determined their identity and criminal background. Some of these detainees were found to be robbery offenders and were facing capital punishment or serious time behind bars. We could have easily been among them if conditions or personalities had been different, and the Peace Corps would've had a difficult time bailing us out.

I speculate we were detained not because we were feared as an unlawful sort but because we were Americans who weren't employed by the influential or diplomatic and we could be harangued for money. We should have been an easy source of revenue. I speculate we were also released because we were American in a country that regards Americans in a favorable light, not with disdain for a history of unwelcome political, judicial, or military involvement (not as of

1995, anyway). Despite this valence of protection, anything could still happen. The social climate in the Ivory Coast was unpredictable and unfamiliar, not a place to champion all of one's idealistic causes. It was evident I would need to make adjustments in my behavior, or end up a displaced martyr in a foreign land.

* * *

When I filled out my Peace Corps' application, one of the questions was: *Do you have a placement preference? Check the box next to those regions or continents you are willing to serve.* Conventional wisdom told me there was only one correct answer if I wanted to compete with the traditionally heavy volume of applicants. By checking "no preference," with my technical background and the understanding that flexibility was the highest attribute sought by Peace Corps officials, I was all but assured placement somewhere in the world.

I was asked this same question during a three-hour interview with a Peace Corps recruiter in Boston to determine whether I was truly flexible or just apathetic. Instead of defaulting to "no preference" as I had done on my application, I expressed a desire to travel to the African continent above all other locations. My request was sincere. I have always wanted to go to Africa and experience the mystique and hardship as portrayed in books and television and movies. I also thought, by proclaiming a preference, I might exclude locations that were not as appealing to me.

My recruiter was a young, thin, African American man named Anthony who'd recently returned from an extended three-year term somewhere in southern Africa. During the interview, Anthony would raise his left hand and snap his fingers when new ideas emerged or when I said something noteworthy. He wrote furiously in the margins of my application, charged with an excitement beyond what his new office job warranted.

Pausing from his notes, he asked, "How's your French?" This being the same French I'd last uttered eight years previous as a high school junior.

I responded, "Not so good."

Another snap of the fingers "That's alright! That's alright!" he assured me, still focused on his train of thought. "How would you feel about serving in Côte d'Ivoire?" he asked, escalating his inquiry and my hopes beyond the application process.

"Côte d'Ivoire. Sounds good," I muttered, not sure what place on earth he meant or if he just now decided to conduct the interview in French to test my skills.

"Côte d'Ivoire. You know, the Ivory Coast," he confirmed.

"Yes," I acknowledged with confidence, as if there were no need for his clarification. "Where along the Ivory Coast?"

Another snap of the fingers, Anthony spun around on his swivel chair to a corner of the room and pulled out a large rolled-up map of Africa from a cardboard box full of maps. He spread it out on the desk, weighing down the top two corners with his office supplies while the rest of the map unraveled at our feet.

"Here's Côte d'Ivoire, between Ghana and Liberia," he said, pointing. "I'm not sure where you'd be placed. That would depend on the program. Côte d'Ivoire came to mind because we are starting a new Rural Sanitation program in the villages, but you're also qualified for the Urban Environmental Management program."

I pulled my chair closer to his desk while the word "qualified" reverberated through my ears, and I looked carefully at the whole of West Africa. Compared with the other countries on the continent, the West African countries were small slivers of land laid out like a developer's subdivision along oceanfront property. Anthony's index finger was still resting on the letter "e" of "Ivoire" when I realized that the Ivory Coast was a full-fledged country, not just a segment of ocean coastline—a country officially named the Republic of Côte d'Ivoire, often translated to English on maps and in documents for us Anglophones.

As I inspected the map further, Anthony read from a synopsis on Côte d'Ivoire with facts and figures so as not to frighten applicants from a potential commitment: *Côte d'Ivoire became a French colony in 1893 after fifty years as a French protectorate. The country is named for its once abundant elephant population and ivory resources. It has a shape and land area about the size of the state of New Mexico, around 322,000 square kilometers, with a population of approximately 14 million. Côte d'Ivoire gained its independence from France in 1960, creating a centralized multi-party government consisting of a president and a National Assembly. The first president to hold office was Felix Houphouët-Boigny, representing the Parti Democratic de Côte d'Ivoire. Felix "Papa" Boigny held the Office of the President for over 30 years and may have endured longer if not for his passing in 1993. Henri Konan Bedie, also of the PDCI party, succeeded Papa Boigny and continues to run the country to this day....*

Partially tuned in to Anthony's narrative, I inspected the country's serpentine boundary with Ghana, Burkina Faso, Mali, Guinea, and Liberia, meandering along a segment of river or cartographer's discriminating pen. A network of roads appeared like thick varicose veins, delivering the lifeblood of trade to thousands of primary and secondary cities and villages, with most of the roads mysteriously terminating at the borders of surrounding countries, marking the differences in development between Côte d'Ivoire and its West African neighbors. The map had both green shaded portions (representing the dense forest areas of the south and west) as well as beige (representing the northern savanna or the migrating desert of the Sahara). Only minutes had elapsed since my discovery of Côte d'Ivoire and I was already excited about its possibilities.

Anthony continued ...*Côte d'Ivoire is made up of over sixty ethnic and tribal groups consisting primarily of the Baoule, Senoufo, and Bété, with clusters of Diola, Bambara, and Malinké, and significant populations of non-Ivoirian Africans, Lebanese, Asians, French and other Europeans. The country's religions include Christianity, Islam, and Animism, and the country's resources and chief exports consist foremost of cacao, coffee, and timber, but also of cotton, bananas, palm oil, pineapple, rubber, sugar, and diamonds. Côte d'Ivoire is the number one producer of cacao in the world.*

"Sounds like my kind of place," I acknowledged.

Once again Anthony raised his left hand and snapped his fingers. He was optimistic I would be accepted into the Peace Corps once my application cleared its respective gauntlets. He was also confident my placement would be in Côte d'Ivoire, matching my skills and education as a civil engineer to the program's needs, despite my shortcomings as a linguist or geography buff. Anthony and I shook hands and parted company. At last, an interview with promise.

In the months to follow, I prepared for the likelihood I would be called to service; only the most fastidious within Peace Corps could ruin my chances now. I was so sure I started telling friends and family about Côte d'Ivoire, trying to find out what they knew. My aunt Barbara, who enjoys traveling and collects traditional masks from different parts of the world, knew a little about the country. As a youth she was fascinated by West African culture and thought about traveling to the region one day, right up until she read a story in *National Geographic* back in the 80s.

Aunt Barbara described an annual ritual of a tribe in southern Côte d'Ivoire to drive "bad spirits" out of town. While possessed by the powers of sorcery, members of this Ivoirian tribe would perform acts of self-mutilation to accomplish an exorcism of the spirits, with both the act and its cure prescribed by "good spirits" whilst entranced. The writer for *National Geographic* detailed how one possessed soul stabbed himself in the stomach, removed a portion of his intestines, pushed them back in, then closed the wound by rubbing it with eggs, herbs, and kaolin, healing it instantly. The writer, still at a loss for what he had witnessed, saw this man in a bar later that day, a picture of health. Asked how he felt, the man responded by saying that his beer gave him more heartburn than the wound.

I looked at my aunt with skepticism. She wasn't the type to embellish, but I didn't entirely believe her story. She insisted I read the article and do more research before I made my decision.

If the story of the stomach stabber wasn't enough to test my resolve, my aunt described another instance where the same *National Geographic* writer was amongst the Wé tribesmen, better known as the Guéré of the western highlands. He was attending the panther-man ritual near Bangolo, celebrating the return of tribesmen who'd spent the last seven months living in the jungle, seeking to become wild animals. The writer was violently attacked by one of these panther-men when he tried to take a photograph of them prowling around the village compound. A man from the village intervened and rescued the writer using a whip, but he was forewarned: the panther-man ritual was dangerous, sometimes fatal.

"Watch, you'll end up living with the panther-men of the Guéré tribe," my aunt said jokingly, not fully aware of her own mystical power to predict my future.

* * *

After a week of redundant health and safety briefings at the Yopogone facility, the time had arrived for our first up-country travels. Trainees were distributed amongst volunteers like kids divvied-up for a ballgame or schoolyard competition. Most of us were sent to cities close to our sites so we could become familiar with the services and transportation we'd come to rely on. Others would not have that opportunity. These brave or unknowing souls were to be posted where no volunteer had been before, to uncharted territory, to villages in the northern hinterlands, far from conveniences. For these few, there was hardly a nearby region to speak of, let alone services to inventory. They were along for the ride, sent with volunteer hosts who could keep them engaged in the experience before their journey north.

I was traveling up-country with my buddy Tim on an all-expense paid trip to a town named Issia, 300 kilometers northwest of Abidjan on the well-developed paved road system. Tim and I, and our volunteer host Dennis, were dropped off at the edge of *le grand gare* in the *quartier* of Adjamé, which serviced most of the country's overland travelers. Though Dennis insisted that the cab driver take us directly to our bus company, he refused, claiming poor road conditions and high crime.

We followed Dennis on foot down a narrow dirt road that led into the heart (or the gut) of Adjamé. The road indeed was in poor condition, rutted and channeled by the previous year's rain and the non-stop bus traffic. Lining the road were market kiosks poorly constructed from wood and corrugated aluminum, and fortified with scrap materials of the same. These kiosks displayed food, clothing, electronics, hardware, gadgets, and gizmos. We carried our bags tight to our backs to discourage theft, fighting through the crowds, and we arrived at one of the many bus companies that traveled up-country to Issia and beyond.

Dennis purchased our bus tickets because they knew him at the counter as a regular traveler and would not augment the price as they would for outlanders such as Tim and I, as indicated by our looks of marvel and dismay. I boarded and sat in the seat corresponding to the handwritten number on my ticket. From the exterior, the bus looked brand new, with new tires, new lights, and a new paint job. Inside, the bus was bastardized with old chairs and flooring, and a dashboard control from the days before independence.

Just like in Senegal, roving peddlers of merchandise and food were clamoring at the windows, showcasing their wares in aluminum bowls balanced on their heads, shouting a product name into the air until someone showed an interest. Make eye contact with one of the vendors and it was as good as calling them over for a sale. If business was slow and there was no pressing need to be elsewhere, the vendor would stand patiently within range, trying to entice a customer into the bargaining process, not with words or a salesman's pitch, but with silence, playing upon an individual's ability to rationalize a need for a product over time.

Our bus pulled out, proceeding with caution, careful not to tear mechanical parts from the bottom as it bucked and swayed with the rolling terrain, navigating the turns, obstacles, and deep channels that defined the path. Once we reached the highway, our bus was free from the quandary of the Adjamé *gare*, capable of speeds in excess of 120 kilometers per hour, sharing the road with other buses and commercial trucks, but rarely encountering automobiles, as they were owned primarily by the upper class. Here, public transport was the only way to travel, quite literally.

In three hours we made it to the junction of Lakota and the first *gendarme* police stop. When we pulled up to the barrier, one of the officers stepped out from a shade structure and dragged a long board perforated with nails from the road and off to one side. He motioned to our driver to pull over up ahead, to make sure his paperwork was in order and to check for taxable items.

This stop was not a surprise to the drivers. It had been there for years as one of the numerous checkpoints around the country, and the drivers knew the drill. For some, their paperwork would get them through; others who were known to be of non-Ivoirian descent had to submit paperwork of a different kind that would yield a profitable day for the *gendarme,* but not discourage the drivers or anger the *gare* chiefs. Supply and demand had reached a balance along the roadside in Côte d'Ivoire.

Born from the *gendarme* stop were two dozen food kiosks that served fruit and fish, omelets and brochettes, and plates of rice with either tomato or peanut sauce. Food was available almost any time of day or night to meet the needs or cravings of passengers to and from Abidjan. Tim selected an avocado sandwich while I purchased a beef brochette sandwich with tomatoes, onions, and avocados on a freshly baked baguette. Little did I know this delectable roadside treat would be the first of many dietary mistakes I would make during my service. Digestive assimilation had begun without the controlled environment of a training facility and its sanitized meals.

Two hours beyond Lakota, we arrived in Issia and walked a short distance to where Dennis lived. His house was like the others—a one-story concrete dwelling with numerous rooms painted all one color out of frugality, familiarity, style, or all of the above. It also had electricity, piped water to the bathrooms and kitchen, and a spacious yard with fruit trees enclosed within a six-foot high concrete wall. Dennis needed only the large living area, the kitchen, and the master bedroom in order to feel at home; that, and the porch outside where he spent many of his non-working hours. Tim and I were offered the two spare rooms, but one of them was full of recyclables and skeletons from small animals, so we chose to share the other.

We relaxed the remainder of the day and into the evening, drinking beer on the porch in slat-back wooden chairs with denim cloth seats made by a local craftsman. We talked with Dennis about life in Africa and that of the volunteer. Dennis was thin, pale, and older than Tim and I by about ten years, and it showed in the recession of his hairline and his idealism. He was well-educated, sharp-witted, and esteemed by his Peace Corps' colleagues. Dennis was a UEM volunteer and had a site partner with whom to collaborate named Peter, a third-year volunteer who'd spent his first two years in the Central African Republic. Peter lived across town with his girlfriend, who had served in C.A.R. along with Peter but did not officially commit to a third year in Côte d'Ivoire despite the hard work she'd put in toward improving Issia's sanitary conditions.

That night Tim and I slept on plastic woven mats on the concrete floor. The mats did not offer much in the way of comfort, but they did separate us from the dust and grime that had collected on the floor over time. In the corner of the room, by the power outlet, an oscillating fan worked to make sleeping and breathing more tolerable in the oppressive humidity. While this may not sound like much, a mat and a fan made all the difference in the world.

The next morning we followed Dennis down to Issia's municipal offices in hopes of observing his work and lifestyle. Dennis maintained an office in the rear of the municipal building, but he rarely spent time there, as most of his work was field-related, coordinating with other agencies and individuals. He was, however, required to make the rounds each day and offer salutations to his municipal colleagues, filling them in on the progress or shortfalls of projects as they listened with feigned interest.

We walked down the road to the landfill where Peter and his girlfriend were overseeing a composting project adjacent to enormous piles of degradable and non-degradable garbage. With them was an African farmer wearing torn and tattered clothing that barely covered his body, and a straw hat with a large brim to protect his head and face from the hot midday sun. They worked together mixing and turning the compost piles, aerating the microbial feast that would become rich soil to be sold to local farmers.

We climbed down into one of three holes, each with a different mixture of fruit and vegetable matter, leaves, soil, manure, and moisture to determine which would yield the better, more rapid, product of soil. Tim, like me, was a recent graduate in engineering. His aspirations were to someday work in the design of space or ocean craft, but for the next two years compost piles and shithouses would have to suffice. Tim looked the aeronautical part with his clean-cut wardrobe and military-style hair cut, resembling Ed Harris as the Gene Kranz character in *Apollo 13*. Peter explained the composting process as we rummaged through the rancid piles with a stick, trying to identify specific items. Dennis, meanwhile, was pissing into one of the holes, adding the urine he claimed was the essential ingredient for blue-ribbon soil. "His only contribution," quipped Peter.

Having learned enough about compost for one day, Tim and I scrambled up the side slope and out of the hole. We returned to Dennis' porch by noon and called it a day. Too much sun could sap us of our strength if we did not hurry back for our two to three-hour nap. When we awoke, we both felt the onset of illness—Tim with flu-like symptoms and me with stomach and digestive pains. Tim showered in the guest bathroom, hoping the cold water would revive his senses, but such was negated when his Peace Corps-issue thermometer revealed a temperature of 103°F which gave way to a slight panic that he had somehow contracted one of the fatal illnesses hyped during training. Meanwhile, I lay curled up on my plastic mat, floored and fatigued by what I suspected were the effects of the bacteria brochette I had eaten the previous day. I'd had a feeling something wasn't right, but I kept on eating it because I craved something different in my diet; meat or something other than rice and sauce. And anyway, how bad could it get?

That evening, Dennis reclined on his porch, drinking beers, listening to his John Prine cassettes. I spent hours in the bathroom in complete and utter anguish. When I was not shitting the vile from my lower extremities, I was retching through my mouth, gasping and heaving in what felt like a precursor to implosion. At times I would prepare myself in a particular position, sitting on the toilet or kneeling against it, only to guess incorrectly, making an absolute mess of the area in front of the toilet.

During my most cathartic moment, however, the rules of bodily function changed completely as the orifices of my mouth, nose, and sphincter all participated, with perfect cadence and co-operation, in an explosive exorcism of all things ingested over the past few days. When Tim had showered earlier, the water soaked the bathroom floor, turning the dust and dirt into a thick paste of mud and slop. Now merged with the biohazards from my illness, the mixture clung to my bare lower legs, my feet, and my hands as I hoisted myself from the floor to a leaning position against the wall and over to the doorjamb. I opened the door with a feeble push to find Tim there laughing hysterically.

In just a few hours, I lost what felt like ten pounds, and my skin had turned jaundiced and pale. The mud mixture began to dry on my limbs, but I was too weak to chip it off. Tim woke me every thirty minutes throughout the night to make sure I had enough Gatorade or re-hydration solution in my system, using everything we had in our light blue plastic medical suitcases. As soon as I ingested anything, though, my bowels would undulate and I'd scuffle away to rid the thirst quencher from my battered body into or near the toilet.

I survived the evening but didn't get any sleep. Tim's sickness subsided, especially when he found out that he was supposed to shake the thermometer beforehand so the mercury would display the true reading of his temperature, which turned out to be 98.6°F. Dennis concocted a voodoo potion he claimed could heal both of our ailments, which was just stock from boiling a leafy vegetable he'd acquired in the market (or his compost heap). The remedy smelled awful and I refused, lest unleash the fury that now monitored my food and beverage intake. So Dennis did what we expected him to do. He guzzled the stuff so it wouldn't go to waste, down the hatch in a series of gulps, culminating in a satisfying belch.

Tim and I later shared our fears that we might become like our host. Not that Dennis was a bad person or led a miserable existence; in fact, he was decent guy and a stellar host. But Dennis had become cynical about development work, which was reflected in his comments and routine. We did not want to believe that this was our only path, that when we reached a certain point in our service we would begin forsaking our ideals (and keeping animal bones in our spare room). Little did we know that Dennis was the quintessential volunteer in many ways, and that life wasn't so bad working partial-days, spending evenings on a porch drinking beer, and listening to John Prine tunes. Life could've been much worse, and, at times, it couldn't have gotten much better.

We bid Dennis a fond farewell, thanked him for his hospitality, and hiked down the road toward the Issia *gare*. As we approached the oil-stained sandlot of idling vehicles, a hoard of teenage boys dressed in shorts and ragged T-shirts hurried towards us, tugging at our baggage in the direction of their employer's bus or van. A fight broke out between the boys as to who among them deserved our business, as if they decided where and how we traveled without our consultation.

Tim and I were continuing northwest 200 kilometers to the city of Man to meet and interact with our Ivoirian counterparts. Buses heading in that direction had already gone through Issia earlier in the day and would not pass again until evening, so we were talked into riding a smaller vehicle called a *gbaka* for the same price. *Gbakas* are essentially minivans with more of a box shape than the sleek, aerodynamic design of their American cousin, generally painted white, unlike the colorful charm of the Senegalese bush taxi. *Gbakas* are used primarily for local travel between villages or towns, back and forth throughout the day until the demand for the service declined around dusk. Occasionally, they travel greater distances, depending on their permit or arrangement with the *gare*.

We were quick to reserve the front seat with the driver. The *gbaka* filled up quickly, with four passengers to a row where three was intended. The passengers gasped and sighed about the overcrowded conditions, about the lack of fresh air in the idling vehicle. I didn't think conditions were bad, but I was not pinched between two large sweaty Diola women reeking of fish from a long day at the market; not on this day, anyway. I got to sit up front by the window, shotgun, the most sought-after place on the *gbaka* for sheer comfort and spaciousness.

A teenage boy was busy tying down baggage on the roof, mostly market goods or travel bags, and occasionally chickens or goats depending on the season or holiday. The *apprenti*, or apprentice, was responsible for loading and unloading baggage, engaging potential passengers, paying off officials, and running errands for the driver in the hope that someday he too would be an owner or driver. When the *apprenti* completed his work on the roof, he hopped down and signaled to the driver by banging loudly on the door with his hand. As the *gbaka* began moving, the *apprenti* ran alongside, reached for a hold on the vehicle frame, and slid the door shut, pulling himself inside with the other passengers.

For entertainment, the driver played music from Côte d'Ivoire and Mali on the cassette player, mostly Monique Seka over and over at a volume that reverberated through the vehicle, trembling the nerves. Not one person asked the driver to turn the music down or acted as if the deafening noise infringed upon their rights as patrons. It was as if Monique's voice was a pacifier of sorts, something familiar that calmed and comforted, even if the blown speakers made it sound like Monique was singing underwater.

Just as entertaining were the decorations inside this *gbaka*. On the dashboard was a swath of thick shag rug trimmed to perfection around corners and vent openings—the same shag rug I had on my bedroom floor when I was a kid in the 70s. On the control panel there were random decals of food and beverage products, anchored by stickers of Maggi bouillon cubes placed in deliberate patterns around the controls. Of all the ornaments, though, nothing compared with the 20-cm plastic Batman doll in its original cardboard packaging, dangling from the rear view mirror by a string.

The topography from Abidjan to Issia was flat and the road was straight. The area had recently been logged out, leaving significant patches of land now suitable for farming. A sporadic patch of tall native trees rose from a grove of pineapples or rubber as far as the eye could see, standing testament to a once thick tropical forest. Further northwest, the road took on different characteristics, up and down hills, over rivers and lakes, around sharp bends where enormous trees loomed large and grass grew until it collapsed under its own weight.

Many villages once connected by a beaten path now have a paved thoroughfare running through its center. These villages use modern transportation to acquire goods and services, but not all have adapted to paved roads in Côte d'Ivoire. The chickens and goats have definitely not adapted, losing many of their brethren to full-size buses and *gbakas* traveling at breakneck speeds. Some residents have not adapted either, walking without a care in the world across a highway that didn't exist when they were children, only to be overcome by absolute terror when they look up and realize a fully loaded bus is driving through their village and heading straight for them.

I too had not adapted to the ease of travel in Côte d'Ivoire. I expected, prepared for, and even desired to endure long hours, days if need be, to reach my site from Abidjan for the sake of the voyage, the adventure, and the post-service bravado that Peace Corps volunteers seem to share. Alas, I could reach my site from Abidjan at an average rate of 100 kilometers per hour, which seemed too fluid to claim the hardship my ego desired.

One hundred kilometers beyond Issia, at Duékoué, we turned due north, where the road seemed to straighten out but the hills grew more pronounced. Farmers walking or riding one-speed bicycles on the shoulder of the road shuttled back and forth between their village and the field, carrying bundles of wood, baskets of manioc, and large containers of the highly touted palm wine on their handle bars.

On the east side of the road, we passed the town of Bangolo, my home for the next two years. Bangolo was not located in forested terrain as I imagined or as suggested by its inclusion within the dark green sections of my topographic map. Bangolo didn't appear to be very populated either, and it did not resemble the other UEM sites. Bangolo was more of a village, or a series of villages, that met one day in a broad valley by the road. Houses were built from mud and thatch, concrete and aluminum—a clash or concord between traditional and modern. However, it took no time to spot the conditions that justified my assignment. There was trash everywhere, in piles and strewn about open spaces. Heavy rains had eroded the dirt roads, with massive channels that cut deep through the right-of-way. And men were frequently seen urinating by the roadside. Though these conditions may not have signified an environmental disaster, sanitation improvements were definitely in order.

Fifty kilometers beyond Bangolo, Tim and I arrived at the *gare* in Man and parted company with our driver and his caped-crusading co-pilot. We braved the main street, thick with workers, vendors, travelers, and loiterers-turned-travel-agents in this semi-tourist town, and flagged down a taxi to take us to the Collège Moderne for our teambuilding seminar. On the way, we were treated to a spectacular view of the city nestled within a lush green forest against the backdrop of the Monts de Dan mountain range.

In the days that followed, we swapped stories with trainees still traumatized from their site visits. Megan and I became acquainted with our African counterparts, who had been sent from the municipality of Bangolo. We discussed our roles and what was expected from both factions for a successful alliance. Megan's counterpart was about thirty years old, with a typically round, rich brown Ivoirian face, a handsome smile and pleasant disposition. His name was Dogbo and he was assigned to the town's Social and Community Services. My two counterparts were both agents with Technical Services, field supervisors of minimally skilled labor teams. Their names were Charles and Dao, products of Bangolo and the local Guéré tribe. Charles was about thirty, tall and meaty; his scalp was shaved clean, which enhanced his cool calm demeanor. Charles had a good sense of humor and he'd laugh at our humiliating stories of adjustment. Dao, on the other hand, was short and deviant, his hair nappy, his teeth yellow and black from years of neglect.

Our counterparts seemed fond of Megan and the other female trainees as demonstrated by their overt gawking and flirting. At first I dismissed their behavior as harmless, the innocent craving and ardor for unique and attractive American women. But their innocence didn't last long. The contingent from Bangolo repeatedly made crass comments, and Dao kept grabbing at the breasts of an Ivoirian employee of the college without any shame or consequence.

The Peace Corps warned female trainees that they might experience this type of behavior in their assignments, as Ivoirian men were not accustomed to working with women, especially American women in technical and supervisory positions. It was too progressive for them. Unfortunately, it looked as if Megan might be a victim of this behavior unless adjustments were made, either in their deference for women or our tolerance for chauvinism. A compromise of values would need to be reached for everyone's sake.

Following the seminar, Megan and I and our new companions left Man together and we caught the next *gbaka* to Bangolo. There, we were subjected to an array of blank stares, wondering why a tall bearded white guy and a small red-haired white girl were clinging to Bangolo's native sons, following them around like ducklings or newborn calves. We paraded from the *gare* down the one paved road until we reached Main Street and the town's lowland *bafon,* or swamp, then south a short distance to the municipal building.

According to Charles and Dao, the first order of business was to meet the mayor and his staff, which was considered custom and courtesy for new arrivals. But our tour was anticlimactic, even somewhat disappointing. Not a lot of the offices were occupied. The only ones who had shown up for work that day were the secretaries and typing pool employees. The rest of the staff, including the mayor, was occupied or out of town, unaware or uninterested in attending our prodigious arrival. Custom and courtesy appeared to be optional in Bangolo.

Without an itinerary or supervisor's directive, the guys could only think to show us around town, introduce us to the people they knew and the places they hung out. Our first stop was to Dao's favorite open-aired *maquis* called Parrain II (translated as Godfather II) for an afternoon beer. Likewise, our next stop was to Dao's second favorite *maquis* called Chez Becky for another afternoon beer; and so on, accompanied by much of the same harassment and unruly behavior we'd witnessed at the seminar in Man. By the end of the day, the only places we patronized were the bars, and the only people we knew were the town's barmaids and barflies.

Eventually our chaperons grew tired of us, and we grew anxious to find a place to stay for the next few days, to unwind in the seclusion of our own space and collect our thoughts. Both Charles and Dao recommended L'Auberge Kamonda, not far from the northern terminus of Main Street, a hotel they claimed to frequent, which seemed strange considering they lived in Bangolo.

Up until this point, we hadn't paid for anything except transportation. Part of the arrangement was that Bangolo would provide lodging for their volunteers. As we checked in, I noticed there was no exchange of currency for our room. There was also no exchange of currency for the beers we drank that afternoon. Not that I was complaining. The municipal staff seemingly paid for goods and services with credit and political clout, selecting only establishments that honored such payment.

The primary manager of the Kamonda was a young Guéré man named Jerome, originally from Duékoué. Jerome welcomed us to Bangolo ceremoniously, ecstatic to show off his place to, perhaps, the first Americans to stay at his hotel. His partner, Mathias, was also a young Guéré man eager to make our acquaintance, but he was shorter in stature and with a fraction of the energy and charm as Jerome. They gave us a tour of the one-story hotel, showed us the ten small rooms, the shared bathroom, the bar and nightclub, and the common TV room, built like a square fortress around an open courtyard where the owner parked when he came to collect his profits. But there were two rooms they did not show us—large rooms with air-conditioning units hanging from windows, accessible only through the TV room. These were reserved for *les notables, le grand types*, big shots from the government or from money that might pass through Bangolo one day without notice.

I retired to my small room and sprawled out on the bed, partly because I was tired but mostly because the bed monopolized the entire room and there was no place else to go. I thought about my commitment to the Peace Corps and the people of Côte d'Ivoire. It was the first time I questioned whether this was really what I wanted to do for the next couple of years. The twelve weeks in Senegal was a breeze, with African culture being spoon-fed to us from our comfortable confines, affording little opportunity to realize what we had gotten ourselves into. After spending a couple days with my Ivoirian colleagues, my goal to be a catalyst for change seemed daunting, if not impossible. What contribution could I possibly make with my colleagues drunk by early afternoon and their hands full of barmaid instead of shovels and trowels?

I went outside to the courtyard to get some air. Jerome came out of his office and sat with me on a concrete stoop at the end of the driveway. We were talking about America, about Bangolo, about how the municipality is months behind in paying their bills, when a man walked in through the gates and introduced himself as Monsieur Assis, Chief of Finances for the municipality. Jerome rushed off to a room and returned promptly with a young girl in her teens, presenting her to Assis for his approval. I watched with skepticism as the man and the young girl retired to the room.

"What was that all about, Jerome?" I asked.

All he said, with a big smile, was, "Ahh, Monsieur Scott!" as if my question was rhetorical to bring attention to the young girl's company. The Kamonda was a brothel and the municipal staff were their most frequent customers.

The following night I decided to leave for Abidjan one day earlier than scheduled. My demonic stomach ailments had barely subsided and now they were raging once again, so I felt that medical treatment was in order, *toute de suite*. Jerome accompanied me to the *gare* by the two-lane highway, showing me the shortcuts from the Kamonda through the *bafon*. The next bus was scheduled to arrive into Bangolo at 1800 for the eight-hour trip to Abidjan. But 1800 came and went without a bus.

Jerome waited with me in the sharp florescent glow of the station depot despite my plea for him to return to work. Insects were thick, bombarding the lights under the pavilion until they got hung up on the lights and fried. During the wait, I anguished over whether the Peace Corps was for me. An idea of my service had been cast long ago, enhanced by the splendor of my recent experience in Senegal; now I was forced to confront the bitter end of my expectations, shattered by residents who did not need or want my assistance.

I insisted to Jerome that he return to the Kamonda, that I was healthy enough to endure the wait on my own. Jerome, with his cheerful face and friendly nature, responded that if Megan asks him if I got on the bus safely, how could he honestly answer unless he sees me get on the bus with his own eyes. It would be a lie he could not convey.

The bus pulled up to the *gare* three hours late. I handed my baggage to the *apprenti* and took my seat as I watched Jerome slowly head off under the streetlights, turning every so often to ensure the bus was moving. In a moment that transpired unexpectedly, Jerome, a young hotel manager and novice pimp, reversed my attitude about the Peace Corps by exhibiting the values I had hoped to discover, and restoring my faith in custom and courtesy. Perhaps the Ivoirians did not require my assistance, but I would require theirs to learn and to prosper.

CHAPTER SIX

HISTORY

The Peace Corps got its notorious start as an election-year initiative put forth by John F. Kennedy during the 1960 presidential campaign. However, Kennedy was not the only politician to promote the idea of an overseas volunteer corps. The concept had been broached by politicians from both parties during the mid-to late-50s, but it never gathered much traction. When Kennedy spoke of a *Peace Corps* in the days leading up to the election, it intrigued a nation, resulting in votes that helped him win the presidency. During his inaugural address, Kennedy's emphasis on public service was evident with his now famous call for Americans to: "Ask not what your country can do for you; ask what you can do for your country." And the Peace Corps was born.

While Kennedy is credited as the program's founder, fewer people know about Robert "Sargent" Shriver, Jr.—political advisor to Kennedy; husband to Kennedy's sister Eunice; and father to journalist Maria Shriver. As the Peace Corps' first director, Sargent Shriver was the driving force behind the program from March 1961 until February 1966, under both the Kennedy and Lyndon B. Johnson administrations. Shriver was also the founder of such programs as Head Start, VISTA, and the Job Corps, and he was active in the Special Olympics, founded by his wife Eunice.

When the Peace Corps was in its developmental stage, Director Shriver convinced Kennedy to keep the program apolitical. In his report to the president dated February 28, 1961, Shriver emphasized: "The Peace Corps is not a diplomatic or propaganda venture but a genuine experiment in international partnership." While Shriver believed this was the key to the program's long-term success, statesmen from the United States as well as host country leaders from around the world would test his design time and time again.

The following day, on March 1, 1961, the Peace Corps was established under Executive Order 10924. And later that year, on September 22, 1961, Congress authorized the Peace Corps Act, declaring its purpose:

> *To promote world peace and friendship through a Peace Corps, which shall make available to interested countries and areas men and women of the United States qualified for service abroad and willing to serve, under conditions of hardship if necessary, to help the peoples of such countries and areas in meeting their needs for trained manpower.*

During the Kennedy presidency, the Peace Corps had no problem filling assignments with qualified candidates, led in part by recent graduates from the Ivy League schools. And by most measures, the program was a bona fide success. Then in the late 60s, as the Vietnam War was ramping up, the Peace Corps became a haven for draft dodgers, and volunteers became more active speaking out against the actions of their government. Volunteers take an oath to defend the U.S. Constitution, but they also maintain the right to free speech under the First Amendment. Still, some members of Congress questioned whether the U.S. should be financing anti-war protests, and volunteers were reprimanded or dismissed for offenses related to their candor. In the early 70s, the early termination rate amongst volunteers was at an all-time high, and there was a marked drop off in new applicants. The Peace Corps attempted to recruit older, more technically skilled labor in lieu of the typical liberal arts graduate, but this approach had mixed results. Also in the early 70s, the program was obscured under a new agency called ACTION, which signified a shift away from Kennedy's Peace Corps. For Peace Corps purists and others alike, this was a huge mistake. Volunteers already had a difficult time promoting the agency, now they had to explain the subtleties of their own country's divisive and pendulating politics. Fortunately, the Peace Corps was restored to prominence in 1979 when President Carter made it a fully autonomous agency and rededicated the program to its apolitical humanitarian causes. In the 80s, the program advocated small business development and strategically placed volunteers to advance democratic principles. And in the early 90s, as the Soviet Union dissolved into separate states, the Peace Corps found its way into Eastern Europe and Central Asia, angling for an opportunity to promote world peace before these areas had a clear identity.

The Peace Corps' first involvement in Côte d'Ivoire was in 1962, when volunteerism across the U.S. was on the rise with Kennedy's call-to-service, but the program was discontinued in 1981, mainly because the country was doing so well economically.

In 1985, the Ivoirian government increased the number of self-governing cities from 27 to 125, and decentralized government responsibilities such as trash collection, enforcement of various sanitation codes, and infrastructure development. It also shifted many burdens to the municipalities at a time of an economic crisis linked to declining cacao and coffee prices, which resulted in a recession and a devaluation of the currency. As jobs in the cacao and coffee industries dried up, people flocked to the cities in search of job possibilities, straining the fragile sanitary infrastructure by the weight of their numbers and by sanitation habits not suited to a dense urban setting. Not only were Ivoirians on the move, struggling to meet their economic needs, but there was also an influx of refugees from neighboring Liberia (a country founded in 1822 by freed American slaves) fleeing the hardships of a bloody civil war.

With dwindling government funds and increased responsibilities, Côte d'Ivoire faced serious sanitation and solid waste problems. Against this backdrop, the Peace Corps designed the Urban Environmental Management (UEM) program to help fledgling municipalities, and they returned to Côte d'Ivoire in 1990, supported by the traditionally successful Health program in the rural areas and the upstart UEM program in the urban centers.

By all accounts the UEM program was a success, resulting in an expansion into new cities in 1995. Bangolo was selected as one of those new cities, possibly because the Minister of Interior hailed from the Bangolo region, as there seemed to be areas in much worse condition that did not have volunteers.

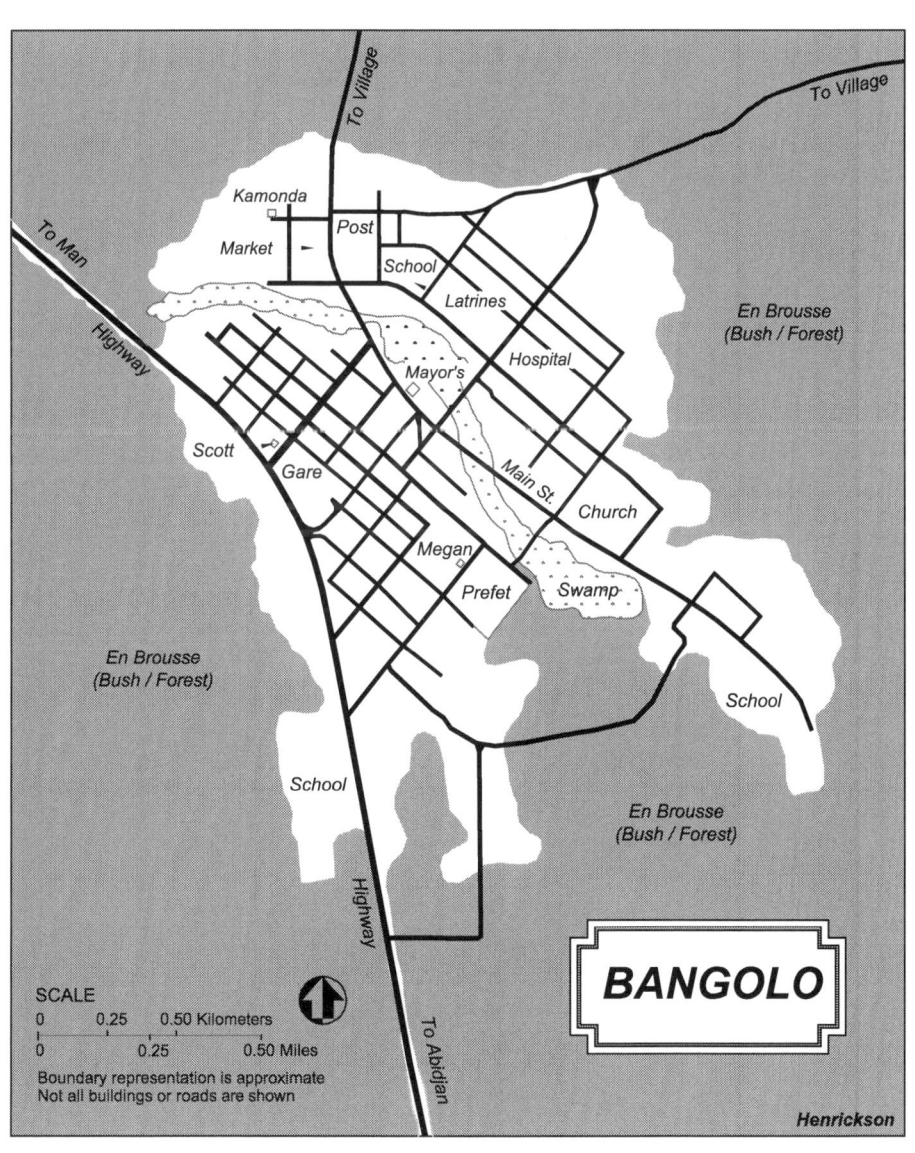

CHAPTER SEVEN

INAUGURATION

I arrived in Abidjan early in the morning and took a cab from Adjamé to the Peace Corps hostel. I was anxious to meet with the medical staff, but I first needed some sleep after a full night of travel. I crashed in a bed on the second floor, but I had to search to find one not already occupied by someone ill or distressed. The sun's rays were beaming through the windows, heating up the room; it was impossible to prolong my rest without inundating the sheets with perspiration. I went downstairs to find that others had gone through similar periods of purging and had also cut their site visits short by a day or two.

All morning, trainees lounged on couches in the living room until summoned to the medical office. We described our symptoms to an unabashed medical team comprised of an Ivoirian physician named Dr. Lomo and an American nurse named Jan. These women had seen their share of sickness in developing countries, and our afflictions were nothing new, putting me at ease that they could handle the most wretched of African disorders. They were caring maternal types who reminded me of the mothers of my childhood friends, so I felt comfortable discussing almost anything with them.

For those of us with stomach issues, the true culprit would not be revealed until our feces were examined in a medical lab at the U.S. Embassy. To ensure a fresh sample, a supply of Styrofoam cups was placed next to the toilet for us to fill, label, and place in a cardboard box for daily delivery to the lab. However, shitting in a ten-ounce cup posed a significant challenge. My accuracy since Issia was highly erratic. I was lucky to keep everything moving in a downward direction and into the toilet. Then there was the problem of volume. Not since living in the States had I experienced a regular bowel movement. Everything now came out in a liquid torrent. There was no way I could get fifteen ounces of loose stool into a ten-ounce cup without a skillful maneuver or by making a horrible mess.

Volunteers explained the situation was futile. Making a mess was inevitable, which could lead to per diem and a few days at the hostel if something was found. The charlatans in the group took it one step further. They suggested we fill the cup to the brim until capillary action was all that kept the contents from spilling out, and then cautiously place the lid on the cup. When the Embassy lab technician pulled the lid away, the sample would overflow onto their gloved hands and workspace—a small reminder to the expatriate community of what we had to endure in the bush that they did not with their mansions and maid service. As it turned out, I spared the lab technician any deliberate mess or message and was rewarded with a confirmed case of Shighella.

For those with philosophical issues, finding a remedy was a bit more difficult. Every trainee had seen or experienced some aspect of African culture that did not meet up to their expectations, the same way my Ivoirian counterparts did not meet up to my own. As a result, the euphoria of living in our perfect Peace Corps Africa began to fade, leaving us with the reality of our true commitment. Trainees realized they could not contribute the way they once thought possible. Some believed they could contribute more to the world at large if they returned home where progress was measured differently. Then there were those who just flat out missed their family and friends and could not bear to be absent for another holiday or momentous occasion. If the trainee could not overcome these nagging symptoms, or could not find solace in their new home, then they returned to the States as soon as possible.

The official terminology for leaving the Peace Corps under one's own recognizance is called early termination, or simply, to ET. This did not include those who were asked to leave for administrative reasons, or those with a debilitating sickness or injury, or those with a family emergency, and it did not include those who totally lost their minds and had to be "psycho-vac'd" as we'd say. It included only those who grew tired of being sick, of eating the same bland starchy foods, of being far from home, of the frustrations of adapting to a new culture, or dealing with too much bureaucracy.

Leaving the Peace Corps by early termination was a decision for the individual to make. If a trainee or volunteer felt they were compromising their goals and happiness by staying, and they wanted to ET, nobody was going to stand in their way. The staff was sensitive and supportive, and did all they could to facilitate the voyage home. A person terminating early could be on a plane within a couple days once their decision was relayed to the administration.

To terminate early, however, did not promulgate a successful stint in the Peace Corps. It's certainly not something one wants on their resume or graduate school application, and not a story one wants to relay to those back home in any great detail. Nobody who aspired to join the Peace Corps and went through all it took to be accepted wants to ever say, "The Peace Corps was not for me," because serving in the Peace Corps is the envy of a great number of warm-blooded Americans who wish to contribute to the greater good, regardless of how difficult or futile the assignment.

This attitude was especially true amongst those who remained. There was veneration for the group as a whole, as an entity, enduring and thriving as a noble cult of idealism. If one were to quit this group, they were given all the support they needed to move on without incurring additional anguish or direct ridicule, but as soon as they were gone, they were forever recognized as someone who couldn't hack it, couldn't adapt, and was lesser than the rest of us had to be to continue. For many of us who contemplated the possibility of ET, this burden of failure and humiliation was good enough reason to stick it out.

On April 7th, three months to the day since flying from New York to Senegal, we officially swore in as Peace Corps volunteers, trainees no more, released unto the world to save it from imminent peril. The swear-in ceremony was held on the manicured lawn at the lavish home of Ambassador Hume Horan on the type of hot humid day that exemplified each day in the IC. Most of the veteran volunteers attended the inauguration in support of our big event, watching in comfort from beneath the shade of a large tent while we sat in chairs on the lawn, tormented by the sun and the reality of a new pecking order.

Speeches were delivered by the likes of Ambassador Horan, members of the Ivoirian community, and the Country Director for Peace Corps Côte d'Ivoire. All were very inspirational and motivating. They spoke of the remarkable 34-year history of the

Peace Corps and the first group of volunteers dispatched to neighboring Ghana in August of 1961. They spoke of the qualities and attributes of the volunteer, such as Yankee ingenuity and egalitarianism. They spoke of the Peace Corps mission and the execution of its three goals: *helping people of interested countries in meeting their need for trained men and women; helping promote a better understanding of Americans on the part of the peoples served; and helping promote a better understanding of other peoples on the part of the Americans.*

During the event, I reflected on the legendary account of Peace Corps trainees from the 1960s, subjected not only to language and occupational training but also vigorous physical conditioning and psychological monitoring. I recalled an old *National Geographic* from 1964 that I had read while sick at the hostel. The entire edition was dedicated to the Peace Corps with photos of trainees running through obstacle courses, rappelling down sheer vertical cliffs, and plunging into deep water with hands and feet tied, trying to pluck objects from the bottom with their teeth before returning to the surface. It resembled a watered-down skills-camp for privileged white American kids. These physical tests were not required, but trainees were asked to try, to challenge themselves, to summon unexpected strength from within to build confidence. As a result, trainees were pushed to their physical and mental limits, trying to conform to the expectations of the program, some requiring psychological evaluation and care in the aftermath.

A volunteer's training no longer consists of this probation of one's physical and psychological endurance. Some would attest that the current rigors of training probe far enough. As I looked around at my training group, most wearing sunglasses and formal attire, I wondered how many could hold up to the sort of challenges the Peace Corps used to dish out in their heyday. Who would stand and who would fall if we had to perform harrowing feats of strength and fitness? How did we compare with the coveted volunteer crop of the 60s? Were we as physically and mentally tough? There was no way for me to know, though I speculate if the Peace Corps could maintain recruitment numbers with physical and psychological testing, it would still be a valuable aspect of training today.

With the sun at its apex, we raised our right hands in unison and repeated the words of our Country Director in an oath to our Constitution:

I, (Name), do solemnly swear (or affirm) that I will support and defend the Constitution of the United States against enemies, foreign and domestic; that I will bear true faith and allegiance to the same; that I take this obligation freely, without any mental reservation or purpose of evasion; and that I will well and faithfully discharge the duties of the office on which I am about to enter. So help me God.

We were then strongly cautioned against any subversive activity against the United States, though we were under no obligation to agree with or defend the policies of the U.S. government as part of our First Amendment rights. Membership has its privileges. We were now Peace Corps volunteers.

After an evening of celebration at the hostel, Megan and I loaded our possessions into a taxicab and proceeded to Adjamé for the bus ride to Bangolo. No more formalized training or practicing. It was time to go to work, time to hunker down and get something done. Time to volunteer. For what, specifically, we did not know.

We arrived at the *gare* at sunup and waited in the cool morning shade, keeping a close eye on the spectacle that was our modern bicycles, with gear shifters and brake levers and shiny colors that beckoned for attention. Our bus was late from an overnight voyage out of the northwest. I sat and watched the commotion until midday when all activity ceased for *sieste*. When the sun was directly overhead, I was lulled into a lengthy slumber and did not awaken until 1430 when the *gare* resumed its activity. By then our bus had arrived and was ready for departure, seven hours late.

The road to Bangolo was along familiar territory, having traveled to Man and back once already. We reached the *gendarme* stop in Lakota in three hours as expected. Police officers gave us a hard time about our bikes, accusing us of not paying the tariff on their purchase, but we had all sorts of official-looking certificates and receipts fabricated by the Peace Corps, which meant nothing to anyone except *gendarmes* looking to supplement their salaries from foreign travelers, illegal commerce, or new volunteers.

A half-hour beyond Lakota, our fully loaded bus was in need of mechanical attention. The driver pulled over by a small roadside village and allowed the disconsolate passengers to exit and stretch their legs. "*C'est quoi ça? Vraiment!*" the crowd sighed angrily as they took turns looking under the hood to witness the problem firsthand. The driver and *apprenti* did not have the tools or parts required to make the repair, and it would be some time before we went anywhere in this bus.

The small village by the roadside consisted of a dozen circular mud huts on either side of the pavement, nestled within the dark green foliage of young papaya and banana trees. The village came to life, assisting in any way they could. One group helped by jacking up the front end of the bus and blocking off the tires so the vehicle would not roll down the slight slope. Another group pulled large clumps of tall grass from a nearby field and laid them out behind the bus, staggering them every few yards like prehistoric flares to warn oncoming vehicles of the situation.

The driver sent word ahead to Gagnoa through drivers with other bus companies. They were to contact the *chef,* or chief, of the Gagnoa *gare* and specify the items needed to get the bus back on the road. Skeptical that I would arrive in Bangolo any time soon, I climbed a small embankment and reclined against the base of a tree. I watched as the sun filtered through faraway branches, then disappeared over the horizon. Darkness came fast as there was no electricity in the village, and the driver and his helpers scrambled to put everything in order with the last of the ambient light.

A *gbaka* on its last run of the day between Lakota and Gagnoa delivered the items that were requested, including a mechanic from the *gare*. They worked by lantern light with an audience of sixty tired and frustrated passengers. When the bus came down off the jack stand and was firmly grounded, the passengers re-boarded and went to sleep in their seats, despite ongoing repairs. I remained outside, virtually alone as most villagers had retired for the evening.

A soft glow from a smattering of lanterns revealed the location of each home within the darkness. The lanterns could not stay on all night, not without a significant investment in fuel, and one by one they went out. A solitary light escaped through the window of a mud hut directly behind me, ten yards away. I listened intently to the talk within, eavesdropping on an African language so foreign I could not fathom that actual words or sentences were being conveyed, only garbled noises. The garbled noises were unexpectedly joined by the slow rhythmic beat from a primitive drum. The noises became voices in song converging into beautiful spirited music. And the music translated all that I overheard, all the beauty and sorrow from the soft glow of the lantern light.

At 2200 the mechanic completed his work and we were on the road again. With five hours remaining until we reached Bangolo, our trip would continue but the day was complete. I could have spent every moment held hostage by our transportation woes, writhing with impatience, worrying that my time was being squandered by this turn of events. But that was never a consideration. There was too much to observe, too much to marvel at, from the daily routine of a bustling *gare* to a melodious celebration of austere and difficult village life. My disposition toward change and adversity was becoming increasingly flexible; Peace Corps training was beginning to pay dividends.

Megan and I arrived in Bangolo early in the morning, too early to expect anyone to be awake. Megan stayed by the main highway guarding our pile of possessions while I shuttled back and forth to the Kamonda on my bike, reducing the pile with each trip until we could make one final ride together. Jerome unlocked the solid metal door to the compound when he heard us stirring outside. He had been worried that something had gone wrong or we had decided not to return. Now that we were there in good health and spirits, Jerome's pervasive smile came to life again.

He helped us carry our baggage to the two big rooms with air-conditioning (the rooms reserved for the *les notables*). My room had a large bed, a table and chair, and a shower, and though my air-conditioning unit did not function, I had actual floor space in which to maneuver. Jerome thought to give us the big rooms while we were away in Abidjan. He was frustrated that members of the municipality and *les notables* from out of town rarely paid for their rooms, or for the young girls that kept them company; not that he would receive prompt payment for putting us in these rooms, but at least he felt empowered. This was Jerome's quiet but brave rebellion against the authorities that governed his world, and we had profited.

Megan and I had a unique opportunity in Bangolo. We figured few if any of Bangolo's citizens would recall the volunteers that imposed their beliefs between 1962 and 1981. This was a blessing in disguise. On the one hand, we were able to start with a clean slate and could establish certain ground rules. For example, if we told the community that it is customary for Americans to vacation frequently to relieve the stress of adjusting to a new culture, why shouldn't they believe us? They had no prior basis from which to determine how Americans lived or behaved other than what they saw on the television. I could have lived vicariously as *McGuyver* if wanted.

On the other hand, starting from scratch was going to require a tremendous amount of time and energy to introduce our program and explain why we were there. It would probably take our entire service. As volunteers opening a new site with a projected 10-year mandate, introducing our mission and establishing relationships for the next group of volunteers was about all the administration expected, as they knew it would take months to prove I was not *McGuyver*, and even longer to explain why I had left the riches of America to dig shitholes in Bangolo for two years.

As the logical place to start, volunteers were encouraged to work with the mayor and the municipal staff. The mayor of Bangolo presided over a community of 8,000 to 10,000 people, and his staff carried out his directive for most community services. Without the municipality, Bangolo would still be operating as a large village ruled by a *chef du village*. Another reason to work with the mayor was that he was our sponsor, paying our rent and supporting our program. If we did not coordinate our activities through the mayor's office, we could jeopardize everything and be asked to leave.

Despite all the training, neither Megan nor I had a clear idea what our jobs would entail, and we had many questions. Would the mayor expect us to work as employees of the municipality and abide by the municipal work schedule? Would we be given an office? Would we supervise our counterparts or would they supervise us? We would not find out until the mayor returned from Abidjan.

For the first week we focused on meeting and greeting the staff, making the rounds bright and early each weekday morning to avoid the hot sun. When you entered through the front door, you'd have to pause long enough for your eyes to dilate from the bright sunlight to a large windowless room. In the center of the room, there was an elevated stage with wooden benches resembling the pews of a church or assembly hall. Surrounding the stage was a hallway that led to offices along the perimeter. We'd always start our daily circuit at the first office on the right, and continue counterclockwise, searching each office for a presence.

Dogbo, Megan's counterpart and head of Social and Community Services, claimed the first office and was always on time at 0800. It appeared he had very little work to do each day and we often caught him napping or tired with his elbows on the table, arms supporting his head, hands covering his eyes. He claimed he was not hungover, that his fatigue was related to *palud,* or malaria, which came and went with the sun. As a result, he struggled to inspire the masses, but Dogbo was a friendly guy, genuine, always happy to see us.

Then there was the *chef de technique* named Dago, a Bauolé native from central Côte d'Ivoire, who appeared enormously tall against the small stature of the Guéré. He was responsible for the operation and maintenance of the town. If enough trash collected around the market to be a nuisance, then it was Dago's responsibility to get it cleaned up before the busy market day on Sunday. If there was an assembly, then it was Dago's responsibility to ensure there were enough chairs for *les notables.* If the grass grew high, it was Dago's responsibility to make sure it was razed.

The *chef's* office was often crowded with young Guéré men dressed in bright blue uniform coats and ragged pants tucked in their shin-high green rubber boots. These men were members of a municipal labor taskforce called *Travailleurs de Haute Intensité et de Main d'Oeuvre*, otherwise known as THIMO (pronounced tea-mo). There were seventy members of THIMO in Bangolo, organized into seven teams of ten, employed with federal funds to help maintain the cleanliness of the town. Each morning the seven team leaders gathered around Dago's desk to receive their assignments while team members loitered in the halls or on benches by the front doorway. Most days, all seven teams were dispatched to public spaces to cut grass with machetes. On occasion, teams were sent to the market with the town's dump truck to rake trash, but only if the truck was operational or the municipality could finagle some fuel.

THIMO consisted mostly of young men in the prime of their life, ripped with muscles from head to toe from all the physical labor they performed as *petits*. The older guys, not quite considered *vieux,* or elders, were in great shape but showing signs of wear and tear. You could almost guess a man's age or sanity in Bangolo by the condition of his pants. There were also *infirme* on THIMO, who walked with a severe limp or with assistance of a crutch, the result of some accident coupled with the lack of proper medical attention. Residents often referred to others by their physical condition or appearance such as the white, the small, the fat, the crazy, the disabled, and so on. THIMO even had an albino guy they called the *Africain Blanc*, whom they would tease with accusations of being an American spy.

The presence of THIMO did not give the impression that Bangolo was a serious victim of decentralization or a recession, not with such a large commitment of federally funded workers dedicated to the very services that had been decentralized just ten years prior. In fact, the presence of THIMO sent a different message to Ivoirians, that the economy was improving and the federal government was responsible.

Not everyone in Côte d'Ivoire received this message, however. There were those who believed that the *Parti Democratic de Côte d'Ivoire* or PDCI (the incumbent political party) created THIMO to enchant the masses for the upcoming presidential elections and not out of a true commitment to the community. Some thought this was underhanded; others thought it was righteous, the spoils of an election year. It all boiled down to political affiliation or allegiances, predicated mostly on one's tribal heritage.

My counterparts Charles and Dao were assigned to Dago as Agents of Technical Services. They reported to the office first thing in the morning when THIMO was dispatched. They did not have their own office. Their job was to assist with field supervision and identify areas in need of maintenance for the following day's work. But Charles and Dao were rarely seen in the field, leaving supervision up to the team leaders while they drank in the bars.

At the far end of the building, three offices were consolidated into one large office for the mayor, with expensive furniture and extravagant décor arranged capriciously from the doorway to the large mayoral desk at the far end. In between the hallway and the mayor's office was the secretary's office, where citizens waited on a small bench in a sort of administrative purgatory. Megan and I were always bothering the mayor's young secretary for information, trying to find out if the mayor was aware of our arrival. The secretary quickly grew tired of our visits, either because we were strangers or because we interrupted her from her daydreaming of living a more cosmopolitan lifestyle in the big city.

The next office on our circuit belonged to Assis, *chef du finance* and a regular at the Kamonda. Assis was a proud man, almost arrogant, because he held a prominent position and the purse strings to the town. And he was full of nervous energy, like he had something to hide or something to sell in a hurry, moving and talking with quick reflex, suspicious of others. Assis greeted Megan and I each day as if we were long lost friends returning home from a prolonged hiatus, bellowing our names as they echoed through the building, "Scooattch! Maguii!"

The last office belonged to the typing pool employees. Three women and one man sat behind a counter typing memos for the mayor and his staff. We did not expect to work with the typing pool, but we stopped by their office anyway because they were pleasant and seemed to enjoy the company.

We also paid a visit to the sous-préfecture across the street from the municipality, and occasionally to the office of the préfecture located along Main Street. The sous-préfecture and préfecture are the local and regional representation of the federal government, respectively. Both departments carry out duties for nearby villages not represented by a municipal government. The sous-préfet has *état civil,* which registers births, deaths, marriages, and military registration in addition to issuing the *carte de séjour*. There is also a financial monitor at the sous-préfecture who oversees and approves the budget for the commune (everyone living within five kilometers of the town's boundary) and ensures the mayor is spending funds correctly. The préfet is a political appointee, who oversees the sous-préfectures in the region and spends time attending ceremonies and observances, representing the president in an official capacity.

Initially, we delivered our regards to the staff of the sous-préfecture as often as we visited the municipality. Then we realized they had no real stake in sanitation, so we ceased our regular visits. However, there was one individual from this office who enjoyed our company and made a point to pull over in his small red Toyota sedan whenever he saw us walking around. His name was Konan and he was the Secretary General. Konan was a lean guy with a thin Clark Gable mustache and a jovial personality. He'd supervised Peace

Corps volunteers once before in a town in central Côte d'Ivoire, so he was familiar with the value we could bring as idealistic Americans hell-bent on improving conditions. For that he welcomed us warmly. Not many people in Bangolo owned or drove cars; only *le grand types* could afford them, so for Konan to stop every time he saw us may have lent credibility to our program.

The formality of greeting the municipal staff took about an hour unless we stopped first to talk with the members of THIMO. It was well worth the time listening to the concerns of these men as they provided clues to the problems at hand. Regular greetings are extremely important in the African culture, almost vital, serving as a ritual of respect, family, religion, and traditional values. In Senegal we'd watch in amazement as two elder Muslim men greeted each other like friendly competitors of an age-old rivalry, rapidly trading inquiries without pausing for a response. The greeting went something like:

"Hello."
"Hello."
"How are you?"
"How are you?"
"How is your health?"
"How is your health?"
"How is the family?"
"How is the family?"

…and so on until the greeting sufficiently covered all they held in regard. It was quite a spectacle.

Our greetings with the municipal staff were not as elaborate or redundant, but we did delay business until we had a chance to discuss health and family and the state of affairs. Sometimes we averted business discussion altogether, sensing it was not the time or place, engaging them only on a personal level. Had we not participated in this traditional greeting and forged ahead with our agenda, we might as well have caught the next flight to America, where health and family are perceived by Africans as secondary values behind business and power and commercial pursuits. How else could we explain leaving our families for two years to live in a faraway African village? At the outset, we could not explain; we could only soften this perception by exhibiting similar values, demonstrating we were not so different through our investment in the African greeting.

Living at the Kamonda wasn't so bad, especially with Jerome and Mathias there to keep us company. One time I shared a bag of peanuts with Jerome. After that he would pass by my window each evening, uttering, "Peeeeaanuts....Peeanuts, Monsieur Scott." But this arrangement (and the bag of peanuts) could not last forever. It was not good for my long-term disposition to live in a single room at a pubescent whorehouse frequented by our new colleagues. We reminded Assis that L'Auberge Kamonda was temporary quarters and that the municipality was required to provide separate homes for Megan and I similar to the dwellings lived in by our host country colleagues.

Assis acknowledged our request and took us around to look at available homes. The first one we looked at was on the south side of town, recently constructed and larger than average for Bangolo, with a covered porch that wrapped around two sides, but it wouldn't be available for another month as much of the interior finish work was incomplete. Megan seemed to take a shine to its location across the road from the enormous compound where the préfet lived, guarded day and night by a host of security guards.

We then went looking for my house. My only requirement was that it was located in a different part of town, so we could cover more territory, reducing the amount of time it would take for Bangolo to get to know us. Plus I liked the north side better. That's where the action was—the market, the shops, the restaurants and the *maquis*; activity I would normally avoid to maintain my privacy was now what I craved because it was so new and unique.

We looked at another recently constructed house, tucked away behind concrete walls and beneath the branches of young coconut trees. It would be a fine place to live, certainly nicer than I expected. But when Assis returned from talking with the neighbor, he returned with bad news. The rental price for the house was too expensive for the municipality. I could not stay there unless I was willing to pay for it myself.

Assis then suggested a place near the north *gare* at the intersection of the main highway and the paved road. It needed work, he said, but it was available immediately as he knew the owner and the owner would cut him a deal. Before I got a look, I knew it was a real stinker, a money pit the owner couldn't rent because of its noisy location by the highway where *gbakas* and buses and logging trucks pass day and night. I knew by how excited he got; by the way he tried to sell the idea of living in this house like he was trying desperately to marry off his last available daughter.

I figured I'd humor Assis and take a look at the house by the *gare*. It was, as expected, on the corner of the two busiest roads in Bangolo, set back from the highway about fifty meters. There were no buildings in front impeding the view to the highway, only a small wood-frame pavilion to shelter travelers from the sun and rain, and a lone tree where the *chef du gare* and his assistants spent their time between passing vehicles. Otherwise, the land in front was vacant, a large dirt lot where travelers awaited transport, which would serve as a nice buffer.

The house was indeed in poor condition. Holes were visible in the roof and beneath the eave. Chunks of concrete lay on the ground, splintered from damage to the front porch and stairs. The compound wall in front had a large gaping hole that looked like a truck drove through it, and then backed out for good measure. As walls go, they were useless. Tall grass was growing around the walls, in the front yard, by the porch, and along the side yard, competing with small patches of rogue corn stalks.

Inside, the conditions were just as bad. It looked as if nobody had lived there for years, except the vermin living off the refuse of the previous tenants. I walked around and saw that it could be restored with some minor repairs, a good cleaning, a paint job, and an implement for killing critters. Despite the work it would take to put this house in order, there was something about its location, the front porch, the activity of the *gare*, the dynamic view of the highway, the forested area beyond the road, and the broad sky that captured the red and orange and purple colors at dusk. This house, this location, was where I wanted to be for the next two years. To Assis' surprise, I said yes to the daughter that nobody wanted.

We continued to stay at the Kamonda because it had electricity and running water, whereas our new homes did not. Our plan was to hold out until Assis paid for the utility hookups. We knew if we moved out we'd be living in the dark and forced to haul water from our neighbor's polluted wells. The prospect of living without utilities wasn't all that bad. I certainly prepared for it in all my years aspiring to the great sacrifice of Peace Corps service. But when the only thing preventing service is the conspiring of one man, you do what you must to avoid being slighted. Allowing Assis to take advantage of us at this early stage would establish a precedent. We could not allow that to happen, for ourselves or for future volunteers.

Determining one's role and one's contribution is perhaps the most difficult aspect of Peace Corps service. Volunteers are placed in host countries without clearly defined objectives. Many volunteers do not have adequate resources to pursue projects, or they cannot find individuals in their community who can afford to be involved in extracurricular activities such as development work.

On paper, our objective in Bangolo was to offer our technical expertise; sensitize target populations on the need for improved waste management; and develop project partnerships between community groups, federal government agencies, and municipal authorities alike. UEM volunteers also had the benefit of a host government with resources such as assigned counterparts, federally funded labor teams, construction materials and heavy equipment. The biggest obstacle to progress seemed to be how we defined or measured the term *progress*.

A tool we used for refining our roles and developing projects was the *étude de milieu,* or study of the surroundings. The *étude de milieu* was required of all volunteers, whether we were opening a new site like Bangolo or replacing others in previously established sites. To initiate the *étude*, Megan and I were to canvass the community, conduct surveys, and assess the readiness of the population to collaborate in projects. We would then gather this information and prepare a community master plan in both French and English that could be implemented by the municipality or the citizens of Bangolo.

I also wanted to develop a map that would show the location of streets, public and private lands, and local services. Subsequent layers or versions of the map could address environmental concerns or demographic information. Developing a map would be an excellent way to get out and meet people, so I began my second week by surveying the town, using pace and compass, compiling the information in a notebook as I walked.

I concentrated my efforts east of the highway, as the only development to the west was a secondary school at the southern boundary and a church at the northern boundary. The most logical place to start was at the *gare* by my future house. When I reached the lot, I noticed I had the attentions of the men sitting beneath the lone tree. One of them called me over. He was a young guy with a thin mustache, big straw hat, and a serious demeanor, as if charged with a vital responsibility other than lounging in the shade.

"American! What's going on? Come here! What is it that you are doing?" he said to me, slowly and deliberately.

I explained to him and his cohorts that I was a volunteer for the Corps de la Paix, living and working in Bangolo for the next two years to improve sanitation conditions and the environment. They were expressionless at first, and then they looked at each other like they had no idea what I said. But I was sure I had said the right words in the correct order. Was my French that bad? Do they not want a cleaner environment? I looked around the dirt lot cluttered with plastic *sachets* that once held drinking water. Everyone was working or moving in some fashion, carrying heavy loads balanced on their heads or pushing homemade carts full of luggage or a builder's material.

I realized it was possible that the men under the tree, and the citizens at large, may have never heard words such as "volunteer" and "sanitation" and "environment." Why would they? It's not as if they can afford to volunteer as a profession or otherwise. Why would they need to command words like sanitation and environment? It wasn't as if the people of Bangolo had a firm grasp of the adverse health risks or ecological ruin associated with pollution. Otherwise, why would I be there? There were more pressing matters to think about such as meals and crops and family.

I switched it up by saying I was to live in Bangolo for two years to help clean up trash, build toilets, and improve dirt roads. They immediately responded with gratitude and large hospitable smiles, shaking my hand vigorously as if I had already completed the job. Trash, shit, and erosion they understood. These were a visual and physical encumbrance to their day, and my assistance was welcome.

I parted company with the men at the *gare* and paced through the town. Along the way I noted services such as the water company, the electric company, and the police office. I took notice of the many food and beverage kiosks that served meals of omelet sandwiches, fried spaghetti, and rice with sauce, distinguished from other kiosks mainly by décor as opposed to the meals' peerless qualities. There were also boutiques or general stores that sold sundries such as cooking oil, cigarettes, candy, cookies, condiments, flour, sugar, coffee, cocoa, tea, plastic buckets, pens and pencils, and notebooks graced with American icons on the cover such as Larry Hagman from *Dallas* or Cindy Crawford. If the boutique owner could afford a refrigerator-freezer, they would also sell cold drinks like Coke or Fanta and chocolate-covered ice-milk bars called Popitos, sometimes peddled in the streets from insulated handcarts.

Along Main Street, carpenters, tailors, and hairdressers leased space in a long one-story building, like an African strip mall. Workers would perform their craft outside in front of their shop to escape the intense heat trapped indoors. They were remarkably skilled tradesmen and women who could produce merchandise as durable as any U.S. or Chinese factory for a fraction of the cost.

Every village, town, and city in Côte d'Ivoire has some form of community *marché,* or market, where fresh foods and durable goods could be purchased or traded. Bangolo's *marché* was located off Main Street near the Kamonda, and it covered two square blocks. It was an open-air affair with a patchwork of aluminum sheets resting on a network of wood framing to direct heavy rains onto the path, out to the streets, and into the *bafon.* The vendors' tables were located on traditional grounds that supported decades, if not centuries, of market ventures by the same tribe or family. On one side of the *marché* was the Guéré of the Bangolo region; on the other side was a mix of Diola-speaking outsiders, who have made a home in virtually every major West African city and town, survived by their skills as exceptional and persistent *marchandes.*

Merchants showed up most days to sell their products at the market, but Sunday was market day in Bangolo *ville,* when people from outlying villages made the journey to purchase stock for their home or market, or to sell items from the bush that were scarce in town. As I navigated through the stalls and alleys, I noted items available for my own provisions, such as onions, garlic, pimento, peanut butter, tomato paste, and bouillon cubes—all the ingredients for a standard African soup or sauce. There was also plenty of rice and dried beans, smoked fish charred until the smell and form was no longer recognizable, and meat from slaughtered cows hanging from the rafters, attracting more flies than customers.

In one day, I had mapped all the streets and services that emanated from two kilometers of paved roadway. With ten to fifteen kilometers of dirt road remaining, I'd be finished within a week, maybe two. But I was mapping more than just streets and services; I had unknowingly begun to map a culture. As a result, I had a better sense of when to use words like "volunteer" and "sanitation" and "environment," if at all; or how to get extra portions or reduced prices at the market in exchange for a smile or a joke; or how not to offer the left hand in salutation, as the left hand is reserved for ass wiping after defecation. Without these skills, I could not know my bearing in the community and a map of streets and services would be useless.

During the middle of our second week, the mayor finally reported to work. Megan and I were still making the rounds together each morning, though we would soon embark on different schedules and pursue our own agendas.

We asked the secretary if the mayor was available. "He is there," she uttered with feigned interest.

"Can we see him?"

"One moment," she instructed, entering his office, walking almost five meters before the mayor was within earshot of the message. "Enter," she commanded, returning to her posturing.

The mayor sat at his desk signing papers, a cigarette burning in a tray, filling the large room with its fumes. "Sit down," he instructed without lifting his head, pointing in the direction of the leathery couches by the door.

We waited for him to finish his work, which we sensed as part work, part pretense for his first impression as the elected chief. A few last drags on his cigarette and he arose to greet us. The mayor was about sixty years old. He had short hair and a thin mustache, physically short for his prominence, about 5 feet, 6 inches tall. Though the Guéré were small in stature, we half expected the mayor to tower above his subjects. He was dressed in the *fonctionnaire's* clothing that high-ranking officials wore in Côte d'Ivoire (dress slacks and a short-sleeved collared shirt, usually of matching color), but his shirt pattern resembled that of a Hawaiian print with colorful leaves.

"Bonjour, Monsieur le Mayor. Our names are Scott and Megan. How are you?" I offered, standing to shake his hand as he approached.

"Welcome, Scoatch and Magui. All is well," he responded. "Excuse me. I must go. Return tomorrow, please. We will introduce you to the people of Bangolo at 1000," he said politely as he ushered us out of his office in haste. Then he walked outside, got in his car, and drove away down Main Street.

The next day we returned for our inauguration with the community. We were excited. This would be our first opportunity to discuss our mission and dispel any early rumors about our presence. But 1000 came and went without any indication of a public assembly, so we waited on benches outside the front door. When the mayor finally arrived, it was after *sieste* and we were not the only ones on the afternoon docket. Citizens came calling on the mayor for promises he had made or appointments he had scheduled, and we sensed there would be no inauguration for the Corps de la Paix that day, or anytime soon.

CHAPTER EIGHT

FAITH

After two weeks at the Kamonda, I was doubtful I'd be moving into my new house any time soon. I settled into the small hotel room, sharing the bathroom with the clientele, and eating out every night. Assis had yet to pay for our utility hookups, each estimated at 60,000 West African francs known as the CFA, which stands for *Communauté Financière Africaine*. Though I hardly knew Assis, or the mayor, I had little faith either would resolve our dilemma.

At 1,000 CFA (U.S. $2) per night for a regular room, and 3,000 CFA for the air-conditioned rooms we now occupied, Megan and I had already tallied a hotel bill of about 40,000 CFA apiece. One more week in the lap of Third World luxury and it would no longer be feasible to keep us at the Kamonda. Assis was not moved by my logic. What my economics did not consider was the relationship with the vendors. The utility companies were privately owned and would require immediate payment or services would not be rendered. While the Kamonda was also privately owned, it was heavily subsidized by the late night conduct of the municipal staff. And the owner knew his establishment would not stand a chance without this revenue, even if it meant excusing the majority of the municipal debt.

I thought to explain our dilemma to the electric company, hoping they'd come up with a payment plan, or bargains for idealistic Americans, or coupons of compassion. A hulking figure of a man in a navy blue uniform rose from his chair behind the counter as if he were expecting my visit. Turns out, he was expecting my visit. Assis must have attempted to strike a deal without success. The man revealed months of delinquent unpaid bills for electric services procured through municipal credit, and he was not about to hook up another person under Assis' charge until the bills were paid. It was nothing personal, he stated. He sincerely wished he could help, as I would need it working with *les incompétentes* of the municipality. As I headed for the door, he made one last cautionary plea to watch out for the likes of the *chef du finance,* wishing me luck with a slightly sinister chuckle.

Hooking up utilities became an issue of contention between us and the staff charged with *l'installation des volontaires.* We hoped to appeal to the mayor, but he was on his way to Abidjan for another session of business and politics and drumming up support for the national and local elections only six months away. Assis suggested we pay for the hookups ourselves and they would reimburse us when the mayor returned. We told Assis that we received only 3,000 CFA per day and could not possibly pay for hookups.

Truth of the matter was, we could afford the hookups if we were willing to use personal finances, but we would never see it again. My goal was to live on what Peace Corps doled out, without dipping into my savings. Furthermore, it would be detrimental to our credibility to succumb to Assis' request. If it were revealed that Peace Corps volunteers had a reserve of cash and were willing to part with it upon request, we'd never be able to sustain our work. So with mixed emotions, Megan and I decided to wait patiently and live at the Kamonda until the mayor returned to Bangolo or things changed. Much like the situation with our SSP project in Thiés, we were going to ride it out, allow them to come up with the proverbial barrel and accept the consequences.

During my spare time, I'd clean or paint the inside of my future house. I ordered chairs, tables, and a bed frame from a local carpenter, and I purchased tools and lumber to make shelves for books, clothes, and kitchen provisions. The neighborhood children helped me out by cutting the grass and sweeping the dirt in my compound, warning me that I must keep my yard neat to avoid the deadly green mamba. All they asked for in return was permission to enter my compound and sample freely from the numerous fruit trees that grew in my back yard. Good trade, I thought, until I went to harvest the fruit and found only husks and rinds of papaya, banana, mango, coconut, and citrus scattered throughout the yard, attracting flies and other kids with machetes wanting the same carte blanche.

While I was working on the house I met both of my neighbors. To the north was a pleasant woman named Valentine, who offered the use of her household supplies and tools but regretted she could not help me clean as her younger brother was sick and needed her attention. I took her up on her offer, using water from her well for cleaning, as the well in my compound had been filled with debris. Out back was the family Baman—a couple with three small children, and the wife's sister and her small boy. Monsieur Baman was a teacher at the high school. Madame Baman took care of the family and ran a small *maquis* in the evenings to supplement their income, serving cold beer and soda outside on a raised concrete slab with three tables. She would also serve dinner if you notified her a day in advance, to buy fresh fish or chicken early in the morning when it was available. They were both decent respectable neighbors and I was relieved to have chosen a house among them.

On Easter Sunday, I awoke late at the Kamonda and took my time getting ready, anticipating a full day of painting. There was a loud pounding at the metal doors. I staggered outside and opened the gates to find Konan, the Secretary General, in his Sunday best, leaning impatiently against his idling red Toyota.

"Why were you not in church this morning? Where is Magui? Get in the car," he blurted in one breath, as if we had arranged to meet in advance of this particular moment.

"I have no idea where she might be. She's not here though," I responded, deliberately evading his first question.

"Let's go, we'll look for her on the way."

On the way to where, I thought, but refrained from asking because I trusted Konan to keep us out of major trouble or boredom. I had no idea what he was up to, but I had come to accept, even enjoy, these fortuitous unpredictable days that began with skepticism and usually ended with an enlightening new perspective. Wherever we went, I would most certainly learn more than if I shut myself in my house to do chores.

I changed into presentable clothing and climbed into the back seat. Along Main Street we spotted Megan and persuaded her to join us. Then, as if receiving a precursory sign from beyond, I thought about the dangerous, potentially fatal ceremonies of Ivoirian tribesmen as told by my aunt Barbara, including the panther-man ritual among the Guéré of the western highlands. Egads! I was in the heart of Guéré country. Is this what Konan had in mind for the day? Would he jeopardize our lives to expose us to such an exhibition, where crazed voracious panther-men wait to ambush and cannibalize curious Americans?

We drove slowly into the south part of Bangolo until we reached the enormous compound of the préfet. Konan leaned on his horn until the security guards opened the gates from within, allowing us to proceed up the long driveway to the house. We were greeted warmly by the préfet with his big round face and cheerful smile. He was dressed for ceremony in a traditional African robe called a *boubou*, draped like a decorative poncho over his tall heavy-set frame. We didn't stay long. The préfet ushered us back out to the carport and into his chauffeured Peugeot with me, Megan and Konan in the backseat and the préfet riding shotgun. I had no idea where we were going and I did not dare to ask. I felt like a bigshot being chauffeured around Bangolo with the local leaders, though I was deftly self-conscious of the town's perception of the Peace Corps. Being seen in the préfet's Peugeot may have qualified us as high-steppers in the eyes of the community, but that is not the image we wanted to portray, not as agents for an obscure grassroots agency with no funding for projects. Our job was going to be difficult enough. We did not need to be classified as wealthy, irreproachable, indignant foreigners who specialized in telling people where to crap.

With my head down, trying in vain to conceal my identity from the people on the street, we traveled northeast beyond the town limits, *en brousse*, where Bangolo *ville* ended and the Guéré villages began—villages with names such as Gueoué, Béoué, Goenie, Gohouo, and Baou. Essentially, put a handful of marbles in your mouth and start talking—that's what these villages sounded like.

En brousse, the grass was thick and taller than most men, soiled brown from the dusty wake of buses and automobiles and mopeds. Large patches of jungle forest still remained, ascending to enormous heights, blanketing the road under an arch or canopy of branches and vines. But these patches were rare, as the once prominent jungle was mostly reduced to grasses and young forest recovering slowly from the continuous logging operations.

During the drive, the préfet had many questions about our program, and he spoke candidly about the troubles with African society, especially those within the small town of Bangolo. He was pessimistic we would succeed in our endeavors with the current municipal leadership, though he was careful not to criticize anyone in particular. He encouraged us to work in the schools or at the market. Our discussion adjourned when we reached a small, end-of-the-road village at the fringe of an old-growth forest about twenty-five kilometers northeast of Bangolo. A crowd gathered around the car and welcomed us warmly, escorting us to a row of chairs on a raised wooden platform facing an audience. As we took our seats, another vehicle approached and the crowd went into a frenzy, reacting wildly as if graced by the presence of a celebrated icon. A handsome, sharp-dressed, middle-aged African man emerged from the back seat of the vehicle and joined us on stage. We rose and shook hands, introducing ourselves. When the crowd was settled, a spokesman cordially welcomed our guest of honor—*Monsieur le Ministre d'Intérieur de Côte d'Ivoire.*

I didn't know much about the Ivoirian politics, but I knew I was in the presence of one of the country's top government officials, not only by the sound of his title but by the way he looked and dressed, the way he spoke, the way the crowd swooned to his every gesture. His name was Emile Constant Bombet and he was one of the president's top cabinet members, hailing from the Bangolo region, maintaining a nearby residence and a stake in local affairs.

Monsieur Bombet was one of twenty-eight ministers, and one of three appointed to look after the internal security and defense of Côte d'Ivoire. His position was nothing like the U.S. Secretary of Interior, more like a domestic Secretary of Defense. Monsieur Bombet was responsible for overseeing the préfectures, sous-préfectures, and local police forces, as well as regulating public associations, gun control, access to public buildings, emigration and immigration, foreign propaganda, foreign visitors, and passport controls. The position also directs the National Security Police, supervises traditional chieftaincies, and administers territorial subdivisions. As far as this village was concerned, *Monsieur le Ministre* was as powerful as the president, and it showed in their hospitality and reverence.

After Monsieur Bombet said a few words about the economy and the upcoming elections, and promised big changes in Abidjan, he presented an envelope of cash to the village chief. I thought this was generous of the Minister, returning to his region to offer financial assistance. I can't imagine that it's in the Minister's job description to give money away to the citizens of the country. The village chief reciprocated by presenting Monsieur Bombet with an African *boubou* from the local tribe. Monsieur Bombet, still commanding the attentions of the crowd, turned to where I was sitting and presented me with the *boubou*, heralding our presence in Bangolo as a sign of real progress. The crowd responded with applause, much attributed to the novelty of a thin white guy wearing an oversized traditional robe meant for large African chieftains and kings. I was honored to receive such a symbolic gift presented by such a prominent man. I even flaunted my attire in front of Megan as Konan leaned over to her and revealed, "This is one of the better *boubous* he's given away at these rallies."

I was aware of the importance of politics throughout Côte d'Ivoire. I frequently observed citizens expressing support for their favorite politician by wearing T-shirts and *pagnes* branded with a politician's face in an elaborate rosette of flowers and optimistic slogans, just like Americans may don clothing to show their loyalty to a particular sports franchise or player. Sitting there on stage, draped in my own personal *boubou*, it was obvious that politics were the primary, if not the solitary, reason for this visit—an advantageous stop along the campaign trail to donate alms for votes.

Not only did I feel self-conscious, but I'd just been cloaked in the politics of the region, present at a rally in support of the incumbent PDCI. While much of Bangolo supported the PDCI and the current president, Henri Konan Bedie, and the majority of the people would look kindly on our visit, I was not comfortable on that platform. It was vital not to embrace or alienate any political party, as our mission was supposed to be partisan to health and sanitation. And there might come a day when President Bedie, Monsieur Bombet, and the PDCI would be on the outside looking in.

Our entourage left the small village in the early afternoon under a hail of cheers. We were invited for Easter dinner at the Minister's house north another twenty kilometers. At the time I wasn't too fazed by the invitation. I was hungry and it didn't seem to matter where we stopped for dinner. However, as we approached the Minister's massive compound, easily the size of a regulation *futbol* field, I began to realize the significance of the invitation.

Imagine yourself in your hometown. The finance manager of the local federal government—let's say your town's treasurer—comes banging on your door and commands you to get in their automobile posthaste. That person then drives you to the home of the regional representation of the federal government. Since there are forty-nine regions in Côte d'Ivoire and fifty states in the United States, let's assume this position is comparable to a governor. So you and your town's treasurer and your state's governor are driving down the road one lovely Easter morning in the governor's luxury car, and you go to a neighboring town to campaign for their party. And then, one of the president's cabinet members arrives at the event—let's say the U.S. Secretary of Defense. He honors you in front of an entire village then invites you to his house for Easter dinner. That would be quite a day, no?

Though this may not be the most analogous of circumstances, and the chances of the same scenario happening to a random citizen of the United States are zero to none, it was possible for volunteers in Côte d'Ivoire to meet and interact with the country's leaders. For one, Côte d'Ivoire is much smaller than the United States, so news and politics were more intimately shared. Also, Ivoirian officials were more accessible, frequently attending events and cultural ceremonies in person because it was the only medium in Côte d'Ivoire (at the time). But the primary reason volunteers were such an attraction at these gatherings had a lot to do with our status as Americans. Though the French are recognized as the former colonists of Côte d'Ivoire, Americans were seen as the colonists of a modern free world, largely due to Papa Boigny's thirty years of global success.

As Monsieur Bombet noted, our presence at these events signified "a sign of real progress," whether we were contributing to the development of their country or not, and that translated into votes. And whether we were ready or not, Megan and I had just been given the inauguration we had requested, just not the type of inauguration we had hoped for.

Dinner at Monsieur Bombet's house was an extravagant affair involving a bounty of traditional dishes I never knew existed (and probably didn't exist for most Ivoirians). There were about a dozen attendees including the four of us from Bangolo and the Minister's family who offered a blessing before the meal. For the most part I was quiet during dinner conversation, intimidated by formalities and my less-than-stellar French, though I did not hesitate to answer Monsieur Bombet when he asked my opinion of Bangolo thus far.

My responses were brief and optimistic so as not to convey my growing cynicism. I made a sincere effort to remain diplomatic about my dealings with the municipality, but I was nowhere near the diplomat as the Minister. I think he could sense that if I had known the French words for *lazy, good-for-nothing, drunkards and miscreants*, I may have been tempted to use them to describe my counterparts.

After dinner we walked outside with Monsieur Bombet through the carport where the chauffeurs and security guards and cooks were crouched around casserole dishes, eating the leftovers. We strolled around the well-maintained property nestled within the southern reach of the Monts de Dan mountain range. We listened as he dispensed similar advice as the préfet about Africa and Bangolo. He even expounded on his beliefs as a Christian as we passed a tall concrete statue of the Virgin Mary caste with her immortal child on a landscaped embankment.

It was an eventful day. We thanked Monsieur Bombet and his family for a wonderful Easter dinner and headed down the road. In the car I asked the préfet about religion in Côte d'Ivoire's western region, curious about the percentage of people who attended church, as I had seen many churches of varying denominations in and around Bangolo. The préfet, an avowed Muslim, turned to face us in the back seat and said, "Religion is the varnish of Africa. When you scratch the surface, it reveals its true animist self." A chill ran up the back of my neck as if the préfet himself was going to mutate into one of those panther-men in the front seat of the Peugeot and pounce on us as we sat defenseless and awestruck in the back seat.

West Africans and others born of the Dark Continent are not alone in their animist beliefs. American Indians and Mayas, as well as those who practice voodoo, sorcery, and witchcraft, are considered practices of animism. In general, animists believe that the vital principle of all organic development is immaterial spirit, that everything has a "soul" or "anima" that is immortal and indestructible. Animists also believe that humans are not supreme rulers but a part of all things including animals, plants, minerals, and natural phenomena such as the sky, mountains, water, and earth. Animism infuses the sacred into real life through one's ancestral spirits as a way of coping with everyday needs and problems. These ancestral spirits are worshiped, offered food or drink, and consulted to help bring about inner strength and guidance. Failure to perform the appropriate sacrifices to ancestral spirits may not only damage one's spirituality, but may summon the wrath of irate ancestors, resulting in a life of unhappiness or even sudden tragedy.

Could it be that the préfet was correct, that modern religion in Africa is a façade for a more indigenous faith? If so, why would the African people practice the tenets of a doctrine they don't entirely endorse? In that moment, the préfet not only scratched the varnish off of Bangolo's true faith but also provoked me to scratch the varnish off of my own.

The day after Easter, Megan and I went out to dinner at Chez Baman, and we processed our day over a couple beers and planned for the morrow. In Bangolo, there were about ten *maquis* to choose from, each with large posters advertising Bock Solibra, "*Bière de l'Homme Fort*" and "Guinness Is Good For You." Each had a similar layout and ambiance, with uncomfortable wooden chairs surrounding crude wooden tables that reached no higher than the middle of your shin, and a harsh florescent glare beaming from the underside of a pavilion or a nearby wall. Though the food was generally good, it was also relatively expensive. We'd spend half our daily allowance on dinner alone; the other half comparable to three big bottles of beer—the gauge by which volunteers measured or rationalized most expenditures. The *maquis* in Bangolo, like the *maquis* elsewhere in the country, catered to certain political affiliations. So when my Madame Baman told us she had the capabilities to cook us dinner and serve cold beverages, we were quick to make reservations, hoping to start an affiliation of our own.

Chez Baman had no pavilion or building to protect its customers from the elements, but the rainy season was months away so we were able to enjoy the fresh air and the night sky, bothered only by an occasional mosquito. Chez Baman did not have florescent lighting, relying on a nearby streetlight to cast a faint, tranquil glow over the entire compound. We were the only customers there that Monday night, maybe because it was a weekday, maybe because we were a few blocks away from the Main Street crowds. Still, we were treated to some of the tastiest *poulet cajunou* since our arrival, and we vowed to come back as frequently as we could afford.

As we were finishing up, we noticed a commotion in the compound across the way where Valentine lived. A procession of people was carrying lanterns, as the ambient light did not reach their house. Everyone was moaning and sobbing, obviously distraught. Madam Baman informed us that Valentine's twenty-five-year-old brother had died earlier in the day of a mysterious cause, and the people were paying their respects. Hoping to catch a glimpse of a traditional mask rumored to be common at Guéré funerals, we paid our bill and walked over to my back yard for a better view. For fifteen minutes we hunkered down in the shadows, but the masks never materialized. All we saw were the mourners filing in and out of a *banco* mud shelter where the corpse was on display in wake, so we decided to head back to the Kamonda where I'd read or journal before lapsing into a Mefloquine-induced coma.

The TV room at the Kamonda was packed with young kids for a showing of *Terminator* starring Arnold Schwarzenegger. Apparently Jerome let the neighbor kids into the compound if something decent was on television, as long as they respected the guests and kept the noise to a minimum. There must have been twenty kids sharing three couches, completely silent. When I entered they vacated an entire cushion for me without taking their eyes from the screen. Who could refuse this invitation? It was hilarious, listening to Arnold speaking in French, uttering *"J'arrive"* in place of "I'll be back." Arnie wasn't so tough in the French language, and *Terminator* seemed more like a comedy.

I had been sitting there for about thirty minutes when I heard the distant roar of a crowd. At first I thought the noise was coming from a competing television set tuned to a late night *futbol* match, but the roar grew louder and louder. The kids continued to watch TV as if immune to the disturbance. Jerome and Mathias were sitting on the concrete stoop at the end of the driveway facing the metal gates as if waiting for the curtains to open on a theater performance. A crowd passed slowly, as indicated by the movement of raised arms over the courtyard wall. Jerome informed me that the crowd was assembling to witness the hunt for the bad sorcerer responsible for the death of a young man who lived near the *gare*.

"Bad sorcerers? We have bad sorcerers in Bangolo?" I murmured with astonishment. I went into my room, threw on my Tevas and grabbed my flashlight, hoping to catch up to the action.

Jerome and Mathias could not leave the Kamonda, so they sent me out with Alpha, the custodian. Alpha lived in a concrete hovel in a corner of the compound with barely enough room for a single bedroll. I rarely saw him aside from the occasional mopping of the public bathroom or when he'd hang the bed linens out to dry. Alpha was in his twenties, with a wiry but toned physique. His face was old and weathered, his voice throaty and fiendish reminiscent of the Gollum character from J.R.R. Tolkien's *The Lord of the Rings*. If anyone in this town knew about the mystical and enchanting world of sorcery, Alpha appeared to be the stereotypical guide.

The two of us followed the stragglers and caught up with the crowd, down a wide dirt pathway with clumps of grass and severely eroded channels. The pathway extended one hundred meters before terminating at the forest *bafon* and the northern edge of town. At the end of the pathway, a lone streetlight flickered to illuminate hundreds of people standing in a semicircle around a small mud hut. Despite the size of the crowd, it was now completely silent except for the buzz of electrical current straining through the filament above.

Alpha and I fought our way through the masses to a clear view of a wooden coffin, stained and polished a shiny dark brown, hoisted above the heads of seven powerful men with beads of sweat glimmering from their brows. One of these men was at the front of the coffin facing the mud hut while the other six supported it along both sides. The streetlight flickered again, which made the crowd stir restlessly. Suddenly, the seven men and the coffin whirled around and came right at us. The crowd scattered in all directions in a chaotic stampede, tripping on clumps of grass, screaming and running. Small children were being trampled underfoot, and springing back up. It was pandemonium. The coffin, still hoisted in the air by the men, traveled about twenty meters before settling in front of a small concrete building with three separate apartments.

As Alpha and I stood alert on the periphery, a safe distance from the coffin, Alpha explained what was transpiring. The deceased young man became sick and it worsened over time to where he lost all his strength and a considerable amount of weight. He died mysteriously. Nobody in his family could understand why. They were sure it had to be the work of a bad sorcerer, poisoned by "bad medicine," which was reportedly common in Bangolo. So they organized a sorcerer hunt to find the guilty party. Animists believe the dead can communicate with the living, so they hired a clairvoyant (the man positioned at the front of the coffin) to serve as a conduit for the thoughts and wishes of the deceased young man. The six men who supported the coffin served as pallbearers, responding to the commands of the clairvoyant. If the coffin touches or hits someone accidentally during the search for a bad sorcerer, that person may be suspected of practicing bad sorcery, hence the concerted efforts of the crowd to steer clear of the coffin.

As Alpha was talking, the coffin was thrust twice at the hardwood door. Boom! Boom! No answer. The crowd remained quiet. The coffin and its pallbearers then moved three paces to the left and knocked once on the middle door. Boom! No answer. The coffin hovered there long enough for the crowd to settle down and start talking amongst each other. Then, without notice, the coffin whirled around and headed back to the mud hut at the end of the road under the streetlight. Its movements were like the hands on a Ouija board, trying to piece together a portentous message from beyond.

The coffin stopped within a half meter of the hut, assessing its next move or waiting its next command. The lone streetlight went off for a few seconds, and then came back on. Suddenly, the coffin turned and raced headlong toward the crowd, creating an absolute frenzy. When it reached a berm along the pathway, the coffin stopped abruptly, swung back around and charged full steam at the hut as if storming a castle with a battering ram. Boooom! Crack! The coffin was suddenly lodged within the small structure, splintering the wooden door into many pieces as the crowd screeched in horror. The pallbearers composed themselves, then charged the hut again, this time destroying an entire section of mud wall. They continued this charge four or five more times until the grass roof collapsed onto a pile of bricks and broken furniture.

Until now, the search to find bad sorcerers seemed almost ceremonial, staged for the amusement of the crowd, especially for me. But when the men carrying the wooden coffin destroyed an individual's home and his possessions, I realized the seriousness of their search. For the first time since being detained by crooked cops in Abidjan, I was frightened and concerned. What would prevent these men from bashing down my door some day, accusing me of committing murder in the first-degree by means of sorcery or other transcendental means? Alpha assured me this could never happen, as the ancestral spirits knew I was not a bad sorcerer, or an accomplice to a bad sorcerer, because I was an American.

The coffin was lifted from the rubble and the clairvoyant and his pallbearers resumed the search, roving down the dirt road towards Main Street. The crowd followed in earnest with hopes of finding the guilty party and bringing him to justice. As Alpha and I walked back to the Kamonda, it was extremely difficult for me to fathom all that I had witnessed. Valentine's young brother died from what could have been any number of conditions, yet the sinister works of a bad sorcerer and his "bad medicine" was the irrefutable conclusion.

When Valentine first told me of her younger brother's symptoms, what immediately came to mind was HIV/AIDS. It seemed like a logical explanation. It's a disease seemingly endemic to the continent, with an estimated three-quarter of the world's HIV/AIDS population living in sub-Saharan Africa (at the time of my service). When I asked my African colleagues about AIDS, I received some startling feedback. Dao, my counterpart who can't keep his hands off the women, told me that AIDS is not real, that it was made up by jealous wives to prevent their husbands from cheating on them. I expected this kind of response from Dao, but I was surprised when Konan explained one evening over a beer that AIDS has a particular smell that identifies whether a woman is infected. "You only need to use a condom the first time you have sex with a new partner," he said assuredly, "...to smell for yourself and determine if she has AIDS without the risk. After that, you no longer need to use a condom." He wasn't joking.

Secure within my room, I couldn't get over the evening's events. It was like a rare and extraordinary ritual as seen only in travel publications or public broadcasting specials. Does sorcery exist? Perhaps. Who am I to determine? But if these truly were Dao's and Konan's beliefs about a disease that has killed so many millions worldwide, I wasn't so sure the collective could identify sorcerers in Bangolo, good or bad. And I was certain Alpha could not guarantee I'd be immune from the fate of sorcery or its bad medicine.

When the moon gave way to the sun, the search for sorcerers concluded, with seven men identified as potential suspects. These men were paraded through town and turned over to the local *gendarmerie* where they awaited trial. According to Ivoirian law, Article 205 of the country's penal code of 1981 (amended in 1995), the penalty for conviction of bad sorcery is five years' jail time and/or a fine between 100,000 and 1,000,000 CFA, payable to the family of the deceased. If a suspect pleads innocent but is found guilty in the local court, that individual may face stiffer penalties, including certain punishments not described in any law, article, or penal code.

Of the seven individuals, one was found guilty and two others were named as accomplices. I don't know how the local judicial system came to its conclusion. Based on reports, these individuals came forth and admitted their guilt before the matter reached the courts. The convicted sorcerer served no jail time, but they had to pay the family 100,000 CFA (U.S. $200). Few individuals in Bangolo have this kind of money. The average worker would be lucky to gross this amount in four to five months. But 100,000 CFA was a small price to pay to be sanctioned by the local judicial system as a badass sorcerer.

In the ensuing years, the community would grow to fear and respect this sorcerer's power. This fear was so prevalent that few would dare collect their debts, while others, devious in their ways, might pay the sorcerer a hefty sum to unleash a similar wrath on their enemies. Being a bad sorcerer in Bangolo appeared to be a lucrative practice—a business so entrenched in the local culture that it was sure to give HIV/AIDS education a run for its money.

Three weeks into our campaign and I had mapped all the services and gathered basic information for the *étude de milieu*. It was time to expand the study area to the residential neighborhoods surrounding Bangolo *ville*. In preparation, I formulated a list of sanitation-related questions. My strategy was to ask these questions to people I met on the street or to families outside in their courtyard who did not seem to mind my approach into their daily lives. I figured I'd get a better response without banging on doors or intruding where I was not welcome.

There wasn't much to survey on the north end of town, just L'Auberge Kamonda and the few houses that remained after the violent search for sorcerers. I already knew what the guys at the Kamonda thought about the environment and politics, and I could reasonably assume that their neighbors had bigger concerns, namely rebuilding their homes.

I returned to the *gare* and sat down on a bench beneath the pavilion where young girls were selling *bisap* (juice made from the stock of boiled hibiscus leaves) in plastic *sachets* kept cool in Styrofoam containers. People approached me with curiosity, as so few Americans or Europeans graced this humble hamlet in western Côte d'Ivoire. They did not hesitate to inquire about my business in Bangolo, as the Ivoirians (especially the Guéré) are not shy people. Some may even say they are abrasive and curt, void of diplomacy. Nevertheless, I engaged in numerous discussions and collected valuable information for the *étude* without ever having to leave the shade of the pavilion or the company of the flirtatious *bisap* girls.

East of Main Street, by the lowland *bafon*, there was a primary school surrounded by a few homes. The school buildings were not equipped with bathrooms, as far as I could tell, and the children relieved themselves in the high grass surrounding the school, sometimes defecating in the middle of the courtyard. If this wasn't messy enough, a large number of cattle were herded through the school grounds each day, leaving their droppings while they fed on isolated clumps of grass. During recess I'd watch as kids maneuvered their way through a minefield of cow flops, slipping every so often on a moist batch hidden from view. As the préfet noted, the primary school was definitely a good place for a project.

The building just north of the primary school was the post office where Megan and I shared *Boîte Postal 111*—a letter-sized mailbox accessed from the exterior, allowing us to check our mail any time, day or night. And we did, sometimes twice per day. Receiving mail from home or from volunteers was exciting, almost vital in maintaining relationships and staying abreast of the news of the outside world. Those who took the time to write were revered over others, and I responded judiciously, putting forth the same if not greater effort in my letters back to them.

Receiving packages from the States was also cause for celebration, supplying us with the essentials of our past, now novelties in our present. I received books, cassettes, puzzles, spices, cookies, and candy. I even received an issue of *Playboy* from my aunt Jean who was under the impression that I was resigned to a term of celibacy and I'd need all the stimuli I could muster. Perhaps the most anticipated package I received was the daily sports section of my local newspaper, bundled and mailed at the end of each week by my ex-girlfriend's mother, of all people, keeping me posted of each cursed Red Sox game for two long mediocre seasons. To those who sent me packages, I am forever grateful. To Miss April 1995, I am forever indebted.

Generally, it took anywhere from a week or two for letters to reach me from the States, and two days to a week for in-country mail. Packages took much longer, from two weeks to two months, if we received them at all. Though we received most of the letters and packages intended for B.P. 111, we presumed a few were intercepted along the way. We were not happy about it but we expected a percentage of our mail to fall by the wayside, consumed by the African postal system.

As evidence, there was an incident that occurred on the last day of training in Senegal. A woman from the Health Program and I decided to make one last visit to the post office in Thiés, as we were both expecting packages that had yet to arrive. While waiting at the end of a long and serpentine line, I noticed my friend staring hard at one of the postal clerks. She abruptly abandoned her place and rushed up to the counter, speaking forcefully to the clerk. Apparently, he was wearing one of her favorite flannel shirts, sent by her parents during the first week of training. The postal clerk was caught off-guard. He dismissed her accusation at first, claiming he'd bought the shirt at the market, but he eventually fessed-up, realizing he could lose his job if his boss or the police found out. He motioned for us to follow him to the back room. In a large pile on the floor were about fifty packages addressed to Americans. Two of them were addressed to me. He was just waiting for our group to depart before cashing in. We left with as many parcels as we could carry out. We reported the incident to Kayego but it went nowhere, not in the short time we had left, muddled in West African formalities.

I finished canvassing the north, central, and east parts of town, then I moved to the south side where the bulk of the populace lived, including the mayor and the préfet. Other than our brief visit to select Megan's house and to pick up the préfet on Easter, this was the first time I had ventured this far south. Roads were laid out in a grid pattern, with a regular occurrence of streetlights as if the neighborhood had been planned in advance.

Along the highway, I met an interesting 92-year-old *vieux* named Prince who claimed to have known former President Felix Houphouët-Boigny. As proof he showed me a fading gray and yellow photograph of Papa Boigny standing with the young Prince in lavish African attire. Prince was outspoken, talking continuously about politics, religion, and the events he had witnessed in his long life. I couldn't get a word in edgewise. His real claim to fame, however, was his family. Prince had nine wives and thirty-two children, and he was proud of every one of them, even though he had difficulty recalling their names and whereabouts. Some of his family members were still living with him in Bangolo, relatively young wives providing for his day-to-day needs. Some were in other villages or had ventured to live in other countries. A few had passed on. Nine wives and thirty-two children! He would've had more, he claimed, if his faculties were in order.

This is not an uncommon occurrence in Côte d'Ivoire. Men generally take on multiple wives or multiple partners, and children are frequently products of those relationships. Alpha, my guide during the hunt for bad sorcerers, was one of twenty-five children himself. More than once I asked him if he really had twenty-four brothers and sisters, astounded that one man could or would engender that many young without being crazed or feral. Alpha always responded the same way, with a smile followed by a head-nod and a drawn-out "Ouuiii" in his throaty Gollum voice. I think he enjoyed the attention, like he was part of something unique, just like the hunt for bad sorcerers.

Where I come from, having this many children would generally be considered outlandish and irresponsible, even if you could provide for them financially. You're liable to grace the cover of a grocery stand magazine or end up on a reality TV show. Most Americans these days attempt to balance career with family, and they strive for a healthy litter of two, three, four kids. Not that the United States doesn't have its fair share of procreators, busy propagating minions for their respective movements.

Prince's rationale was simple: he was a devout and religious man guided by a doctrine that encourages many children from multiple wives. He was a proud and arrogant man, illustrated by the way he hoisted up his pants by his belt-buckle and snorted like an beast, asserting he was the strongest, healthiest man in Bangolo because of his virility. And despite his many years as an elder and friend of the president, he never led me to believe that the adverse impacts of his lifestyle ever weighed on his conscience. Most of all, he was an African man living in Côte d'Ivoire, where women don't have much of a say in the matter. Their role is the rearing and bearing of children without restraint, be that as it may. Nine wives and thirty-two children!

After meeting Prince, I couldn't help but wonder: what is our responsibility with respect to the earth's population and its limited resources? Are we to exercise any kind of restraint? Do we conserve anything for others? Who's providing the oversight to ensure the earth's resources are not polluted, destroyed, or consumed in a way that would jeopardize human survival: World leaders? Politicians? Government agencies? Corporations? Individuals? They all play a role, but who is in charge? It's no mystery that our primary driver as humans is to procreate, and the progeny require food, clothing, shelter, and other extravagances. When do we, as the stewards of the earth, draw the line? Do we just keep living, consuming, surviving, consoling, and rebuilding until something gives?

Our ancestors produced doctrine instructing us to be fruitful, to multiply, to fill the earth and subdue it. Subdue the earth? Like one would subdue a bitter enemy? This seems like an existential paradox. Couldn't we have tempered this edict a bit so that future generations weren't so reckless? The earth responds in myriad ways to human activity, and there's evidence that the earth isn't particularly thrilled with our choices. In the grand scheme of things, I doubt if Mother Nature is ultimately concerned with an individual's faith, beliefs, good intentions, projections, or last-minute pleas.

Maybe I'm wrong. Perhaps the ancient doctrine is righteous and insightful and the authors had a Grand Plan, or the authors are simply prescribing what is in our nature, and good citizens like Prince and others around the world are just doing their part to ensure the continuation of the species during times of attrition and cataclysm. If that's the case, why did I waste my time volunteering to improve Africa's environment? I should have been humping like a dog in heat, preparing for the Rapture; me and my nine wives.

I finished my mapping project, but not without another trial of faith. Near the préfet's house, I happened upon a large compound bordering the eastern edge of the forest. The compound was twice the size of the préfet's palatial residence. I was certain I had accounted for all major commercial services, so I ignored my better judgment and entered through the open gate without an invitation. A wide dirt path led down the center of the compound to the front stairs of a two-story rose-colored building enveloped in construction scaffolding. On both sides of the path were smaller buildings interspersed amongst tall tropical trees. It was as clean a compound as I had seen since the training facility in Thiés.

As I walked closer, I noticed wooden pews through the open front doorway and colorful stained-glass windows that allowed light to pass through on both sides. Locals were painting the exterior walls from the planks of the scaffolding or trimming the hedges with machetes. It was the most physical work I'd seen since my arrival. If I could only harness their energy for sanitation projects, the entire town might resemble this immaculate enclave. Not ten minutes had elapsed before I was approached by an older white man (the first I'd seen in Bangolo) resembling Colonel Sanders from the Kentucky Fried Chicken franchise. Though he did not know my name, he knew the details of my assignment.

The 'Colonel' and I walked over to his office where he made tea and gave me a brief history lesson on mission work. The story goes that Jesus instructed his apostles to propagate his teachings. That includes not only the twelve apostles from the last supper but also messengers from the early Christian Church, missionaries sent to canvas a new territory, or anyone spreading *the word* for that matter. Christian missionaries began moving into Africa during the Age of Discovery between the 15th and 17th centuries, and they continue to do God's work today, converting the indigenous people into disciples, and disciples into apostles.

I learned that the Colonel was originally from France, called to the Bangolo region to spread the Christian faith and convert the local heretics of the animist religion into children of God. He seemed pleased with my admission to having been raised Catholic and invited me to worship on Sundays. I didn't have the heart to tell him that I had strayed from the church since my Confirmation. After all, he was a clergyman whose judgment I had been conditioned to fear.

After tea we stepped outside onto the porch. The Colonel gave me a tour of the grounds by pointing to various projects underway. He was proud of the work they had accomplished, all completed with local volunteer labor. I asked him if he and his parishioners would be interested in coordinating with me and Megan to improve sanitation conditions in the community. I didn't expect him to pledge much if any time to our Peace Corps mission, for I knew he was a busy man, but I certainly did not expect his reply, proclaiming with a slow, backhanded sweep of his right arm that there were no sanitation improvements needed in *his* community.

I understood the pride he must have felt, working hard each day to maintain God's law and order, transforming primitive heathens into an obedient flock of Christians to maintain a sense of utopia. I would eventually come to feel a similar pride in convincing a handful of Guéré that it's more hygienic to shit in a deep hole in the ground than on the ground itself. I could not understand why this older Christian missionary—an alleged community leader with divine and moral obligation—held to the belief that improvements, whether sanitation or spiritual, should be exclusive to the confines of his compound. Every day, faithful citizens of Bangolo were showing up at the church and working hard, not for money or food or surplus hedge clippings, but for the church and its promise of salvation. And when their work was complete, these citizens were not duly compensated or offered shelter within the enclave, but forced out to survive in an unforgiving world.

I am certain that there have been a great number of missionaries who have made generous and lasting contributions to the world at large. What I resent is when salvation is brandished as currency by zealots in the business of evangelism. Or when salvation is dangled as the carrot that cajoles us to do good but is often the apple that tempts us to be pious and ignore our fundamental obligation as Samaritans. From that day on, I rarely saw the Colonel despite living in the same small town. Not because of any ill will, but because there was hardly a reason for him to leave his community. For there was work to be done, not only repainting a church but also varnishing a community from the inside out.

I stopped at the mayor's office early the next morning before THIMO was dispatched to cut grass. While making the rounds, Dogbo informed me that Miss Eliane from the Corps de la Paix was on her way south from Odienné, and she requested to have a meeting with me, Megan, and our counterparts. The Eliane that Dogbo was referring to was the Associate Peace Corps Director for the Health Program. We'd received no previous notice of Eliane's visit. We weren't due for a formal visit from our own APCD for another month. We figured Eliane was returning from a *tourneé* up north to visit with the new health volunteers and thought to check in with us on her way back to Abidjan. It was a surprise, but a welcome one. Eliane was a pleasant woman, an Ivoirian with tremendous presence, and she would bring news including that of our group's attrition.

I'm not sure what else Eliane said to Dogbo, but it sure put everyone on notice at the mayor's office. It even brought out the mayor himself, last seen in Bangolo sometime before Easter. All the key players were in attendance: Dago and Assis were present, Charles and Dao came in from the field or wherever they were hiding, and Dogbo put off his mid-morning nap until later that day. It was a regular reunion.

Eliane and her driver arrived just after lunch in a white Pajero. Though I knew this was how our Peace Corps staff got around, it half surprised me to see the new sports utility vehicle in Bangolo without a president or an ambassador, or without a decal on the side signifying one of the many non-governmental organizations aiding the refugees from neighboring Liberia. Eliane greeted the staff at the mayor's office in traditional Ivoirian fashion, slow and thorough, apologetic for her late arrival. The mayor directed us to meet at the Parrain II for a cold drink. Megan and I rode with Eliane to brief her on our first few weeks, including our difficulties with the housing situation, though we scarcely had time to cover anything in depth.

We convened to a pavilion where a young waitress brought out an array of refreshments including Coke, Orange Fanta, and beer: "Compliments of the municipality," said the mayor with such decorum. Eliane politely refused. Charles, Dao, and Dogbo opened a few bottles of beer. Dago, who is normally quiet, broke out of his shell and joked of how Megan and I were not drinking because our boss was present and she would not approve of alcohol on the job. He said it in such a way as if to mock our restraint as one of the peculiar qualities of an American. And everyone shared in a big laugh. Except for Eliane. She was all business now that she had them together, and their smiles didn't last long.

The first thing she asked the mayor was why we were still living in a hotel after almost one month. She even threatened to pull our presence if something wasn't done soon. Charles and Dao immediately went for their softbound notebooks (one with Alf on the cover, the other with Speed Racer), sensing the shit was about to roll their way. The mayor looked at Assis; Assis looked at Dago. Nobody offered an explanation because they didn't know what to say. After an uncomfortable pause, the mayor apologized to Eliane and said he would make our installation a priority. He instructed Assis to champion the cause and pay for our utility hookups so we could move into our houses as soon as possible.

For the rest of the meeting we discussed our working relationship. I would work with Dago, Charles, and Dao on sanitation projects, possibly using members of THIMO as labor, but I could also work with the schools or local businesses at my discretion. My immediate supervisor would be Dago, as he was the closest to a technical peer as anyone. I would not be required to report to the municipal office, and I could work from home as they claimed there was no place to put me in the office.

Megan would work with Dogbo, the schools, and various women's groups. She too would not be required to report to the office. Megan had a small room with a separate entrance on the side of her house that would make a good office. Once our roles were defined, Eliane got up, thanked the mayor for his hospitality, wished us luck under her breath, and departed for Abidjan with her driver.

It was remarkable to watch Eliane orchestrate such a productive meeting. But that's why she came. She'd probably confronted the likes of our counterparts throughout her career, maybe multiple times on this trip, and she knew just how to respond, even with the little background information we'd provided her in the Pajero. In the days that followed, Assis fronted the money needed for our hookups and we had electricity and water like everyone else in Bangolo *ville*. I knew it would happen eventually. I just needed a little more faith.

CHAPTER NINE

SANCTUARY

Megan and I moved into our houses on a bittersweet day in the middle of May. On the one hand, we were moving into our own space at last, enabling us to get on with our assignments. On the other hand, we were moving a good distance from our friends at the Kamonda, and although we would visit with them frequently, we would no longer benefit from their daily care and refuge.

Megan's house had a new paint job and plumbing fixtures, but it lacked the protective wall the culture found so comforting. In contrast, my place was old and decrepit, but I did have a wall if you could overlook the large gap in the front yard, which I chose not to rebuild for practical and symbolic reasons. Each day a herd of free-range cows fed on the tall grass within. Rebuilding the wall would require I do the mowing; plus, it didn't feel right to rob the cows of a dietary source on their daily plod before the inevitable slaughter.

With regard to security, rebuilding the wall would not protect me from the local rabble. If the criminals did not enter directly through the hinged front gate, they could climb the one-meter high wall with ease at any number of locations hidden from view. For the wall to provide any real deterrent to crime I would have to build it up another five or six feet, then line the top with glass or concertina wire, as was common for dignitaries. I'd take my chances.

All in all, my house was habitable, not only for me but for the resident mice, spiders, and flying cockroaches that hid in the recesses of concrete and wood by day and feasted off my refuse at night. There was nothing fancy or modern about it, and it would more than serve its sheltering purpose. Through the front door there was a large living room, and if you kept going straight, you'd enter a small kitchen with a back door. Off the living room was a hallway six feet wide that led to three bedrooms and two bathrooms with actual toilets and showers. Toilets? Showers? I would be the envy of my colleagues who crapped in bug-infested holes and washed with water they had to hoist from the depths of the earth.

My new house was larger than I would need, though I was not about to complain after living on a bed in a brothel for a month. A smaller house would have suited me fine, but you'd be hard-pressed to find one in Bangolo. Houses in Côte d'Ivoire were not built for single American bachelors; they were built for large extended African families with income from employment in town or in Abidjan.

One could describe my house as blue from the inside out. Both interior and exterior walls were painted a Smurf-blue color, now faded and worn, dirty like an urban skyline on a cloudless day. The trim on the doors and windows was a dark blue for contrast. When I visited Jerome for the first time since moving, I yelled out *"chef du Kamonda!"* over the gates as I approached. Jerome bellowed back, *"chef de la maison bleue!"* with a chuckle.

The floor throughout was a slate tile of deep red with swirls of white. The ceiling tiles, originally painted white, were now marbled with brown stains from the leaky roof. I repainted the living room with the same blue and white shades, so any omission of paint was not so obvious, but I limited my labor to the living room as I didn't figure to spend much time in the other rooms, and I had no vested interest in the property or the absentee landlord.

Another feature of my house, and every other house in Côte d'Ivoire, were the metal *anti-vols* or theft bars embedded in the concrete at each window to keep thieves at bay. *Anti-vols* were definitely a good idea as theft was the most common crime. Windows were not made of glass; they were made of horizontal wooden slats angled like louvers, framed and hinged at the top. Exterior doors were made in a similar fashion, with open slats instead of a solid material, to allow airflow through the house when windows were latched and doors were closed. Mosquitoes were a big problem, so I fastened a fine mesh netting to the slats on both windows and doors. That generally worked, but if the windows and doors weren't closed by sundown I'd end up with a steady stream of the little buggers in the house, always keen to my whereabouts.

My furniture was basic and inexpensive, made by a local craftsman. I procured a desk, a table, two wooden chairs, and two slat-back chairs of denim cloth for the living room. If visitors came by, I'd drag the chairs out to the porch, as it was considered rude to enter someone's home without being invited and customary to gather outside. I also had a wooden bed frame inserted with a thick foam mattress. The alternative was to sleep on a mattress made of straw encased in rice sack, which was better for the lower back but a bit scratchy on the skin. I erected makeshift shelves in the bedroom and kitchen, and I bought an oscillating fan, an electric fridge, and a two-burner propane stove. Life was good.

When I was settled, I learned from Madame Baman that there were two high school-aged boys living in the storage shed at the back end of my compound. She asked if I had any plans for the shed because the two boys were worried they would need to find another place to live when I moved in. I had no intention of tossing them out. Madam Baman said they were good boys from Duékoué who needed a place to stay while attending school in Bangolo. I considered making a scene, telling them with a straight face that I had big plans to use the shed to store the surplus of my possessions, but I had no idea how they would respond to that type of deadpan humor. They didn't know me, and if I couldn't pull it off I didn't want my failed attempt at humor to be their first impression of their new neighbor. Who knows what they'd been through as kids if they had no family in Bangolo and were living in a vacant shed.

For a week the two boys managed to steer clear of me, concealing their identity, but now that I was on the lookout I managed to spot them one day hopping over the wall. I called them over to the porch and we talked at length. I assured them they were welcome to stay as long as I lived there, and in return they offered to care for the yard and keep an eye out for *les voleurs*, aware that the color of my skin and the riches of my heritage made me a target, made us all a target.

Their names were Maseem and Ernest, and their presence paid dividends immediately. I was putting the last coat of paint on the living room walls. The front door was open for ventilation and the neighborhood children were coming and going for the spectacle of an American. Most of the kids I recognized. Some I did not. When I looked down into the plastic bucket where I kept my tools, I noticed that my Leatherman was missing. I was certain it was in the bucket just minutes prior because I remember thinking how uniquely modern the multi-purpose tool must look with its pliers and folding blades and shiny chrome finish.

I approached Maseem, who was in the side yard practicing his footwork with a miniature soccer ball, and I mentioned that one of the kids may have taken a tool from my house. Maseem was young himself, sixteen at most, with a round face, hair trimmed almost to the scalp, and a big carefree smile. Adults referred to him as *petit*, as they did most every child, not acknowledging him by name until he graduated high school or turned eighteen. Despite his age, Maseem was mature and determined not to allow this kind of behavior into our compound.

I never expected to see my Leatherman again, but less than an hour later, Maseem was hauling a young child by the nape of the neck, his tiny feet dragging behind, failing to keep pace with Maseem's long angry strides. They approached while I was sitting on the porch cleaning paint off my hands. Maseem delivered a swift slap to the back of the boy's head, which prompted the return of my Leatherman and an apology under duress. The little boy's name was Herman, wearing a ballcap on sideways, tattered shorts, no shirt, and a wide, shit-eating grin. If I had to pick a guilty party out of a lineup of neighbor kids, he would've been my first choice. But Herman had no parents. He lived with his uncle, and his uncle didn't have a job, so I put him to work in the yard, and over time he became my little confidant, and he never stole from me again.

If I actually owned or were paying rent on my house, I'd say Maseem earned his keep by tracking down our young culprit. But I was as big of a freeloader as Maseem and Ernest, living without bills, mortgage, or financial responsibility, and my debt to them for their hard work was far greater than their debt to me for my phony allowances. Still, it was good to get my Leatherman back.

Months later there was another incident, this time without Maseem or Ernest around for surveillance, as they had returned to Duékoué for the school break. It was a hot afternoon, late into the *sieste*, and I was reading in one of my slat-back chairs in the living room. Though the windows were wedged open as far as they would go, and the oscillating fan was on high a few feet from my chair, my bare back was sweaty against the thick denim backing. I kept thinking that I heard noises in the kitchen, but with the clamor of the fan and the grumbling of the old fridge and the clatter of an expanding metal roof, it all sounded the same.

As I rose to get a drink in the kitchen, I saw two wooden poles the size of broom handles stuck through the *anti-vols* in the open window. At the end of one pole was a small woven basket. The other pole was knocking dried goods off the shelf and into the basket. Taken aback by the nerve of this thief, I yelled and rushed to open the back door. The poles fell to the floor. By the time I got the door unlatched, my adrenaline was flowing and I shouted *"Voleur!"* before the door was fully open, loud enough for Madam Baman to hear me, as the suspect jumped the wall into the Baman compound. She rushed toward him with a handheld broom, but he got by her and into the side street. Others within earshot took up the chase as Madam Baman pointed in his direction.

As *"Voleur!"* resonated though the *quartier*, growing more distant but gathering participants, I realized the severity of the situation. The thief was a small boy, maybe twelve or thirteen years old, and he had been caught stealing red-handed. At a minimum his act would bring shame upon himself and his family for a long time to come. By American standards, it was but a prank, a dare perhaps, barely enough to elicit the law or even serious punishment. Was it a mistake for me to yell '*voleur*' so quickly? The boy certainly did not deserve to be beaten by frantic strangers for his petty crime. But it was too late. I had accused a boy of stealing in dramatic fashion, and he was going to pay a price. When I asked Madam Baman about the boy's fate, she said it was not my concern, that he would receive the proper punishment to ensure he never steals again.

In America, kids have been known to bring weapons to school, using or threatening to use them on their classmates and teachers. Gangs are present in every city and town, selling drugs and perpetrating violence. And common decency and respect towards adults has become a rarity, a value lost in the distractions of progress. These transgressions often go unpunished or even ignored, mired in legal red tape. It used to be that a measured wailing by one's parents or a degree of consequence was an adequate means by which to discipline a child. That is no longer the case. Today the notion of such discipline is considered abuse, upheld by a new interpretation of the old laws.

In Côte d'Ivoire, punishment is dispensed daily by family and community who do not wait for police or lawyers or courts to intervene (not that they have that option). As a result, or by chance, violent and perverted crime seemed to be negligible in Côte d'Ivoire. During my time in Africa, I rarely heard of an instance where someone was raped or murdered (unless the murder was by way of bad sorcery). There was no such thing as serial killers or pedophile priests or drive-by shootings or murder-suicides. The local jails were almost always empty while the police reposed on chairs on the jailhouse porch, growing fatter by the day. Crimes common to Côte d'Ivoire were theft, corruption, and various manifestations of poverty, but these crimes were seemingly manageable compared to the deluge of crime in America.

With respect to my own personal experiences in the U.S., I've had my apartment and car broken into, and my television, VCR, money, and other valuables stolen, never to be recovered, as police were purportedly too busy with major derelicts. I've encountered people who want to hurt you just because you looked at them the wrong way. And I've witnessed random acts of violence in various forms. These are hardly the most egregious crimes that America has to offer, but if you live in a major city or town, they are almost obligatory. In Côte d'Ivoire, my Leatherman and some dry goods were stolen (both ended up back in my possession), and the *gendarmerie* managed to extort a few bucks from my per diem to supplement an income not always guaranteed by the préfecture. But I hardly ever felt my physical well-being was in danger by the deliberate hands of others.

One could attribute these differences between crime in America and crime in Africa to any number of distinctions or circumstances. It's possible that America's criminal transgression is the price to pay for progress and development. It's possible that there is no criminal transgression in America, just an increase in how criminal acts are publicized or psychoanalyzed; and it's possible there's no difference between our culture's innate potential for criminal activity, just different opportunities. There are far too many variables to consider.

Whether real or imagined, I did feel more secure living in Côte d'Ivoire than anywhere else prior to joining the Peace Corps. If I had to venture a guess as to why, I'd say it had something to do with a strong sense of community. Despite the concrete walls, the people of Senegal and Côte d'Ivoire looked out after each other, shared their food and possessions, however meager, policed their youth, respected and honored their adults and elders, and welcomed strangers like one of the family. This is not to say that Ivoirians do not discriminate, especially when it comes to tribal affiliations or politics. But as a stranger I could pretty much walk up to any house or hut, start a conversation, and almost always receive an invitation for lunch or a place to sleep without anything in return, less a few stories about my hometown and my family. Hospitality was fundamental. Try approaching a random house in America as a foreigner or stranger. You'd be lucky to make it past the front gate without being turned back, attacked by dogs, or riddled with bullets. There are exceptions, of course, but on the whole, American has become a defensive, untrusting, panic-stricken culture that pardons instead of punishes its *voleurs* of community.

With a new house came a new routine. I usually awoke before 0800 on weekdays, fighting the urge to stay in bed to resolve a night of bizarre, unnerving Mefloquine dreams. I'd shower, dress, and walk to the municipal office where I'd catch up with THIMO mobilizing for a half day in the fields and empty lots. Then I'd make the rounds at the office. As usual, Dogbo was tired, still suffering from malaria; Assis was still anxious, eyes fixed in the same thousand-mile glare; the mayor was still absent; and our Peace Corps protagonist (or antagonist) was becoming as cynical as ever.

Within a rock's toss of the office, there was a small kiosk where I ate breakfast each day. I'd sit at one of the six stools along the counter, joined by staff from the nearby offices, and we'd talk about current affairs over coffee or tea. The roof of the kiosk extended over the stools just enough to keep the sun off our faces in the morning, but not off our backs in the afternoon. On the business side of the counter, there was a large fridge and a two-burner propane stove on a table, with condiments and cookware carefully arranged so the cook could operate efficiently in the tight space.

The owner's name was Diallo, a Muslim from Guinea northwest of Côte d'Ivoire. Diallo was thin and tall, unlike the small stout Guéré, and he stood out as much as I did. The Ivoirian men barked orders at him. "Diallo! Give me bread! Diallo! It is necessary to make me a coffee! Diallo! Hurry! Hurry!" ordering him around because they were late for work, they claimed. You'd think by listening to these men that Diallo was responsible for all their failings, but Diallo accommodated them in every way, moving as swiftly as anyone should, always addressing his customers as *"patron"*—a reverence they neither earned nor deserved. They were belligerent to Diallo because he was in the service industry and not a politician or government employee, because Diallo was a Guinean and their numbers were growing throughout Côte d'Ivoire, threatening the stability of the region's politics, and despite Diallo's friendly and humble nature, he had a look of contempt for men who did not treat him as an equal, as a man.

When the morning rush was over and the customers had gone elsewhere, I'd order food and hang around, talking to Diallo and his family, especially his young boy, *petit* Diallo. At first Diallo did not know what to make of me, and he remained reserved. Over time, horsing-around with *petit* Diallo at the counter, he warmed up to me as someone with whom he could discuss his affairs.

The regular fare at the kiosk was an omelet sandwich with freshly baked bread sliced from a long baguette. Diallo would light a messy grease-stained stove under a charred black frying pan half full of palm oil. Once the oil was hot, he'd scramble the eggs in a bowl, add onions and tomatoes if available, a touch of salt, and pour the contents into the hot oil. The eggs immediately grew in size, like an air bag being deployed from a crashing automobile, like a science experiment, cooked in seconds flat without any flipping or stirring—essentially, deep fried eggs.

The first time I ate at Diallo's kiosk, he poured the entire contents of the pan, oil and all, directly into my bread, saturating the sandwich. "The oil is where the flavor is," I was told. If I were going to eat eggs for breakfast as often as it seemed, it would have to be without this massive quantity of oil or I'd be dead before my two years were up. Diallo did not comprehend my request to cook the eggs with only a dab of oil, for the oil is the healthiest part and it keeps the eggs from sticking to the old pan, he claimed. Eventually we compromised. He could cook my eggs in the oil as long as the excess was drained off, and I would agree not to complain about the lack of flavor I sacrificed for *la santé Américaine*.

After breakfast I'd continue walking through town, stop in most stores as a courtesy, see if I had any mail, say hello to the boys at the Kamonda, pick up supplies at the market, and head back home, engaging as many people as I could about their business or pursuits. By then it was usually lunchtime, so I'd walk from my house to the *gare* with my plastic bowl to get rice and sauce. For about ten cents, I could buy a heaping portion of rice with peanut sauce, which I gladly ate most every day. After lunch, I'd try my best to stay awake and read all the handouts and manuals from training, but at some point between noon and 1300, I conceded to a nap. In the late afternoon, I'd usually do some sort of exercise. I frequently rode my bike north on the paved road then back to my house to watch the sunset from my porch, which dropped over the horizon at 18:30 each evening, as Bangolo is just seven degrees north of the equator.

I exercised in the house to the sounds of Dave Matthews, Weezer, Red Hot Chilli Peppers, Blues Traveler, Neil Young, and the Presidents of the United States from a cheap cassette player. In my cavernous space, the tunes echoed through each room and out through the window slats. I often wondered what my neighbors thought. Nobody ever stopped by to complain, and they never said anything about the volume or my taste. Maybe my neighbors enjoyed the music, or perhaps the tempo helped inspire them while pounding maniocs into mush.

Megan and I were now living and working independently, with a different approach to development work and life in general. If I didn't have something planned for dinner at home, I'd wait until dark and walk down to Main Street. I could usually get decent street food such as grilled fish over *atchieké*, or skewered beef, or a hodgepodge of items ranging from fried plantains to fried beignets. If I wasn't in the mood for street food, I could mosey up to the counter of a kiosk and get spaghetti, fried in the same oily manner as Diallo's omelet, or I could spend my money at a *maquis* and get a chicken. I was definitely not in want of nourishment or variety as my colleagues were in rural Côte d'Ivoire. They often ate nothing but gruel, porridge, and pounded-up starch, two to three times a day for two years—the "real" Peace Corps I was told by volunteers who sacrificed in this manner.

After dinner, with no television or short-wave radio, I'd usually write in my journal or read from the many books I brought or smuggled from the hostel, pulling a slat-back chair beneath the overhead florescent light until I grew tired around midnight. Journal writing was therapeutic, but when I reread the contents I felt it was mostly garbage, full of ruminations about my past, promises for the future, and other such flatulence. As far as books, this was the first time in a long while I actually enjoyed reading, having spent the last six years with my nose in engineering textbooks. While I was not a swift reader (averaging around twenty pages per hour), I must have read nearly one hundred books during my time in Bangolo. My favorites were works of fiction from Steinbeck and V.S. Naipaul, and non-fictional accounts from Thoreau, Twain, Colin Fletcher, and Edward Abbey; none so eagerly anticipated than an unread Abbey. These authors, philosophers, and characters were there when no one else was, and they became loyal companions, waiting patiently on a shelf or a stack for when the time was right.

Around 2000 the *gbakas* and the majority of the bus traffic ceased for the evening, and around 2100 most everyone was off the streets and fast asleep. Even on weekends there were only a few diehards out past ten or eleven at night, roaming drunk between the *maquis* or brothels. The absence of noise and commotion in the evenings was pleasant, and I reveled in my newfound solitude, but those few hours of silence could be somewhat disturbing. The drone of the florescent bulb and the rattle of the old fridge with nary a sound outside made me restless at times, and made the evening seem like an eternity. If I were not totally engrossed in reading or writing, thoughts from my past or the longing for love and companionship would creep in with a pang of regret and loneliness.

On occasion, I'd be perfectly content to sit alone on my porch, lights turned off, jazz playing softly on the cassette player while Africa played itself out on the stage in front of me, and I'd drink myself into a glorious stupor. In some artificial fashion, this concert of stimuli helped suppress the loneliness and introduced me to a heightened state of joy and sorrow, of obligation, of prospects, of the future. Factor in the cacophony of a driving rainstorm against a tin roof and I was damn near enlightened. Dennis from Issia was on to something and I was a willing convert, though I was careful to limit these occasions for fear of abusing them or squandering the moment.

To combat the loneliness, I forced myself to put down the books, go outside, and participate in the discourse of life. Generally I interacted with men my age at the kiosks and *maquis*. The great majority of them would steer the conversation to their need for money, clothing, or a correspondent with a stateside address for their visa application. Aside from the boys at the Kamonda, Maseem and Ernest, and Diallo, it was difficult to find men who were sincere and undemanding. I was frustrated that I was failing to relate to Ivoirians the same way I had failed to relate to my homestay brother Sylvean and his friends in Senegal.

As far as interactions with women, it was generally limited to the older *marchandes* who sold goods at the market or a street side table. I'd engage in friendly, flirtatious banter about marrying one of their daughters, and I was usually rewarded with extra portions of their product. Women my age, even much younger, usually had three to four kids and were working to sustain their families, or they were one of the few who'd succeeded in school and moved to Abidjan to pursue a career. Either way, I pretty much ruled out getting involved with local African women from the outset since I'd have to prey on teenage girls in high school before they flunked out or started a family. I was not that lonely. There was also the language and culture barrier working against me, and the need to uphold a reputation as a solid citizen in a community where I was a celebrity mascot of sorts. If this wasn't enough, the HIV/AIDS epidemic in sub-Saharan Africa was constantly on my mind, ensuring my abstinence and a callused palm.

Dinners and visits with Megan were pleasant, sometimes essential in the scheme of our day, but if we hadn't been incarcerated in Bangolo, there was no telling if we would've hung out. Others from the UEM group expressed a similar sentiment about their site partners. Megan was a good person; we were just cut from different molds. Even during our most desperate times, our relationship remained platonic. Too many complications, I reasoned. Despite all that, I did feel a certain fraternal responsibility for Megan, like a younger sister or cousin who relied on me for support and protection in an aggressive, male-dominated society, and we shared many a laugh, meal, or moment over our shared circumstances.

For supplies and camaraderie, I traveled to Man about once a week, usually on the weekend. There were eight volunteers within a 100-kilometer radius of the city. At first we'd meet by chance, run into each other on the street or in a restaurant. As we got to know each other better we'd arrange our meetings in advance, or I'd rely on the local shoeshine boys as my secret informants. They would tell me which *toubabs* were in town and where they were last spotted for the same price as a shoeshine, which amounted to pennies. They even buffed the straps of my Tevas as a bonus.

Of all the volunteers in the region, I was closest to Russ and Stephanie from my training group. Russ was posted in Biankouma, a town of 15,000 located fifty kilometers north of Man. He was a couple years younger than me and had the same tall thin build. People said we could've passed for brothers, aside from his blond thinning scalp and my dark ratty hair and beard. I don't think it was so much our physical attributes people thought so akin. Russ and I were both born and raised in central Massachusetts, about thirty minutes away as the car drives, both interested in the outdoors, and we'd spent a lot of time together as UEM trainees in Senegal. We'd often reminisce of our lives in Massachusetts, of food we craved from such places as Hot Dog Annies and Ronnie's Clams, harkening back to a time when Fenway bleacher seats were an affordable $6. While others from our training group were just getting to know each other, Russ and I were bound by our familiar past.

Stephanie was posted in a village called Gotongouiné II, west of Man, about ten kilometers off the main road to Liberia. Stephanie was my age, a Stanford grad with long brown hair, a bright smile, and the thin toned body of a long-distance runner. She was well liked, marked by her California optimism. In Senegal, we had been residents of the same dormitory building, otherwise known as *bâtiment huit*, reserved for the eldest of the lot. Though we were in different programs, we often went running after class, processing our dynamic lives as we ran. Stephanie was not convinced that the Peace Corps would serve her needs, and she deliberated more than most whether to swear in as a volunteer.

One weekend I met up with Russ and Stephanie, Russ' site mate Doug, and Eric (a.k.a Monkey Boy because he cared for a young chimpanzee in his village) from the village of Gouéssesso. Doug and Eric had been in-country more than a year already, so they gave us a tour of Man, showed us the best *maquis*, the best places to get sauce *arachide*, and the best places to stay overnight. For eight dollars plus taxi fare, you could stay at Centre Bethany, a hotel in the mountains operated by Catholics as a part-time retreat center. The area was quiet and the views were amazing, overlooking a city nestled in the foothills of the Monts de Dan mountain range and its most prominent feature: an 881-meter-high mountain named La Dent for its rocky, incisor-shaped appearance rising starkly from the bold green landscape. Eight dollars was more than a day's per diem, so the only time I stayed at Centre Bethany was when I really needed to get away. There were cheaper hotels in town within walking distance, but Doug and Eric reasoned that if you stay in town you might as well stay at Khaled's house for free.

Khaled was a young Lebanese merchant of groceries and household items who lived above his store in a relatively plush air-conditioned Main Street apartment. He seemed genuinely pleased to meet a new group of Peace Corps Americans, and he welcomed us to stay at his place whenever we were in Man. I should have appreciated his generosity more, but I was suspicious. Why would this Lebanese entrepreneur invite a bunch of strangers to stay with him, share his food, and put him out? What was his ulterior motive? Was he trying to court *our* women by offering them sanctuary from the village? Was he a Hezbollah operative, luring us loathsome Americans with air-conditioning and amenities to hold us for ransom or punish us for our indulgent ways?

Later that evening, Khaled joined us at a carnival in a vacant lot by the *gare*. A carnival was a rare event and a most surreal spectacle in Africa. The rusted metal rides and neon lights were the same as carnivals in the U.S., but watching small African kids with distended stomachs eating cotton candy was altogether new. A row of booths with games of chance and stuffed animal prizes was idle without patrons willing to throw away their earnings. There were even bumper cars, where young Africans did all they could to avoid bumping into each other. I watched three cycles go by without any accidental contact. I remember thinking that if I could figure out why these kids intuitively avoided each other on bumper cars, it would provide insight into the African plight. Then I noticed the kids were all smiles from the time they boarded the small electrically-powered cart until long after their turn had ended. So much for figuring out their plight.

While talking with Khaled, I learned he had been living in Man for ten years and he was ready to go back to his home in Lebanon now that he'd saved a considerable amount of his earnings. Khaled, like many of his countrymen, sought out opportunities in the urban hubs of the developing world where labor was cheap and competition was sparse. In addition to being merchants, the Lebanese also operated restaurants, grew and harvested coffee and cacao, and dabbled in the logging industry. Though they were living abroad to earn wealth, they were not sacrificing by any means. They had fully-furnished, air-conditioned apartments and hired help to clean, run errands, and cook great Lebanese feasts with imported foods. They had cars and chauffeurs and gorgeous young African mistresses. They even had their own club with a restaurant and bar, tennis courts, outdoor swimming pool, and a riding stable. If anyone were to be punished for their indulgent ways, it certainly wasn't our band of relative indigents.

    I stayed with Khaled only a few times before he realized his plan to move back to Lebanon for good, but before he left, he introduced me to his friends, Fardi and Samir. Fardi and Samir were brothers who ran one of the largest coffee and cacao operations in western Côte d'Ivoire. During harvest, their enormous warehouse was filled to the ceiling with heaping burlap sacks to be loaded onto semis, destined for Abidjan and export to world markets. I was amazed to watch great hulking African men carry one of these hundred-pound sacks on their heads, whereas I had a difficult time dragging one along the smooth concrete floor without over-exerting myself. If they'd placed one of these sacks on my head, I would've crumpled like a brittle old corpse.

    Fardi was about my age, the younger of the two. Samir was ten to fifteen years older, a paternal figure to many of the younger Lebanese men in the community. They had been living in Man for almost as long as Khaled, with a house and depot in Bangolo, and they welcomed us to stay with them as Khaled had done. I became friends with Fardi, occasionally eating at his house in Bangolo, and I found no ulterior motive to his generosity. Fardi, like Khaled, was just bored with his small circle of Lebanese friends and craved a different perspective not offered by the local population.

    Whenever I was in Man, I made an effort to hike La Dent or at least explore the jungle area at its base. Nine times I found my way to its rocky summit; six of those times accompanied by other volunteers, usually Russ and Stephanie. To get there from town, we'd take a taxi from Main Street three kilometers to a trailhead at a touristy little village in an outlying *quartier*. The proclaimed *chef du quartier*—a different man every time, each too young to be the actual *chef*—would ask us to pay a fee in order to proceed, which allegedly went to pay our young guide to keep us on the trail. We could haggle this fee down from 1500 to 500 CFA apiece, but we knew the money would not go to our guide, as *petits* were not given allowances.

The hike started with a gradual ascent along a trodden path, a working path, through a series of cornfields. At the apex of a hill on the backside of La Dent, you'd veer from the path at the mandarin tree, bushwhack twenty meters through thickets and nettles to a rocky trail, which rose abruptly in a counterclockwise spiral once around La Dent beneath a thick jungle canopy, up a wooden ladder, and finish with a scramble over a rock breakdown to the summit. The round-trip hike was about eight kilometers.

When I hiked alone, I set out from Main Street, forgoing the taxi. Some of the children along the route were afraid of me, cowering behind their mothers, while others rushed to hold my hand or follow behind in small packs, chanting *"Quee, quee, quee,"* while clapping their hands in unison (the word *"quee"* is both a Guéré and the local Dan word for white man). Some of the volunteers were bothered by the chanting, perceiving it as a racial slur, and they would verbally lash out at the children. But children in Africa, honest as children anywhere, pointed out the obvious: the rarity of a white complexion strolling through their lives, perhaps for the first time. And they did so without hatred or the notion of racism.

Only young children engaged in the chanting. A formative child typically learns that elders, regardless of color, are to be treated with respect. I was addressed as Monsieur, or Monsieur Scott if they knew my name. Still, Africans referred to me by color in conversation with other Africans the same way one would refer to any number of distinguishing characteristics to describe someone unfamiliar or distant. I was the *quee*, the *toubab*, the *toubab bou*, and *le blanc*. And the only time it bothered me was when it was said with obvious disdain. To my knowledge, that only occurred once during my tenure when the mayor introduced Megan and I to one of his staff as *"Magui et Le blanc là"* with a flippant nod. Even though the mayor had failed to learn my name, or he momentarily forgot, he of all authorities should have known better. He could have at least referred to me as *Monsieur Le blanc là.*

Not far from the trailhead to La Dent there was a river that originated from the high country of the Monts de Dan. Women washed their clothes in this river, bent over, knee-deep in water festering with the guinea worm, schistosomiasis, and suds from their

Omo laundry detergent. Clothes were scattered about, draped on large rocks, on tree branches, hovering precipitously on the strength of tall elephant grass. Directly adjacent to this river, continuing up into the mountains, there was a dirt road rising abruptly at the edge of the *quartier*, washed out in numerous places where the river had raged beyond its banks in the torrents of the rainy season. It was on this dirt road that one gained access to a network of clandestine trails, discovered by straying from the trail on previous descents or by following a cacao farmer down a path to civilization.

Now each time I went hiking, I'd avoid the trailhead at the touristy little village and I'd hike up that dirt road and around La Dent via these other trails. It was the long way around, but I loathed forfeiting my hardly-earned salary to random opportunistic men posing as the *chef*. Still, I was usually stopped to find out where I was going or if I were lost and needed a guide. "Nowhere in particular," I would respond. "Just a hike *en brousse* to exercise my mind." This always drew a blank gaze. Ivoirians don't travel without a destination and a purpose. Farmers walk to reach their fields and attend to their crops. Tourists hike to claim the summit of the famed tooth. Who is this defiant *toubab* who walks to exercise his head? Occasionally they followed me up the dirt road to see what I was up to, which gave me an opportunity to point out the flora and fauna. Either they shared my appreciation for the outdoors or they thought I was loony, but in all instances they would leave me to my business and return to the village.

Another spot in Man offering relief from the city was Les Cascades, a tremendous waterfall some ten stories high, emerging from the jungle at the base of Mont Tonkoui, Côte d'Ivoire's highest mountain at 1189 meters. It was a spendy taxi ride to Les Cascades from Main Street, but only a short three-kilometer walk from Centre Bethany. To access the waterfall from the road, you'd first cross the *pont de liana* over a wide turbulent river. A *pont de liana* is a bridge made of vines constructed in one night by young boys as an annual rite of passage into manhood. According to lore, the boys are bound and blindfolded and taken into the jungle. They work swiftly under the cover of darkness, tying and lashing the vines together, crafting a structurally sound footbridge over a river, gaining access to new lands and facilitating the transport of the harvest. It was an amazing feat for such young hands in a short time under adverse conditions.

There are a number of *pont de lianas* in the Man region, but none as accessible as the one crossing over to Les Cascades. This particular bridge was constructed like no other, not to achieve passage into manhood, but for commercial pursuits, to deliver tourists so they could relax by one of the area's natural wonders while consuming cold beverages and snacks from the *maquis* at the base of the waterfall.

Averting the touristy little village and its fees, and buying high-priced beers at Les Cascades, were not the only occasions for prudent spending in Man. I purchased a great majority of my groceries, produce, clothing, and souvenirs from its stores and markets, all of which was negotiable. I could save a bit of money by monitoring the going rates and negotiating my price. Not that I had to. Even if I paid the initial asking price for every item I ever purchased in Africa, I'd probably have per diem to spare. It was not like I was always targeted to pay double because I was white. For certain items, this was the case, but most of the time it was a difference of dollars or cents between the initial asking price and the market price.

The real impetus behind haggling for merchandise had a lot to do with cultural assimilation. Financial prudence is a part of daily life in Africa, a necessity for survival. To be frivolous or apathetic about spending was an affront to the hardship and lifestyle of the local people. The better we were at haggling, the more respect we gained from vendors, especially if we gave them repeat business. The more respect we gained from vendors, the more pride we developed as a conscientious part of the community. Attempt to overcharge us and that pride was summoned, and we haggled with passion and persistence like our lives depended on the outcome. Not all volunteers engaged in haggling for merchandise. There were those who preferred to redistribute the wealth, pay a little extra to avoid the chore of haggling, even give money away. I applaud their generosity, but I did not share this same obligation.

Any productive trip to Man commenced with a visit to the bank. The Peace Corps wired our cost-of-living expenses to the institution of our choosing on a quarterly basis, which amounted to $6.00 per day, $180 per month, or over 500 big ones per quarter. Regardless of the time or day, there was always a long line at the bank. The true extent of the line was not always apparent by the number of people in the queue. I found out the hard way that it is not your person that signifies your place in line but the position of your bankbook on the counter in front of the teller's Plexiglas.

When I first went to the bank, throngs of men in *fonctionnaire* suits were loitering outside on the stairs, smoking, eating, and talking with friends. There were only a few men in the actual line, so I wondered if the men outside were thieves spying my withdrawal. After a customer's transaction, these men rushed the line to physically advance their bankbooks as close to the preceding bankbook as possible, even if only a few centimeters, eliminating the gap in between booklets for fear someone would cut in line. Fights always broke out, mostly verbal but some physical, when someone's bankbook touched another or when someone blocked access to the bankbook queue. It was a most obsessive spectacle. The physical line was for those who felt the need to guard their bankbook, or for an American who did not trust the new process.

More cautious now with a moneybelt full of cash, I'd start my shopping on the bottom floor of the market in what amounted to the produce section. There were two dozen African women sitting behind concrete benches, each with identical displays of fruits and vegetables such as lettuce, tomatoes, potatoes, carrots, cucumbers, purple cabbage, bananas, mangos, onions, garlic, fresh basil, and so on. I never wanted for variety. The market in Man made the market in Bangolo look like an abandoned lot of refuse and tailings.

The first few times in the market, I was hounded to no end by the *marchandes* claiming to have the freshest crop, with some of them physically pulling at me. When I investigated, I found there was little difference in the quality of produce and almost no difference in price. With the day reserved for shopping, I spent time talking with the women, searching for a generous soul, asking about incentives if I purchased my produce from them. One offered nothing, a few offered extra portions of garlic or basil, and one offered a big fat ripe mango for my ride to Bangolo. Jackpot! The mother lode! The fruits of my loyalty. Or rather, fruit for my loyalty.

On the second floor were the souvenirs, the work of artisans, handcrafted masks, statues, games, *batiques*, wall hangings, paintings, and African arts and crafts. The vendors who sold these items were relentless, leaving their stalls to surround me with merchandise in hand, shouting until I promised to regard their wares. I was genuinely curious. I had to buy gifts for relatives at some point so I inspected every stall. I got the lowdown on price and found that they varied drastically. Material costs were about the same amongst artisans; the difference was the markup or the value each vendor put on his blood and sweat—the most negotiable of commodities.

Haggling for souvenirs was great fun because I usually didn't need the item for survival. The vendor would give me his price. I would say it was too high and I'd walk away, feigning disgust. Not so fast. The vendor would call me back to ask how much I was willing to pay. If I actually cared to purchase the item, I was careful not to offend the vendor with an outrageously low price, but I was also aware it wasn't going to get cheaper from here on out. I'd start with a price I could afford, a price I could brag about if it was accepted, and I'd see where it went from there. If the vendor wasn't willing to budge, he probably had other income or greater patience. If the vendor was quick to sell at my price, he was probably desperate for a sale, or needed to put food on his family's table. While there was no way of knowing the vendor's situation, I managed to procure traditional masks and large *batiques* for a few dollars each, spotted in Abidjan at four to five times the price, sold in the United States for hundreds more.

Over time I found even more to Man than supplies and camaraderie, hiking and spectacular landscapes. I found a good tailor who could turn a few yards of material into a nice shirt or a pair of pants. I found stores with cookies, ice cream bars, French wine and cheese, restaurants with pizza and pasta, and patisseries with good coffee and desserts. I found a movie theater with American action films dubbed in French (though I regret never attending the famed karate / porno double feature on Sunday nights). These luxuries and modern conveniences were typical of Abidjan, but I had no idea this lifestyle would be available locally in what amounted to a large, faraway, mountain village. In Bangolo I found a shelter, a home, a sanctuary for the long haul. In Man I found relief, an oasis, and a sanctuary from my village when it was needed most.

CHAPTER TEN

FRATERNITY

Every three months, UEM volunteers were expected to travel to Abidjan for another round of immunizations and to update the administration on our progress. Most of us relented and made our way to the big city when duty called; others made themselves scarce, hunkering down in their village, forsaking the city for the true Peace Corps experience. While administrators had all sorts of rules, policies, and expectations for their flock, a trip to Abidjan was not always productive.

Our first gathering was on July 4th to combine quarterly meetings with patriotic festivities with other American personnel including the Marines, missionaries, embassy staff, and random ex-patriots. The volunteer nearest the capital had a twenty-minute commute by taxicab. In comparison, volunteers in the northern villages began their trips two to three days ahead of time, the first leg possibly involving a long walk or bike ride *en brousse* to the nearest road. No matter how long or how far the journey, getting around Côte d'Ivoire was always a high-risk ordeal that took a bit of patience and luck.

At the Bangolo *gare*, I was getting to know some of the workers. The *chef* was Clement, the man with the thin mustache and straw hat I had first met while mapping the town. If Clement wasn't too busy, I'd sit next to him and try to soften his tough guy façade with sarcasm and self-deprecating humor. Over time, he clued me in on the complex world of public transportation and the *syndicat,* or union, that controlled the business. He even gave me pointers to make the travel experience less of a hassle. Little by little, Clement warmed up to Megan and me, and we developed a decent friendship.

I didn't expect the eight-hour bus ride to Abidjan to be as eventful as my first trip to Bangolo, but after talking with Clement I realized I had some choices to make; mainly, *when* to travel. I could leave in the daytime when the *fonctionnaires* and *marchandes* commuted back and forth, pay top price for a ticket, fight the crowds, wrestle for a seat, compete for bag space in the overhead, and swelter in the heat as the road dust settled on my sweaty clothes. Or, I could take the night bus, the redeye, depart around 2200, haggle for a better price, get there faster with less traffic and fewer manned police stops, and possibly get some sleep, as long as the ride was smooth and the passenger next to me didn't nod off on my shoulder. But I would be risking my life at the higher nighttime speeds, not to mention the danger of arriving at the Adjamé *gare* while it was still dark. Clement also mentioned that the drivers at night take strong stimulants to stay alert and awake. "Then again, so do the drivers during the day," he added.

I decided to take the night bus. Not only did I get a better price, which meant more disposable cash in Abidjan, but the *apprenti* insisted I sit up front next to the driver, the seat of honor, with significantly more leg room and unencumbered views of the African sky. It's one thing to sit in the front seat of a *gbaka*, which is like riding shotgun in a pickup truck with your buddies; it's another thing completely to be in the front seat of a big Ivoirian bus moving at breakneck speeds. The front seat was branded as the "death seat" by the volunteers, wrought with excitement and peril, where a pane of glass can become pain from glass in an instant. Fortunately, I made it to Abidjan unscathed, but not all those traveling that night were as lucky. Near Lakota we passed a bus that had gone off the road, flipping on its side. Judging from its mangled condition, there were casualties, serious injuries, or miraculous escapes.

Upon my arrival I learned that a few of our volunteers had left the country in the three months since swear-in. One had a seriously ill dad, one got pregnant and was required to leave, and one decided that the Peace Corps wasn't for him, which could've been anything. I wasn't close with any of them. It's typical of every Peace Corps group to experience some degree of attrition, but the loss of three volunteers in the second most developed country in Africa was notable. Most of us had it relatively good in the IC, though life can upend the best laid plans.

As analogies go, Peace Corps attrition could be likened to a group of castaways floating in an undersized life raft in shark-infested waters. Those who quit are generally close to the edge, scrambling to stay on board but just can't hold on. It's unfortunate they are no longer with us, but you can't dwell on their loss for too long. What matters is that you and your companions are still paddling, surviving. What matters *most* is that you personally make it to shore alive, however you define that shore.

The hostel was packed. Not only did the lion's share of our group show up, but the second-year volunteers were present, entrenched in their favorite sleeping spots, savvy enough not to miss a reimbursed celebration in Abidjan. I found a vacant mattress on the screened-in deck, navigating the open floor space between other mattresses, laying claim like everyone else by spreading my stuff around as if I'd been there for weeks. For the most part, we all found a place to sleep. Some doubled up, looking for any excuse to get cozy. A few braved the mosquitoes by sleeping outdoors. It was the most inhabitants this hostel had seen at any one time, resembling an infirmary for a group whose illness had yet to be defined.

The first order of business was to check out the famed America Recreation Center. Volunteers raved about its nourishing powers, so I crammed into a taxi with three others and headed downtown. It was a short ride, *après le Polyclinique*; $1.50 split four ways. With our poor French and grimy T-shirts as identification, the guards let us in through the gates to the large two-story funhouse we'd come to know so well. We ate hamburgers and fries, drank milk shakes, watched CNN Headline News on the American Forces Network, rented videos, played tennis, and shot hoops. There was also a large swimming pool where we'd find ourselves bobbing around for hours, gossiping about who was hooking up with whom. It was hardly what we expected.

The manager was an older Ivorian man who wore a USS battleship ballcap and tended to the cash register. He seemed to enjoy the company of volunteers, as he could speak to us in his native tongue and we could relate to his world, whereas, the ex-pats seemed to insulate themselves from the world outside, most not bothering to learn French, some downright belligerent to the locals. Still, the ex-pats paid the bills, and we were there by invitation, so as much as we may have resented them, we were also indebted to them.

Abidjan had other destinations that catered to the interests of *toubabs*. There were markets in Cocody and Treichville known for their cheap African crafts. There was St. Paul's Cathedral, which looked like a big church being pulled with cables by a giant concrete Gumby, like a mule would pull a plow, and a nearby iron statue of Pope John Paul II commemorating his visit to the country in 1980. There was the Hôtel Ivoire with its indoor ice-skating rink and bowling alley—a favorite amongst international tourists and visiting family members. There were restaurants and nightclubs, priced so that only those with savings or salaries could enjoy its offerings. Abidjan definitely did not lack for modern convenience. It was a thriving city with European influence in a resource-rich country. It felt much like Boston in both size and density, but its lack of development and sweltering humidity was a constant reminder that I was far from home.

A block from the hostel was the Peace Corps office where the country director, three APCDs, and their support staff could be found. In the mid-90s, computers were fairly novel so we marveled at the three machines that were available to do our quarterly reports. The appeal of these word processing machines paled in comparison to the draw of air-conditioning funneled reliably through the office, evaporating the fresh sweat from our moldy clothes, prompting us to loiter in the library for hours.

There were other ways to cash in on trips to Abidjan. We could join a club such as Women In Development, which sought creative ways to help Côte d'Ivoire's young women advance their education and fund their college dreams, hoping that the country's best and brightest were not squandered on the mortar and pestle. We could work on the third goal of the Peace Corps mission by writing letters or sending African trinkets to American school groups as part of the World Wise Schools program. Or, we could compile and edit the quarterly newsletter *Je Dis,* which translates as, "I say" in English, but means more like, "I just fucking said!" in Ivoirian.

The *Je Dis* was anywhere from ten to fifteen pages long. It was primarily a medium for the administration to pass along information to volunteers up-country such as meeting dates, reminders, public health tips, staffing updates, travel warnings and such, which took up two to three pages at most. After that, the editors had free rein to report and ridicule anything they wanted, and to take liberties with the truth for our entertainment. Most newsletters followed the format of previous issues, which included serious articles written by serious volunteers about a world event, a controversial issue, or a poignant case for change. There were anecdotes from the field as well as humorous cultural observations. There were cartoons with altered thought-bubbles and manipulated photos of volunteers in unflattering poses. Each issue had a section of quotes overheard by volunteers taken out of context, usually sexual in nature, such as: "You can never go down too far," or "I like *Chocomousse* on my banana," or "You gotta rub the pipe until it's smooth," and so on. The *Je Dis* was a newsletter for the people, by the people, insightful and distasteful, and more entertaining than anything in the *Newsweek* magazines that were shoved in our mailbox with regularity.

In the May 1995 issue of the *Je Dis*, the editors created a section called 'Mailbag' where they would respond to real or hypothetical letters from volunteers, kind of like the Dear Abby column. Below are two such letters. The first letter is from a newbie fresh out of training; the second letter is from a volunteer about to finish his two-year term.

Dear Editors,
The moment of swearing-in has arrived and my reservations about the work we are about to start is funneling into the pressing question: Can I raise my right hand to swear in, go live two years in a village, and wake up each morning and feel good about what I am doing? I am writing this letter to you before dawn while waiting for my boss to come into the office so I can tell her I won't be swearing in. Please respond soon.
– Volunteer

Dear Volunteer,
We just got your most recent letter and we want you to listen to our words very carefully...CHILL OUT! Take a deep breath and relax. Normally we would never say what we are about to say, as we truly hate people telling us what to do, but you are a friend and we feel we are talking about sincere and strong fundamental issues. So listen up!
First of all, and we mean this in the nicest way, fuck ideology! It will only get you so far and then it will get in your way. We all know, and everyone with half a brain knows, what the Peace Corps is and what it isn't; what it can do and what it can't. As a large body with a powerful mission, it must be evaluated over time, not on a day-by-day basis. Its worth must be measured not by you but by its collective history, and neither

you nor we can deny that the world is probably better off with the Peace Corps than without it. It will not be perfect, and neither will you....

The reality of what the Peace Corps does or does not do may not be to your liking, and we can understand and sympathize with that, but you are not some multi-national corporation seeking to exploit these people. You are a health worker, and that crosses many boundary lines. You are there to work and give to others and learn about the world and most importantly learn and grow. Maybe in your eyes the Peace Corps shouldn't be doing what it's doing, but for now it is, and you made a commitment. I'd rather you tell me you hate the food and bugs and living conditions than the ideology. Adapt and understand and learn. The world is not a perfect place and will not conform to your views. You are not, we repeat not, defending murderers on death row. You are just one person. Live a little. Give it a year and then reevaluate.

– The Editors

* * *

Dear Editors,

I hope this letter finds you in good health and better spirits. I write you from my own personal hell here in my village. Only four months remain in my two-plus-year sentence. I looked at myself in the mirror today and was startled by the face staring back at me. I saw an old man, grey hair sprinkled through otherwise jet black hair. The whites of my eyes are jaundiced with thick blood vessels ringing the irises like tortured vines. There is something haunted about my expression—one of a man who has suffered something horrific—a shattering of faith, and utter loss of hope. Despair. I smiled into the mirror. My reflection snarled back at me, revealing yellow, decaying teeth, and bleeding gums.

People tell me I stoop. A once erect figure now bends under the strain of the constant burdens of everyday life here. I am so tired sometimes. But that fatigue is as much mental as it is physical. The heat, the ever-present heat, takes its toll, as do the bland monotonous meals, the numerous parasites residing in my gut which wrack my body with frequent bouts of diarrhea. All of my systems are taxed 24 hours a day. Add to this the loneliness, work problems, personality conflicts, nagging moral and philosophical questions, all barraging a man walking on the razor's edge of sanity and you see why I feel a little down. What should I do?

– Volunteer

Dear Volunteer,
 Have a rendezvous with reality, you pathetic loser and Early Terminate. And while you're at it, brush your damn teeth.
– The Editors

A note on the above articles: The editor's response to the first-year volunteer was really an excerpt from a letter by the volunteer's stateside friend; and the letter by the second-year volunteer was fabricated by the editors for levity. Regardless, the discourse above is a fairly accurate characterization of the mindset between new volunteers (young, hopeful, eager, anxious) and veteran volunteers (worn down, cynical, counting the days until the end).

Our first scheduled activity was a co-ed softball game between the Peace Corps volunteers and the Japanese equivalent. It had rained the night before so the field was a muddy mess, but after a few stretches and a shot of courage, we were ready to play ball. We couldn't speak each others languages, but it didn't matter. It was a commendable scrimmage. I'm sure we kicked their asses, refusing even in our little corner of the world not to let America's national pastime be past its time. Nobody kept score of hits and runs, and we conceded that both sides were equally drunk, muddy, and content.

Next up was the Fourth of July picnic at the hostel, with most of the American community in attendance, held under a big white tent in the event of rain. There was volleyball and horseshoes, hamburgers and hot dogs, all the essentials when celebrating liberation from a former colonial master. The highlight of the day was a farewell to Hume Alexander Horan, who had served admirably as the country's ambassador since 1992, making way for Lannon Walker, who would visit Megan and me in the summer of 1996 with his state department entourage.

The day after, a small group of us took a taxi downtown to the Plateau *quartier*. The Japanese volunteers invited us to a trail run with the international community. They would have free food and drink (which we never passed up) along with a commemorative T-shirt. The trail run was instigated by a group called the Hash House Harriers, made up of mostly middle-aged men working in the embassies around Abidjan, whose motto: "A drinker's club with a running problem," told us all we needed to know.

Members claimed there were no rules to a Hash run, that having fun and socializing was the main purpose, but others most definitely adhered to a set of guidelines outlined in what was described as the Hash *Bible*. In a typical Hash run, a trail is blazed by a Hare or a set of Hares. The Hare marks the trail(s) ahead of time, sometimes a day or two in advance, or the Hares are given a head start on the other runners, known as Hounds; the Hounds' goal is to chase after the Hares. The Hounds are made up of different running levels from advanced to inexperienced. Even young children have been known to participate. The distance each Hound actually runs depends on whether they chase a Hare down a false trail or a dead-end. The Hounds will yell "On, On!" to the other Hounds once they find the correct trail. As a result, the advance runners could end up running more than everyone else if they do not choose their routes wisely. The Hash is also celebrated with song, refreshments, and a big feast, not just after the run but at pit stops along the way.

This particular Hash was sponsored by members of the Japanese embassy, meaning it would feature their national food and drink, such as sushi and sake. Our Peace Corps group ran together at a moderate pace along paved residential streets, down alleyways, through swamps and patches of overgrown vegetation, following the choruses of "On, On!" wafting in the humid air. Not far into the race, we stopped and downed a bowl of sake. A few kilometers further along, we were reaching out for paper cups of Kirin beer like it was Gatorade. As we stumbled to the finish line, a grown man was standing on a chair with a mangled toilet seat around his neck singing a song or limerick or college fight song while the crowd cheered in approval. The Hash House Harriers call this post-race ritual "Religion," which can get pretty raucous and vulgar. But I had spent enough time with my head in a toilet seat, recently; I could forgo their Religion and just enjoy being a Hound in the crowd.

An evening at the hostel in Abidjan might be best described by the following passage from *Tortilla Flat* by John Steinbeck:

Two gallons is a great deal of wine, even for two Paisanos. Spiritually the jugs may be graduated thus:

- *Just below the shoulder of the first bottle, serious and concentrated conversation.*
- *Two inches further down, sweet sad memory.*
- *Three inches more, thoughts of old and satisfactory loves.*
- *An inch, thoughts of bitter loves.*
- *Bottom of the first jug, general and undirected sadness.*
- *Shoulder of the second jug, black unholy despondency.*
- *Two fingers down, a song of death or longing.*
- *A thumb, every other song each one knows.*

The graduations stop here, for the trail splits and there is no certainty. From this point on anything can happen.

We weren't always this *spiritual* at the hostel, but there were enough volunteers coming or going, celebrating or commiserating, that it felt more like a fraternity house than a regional medical facility. In the living room there was usually a movie playing on the TV; we'd watch them over and over, memorizing and regurgitating the lines until we could reenact the scenes. If they ever turn *Pulp Fiction*, *Apollo 13*, or *Speed* into Broadway plays, the producer need look no further for a cast of characters; our group has all the roles covered.

If you had your fill of movies, you could read or write in a tucked-away corner of the hostel. But there was no denying the gravitational pull to the big porch overlooking the front lawn. Day and night, there was a sizable group sitting around long tables, talking, reminiscing, and getting to know each other without distraction. The porch was the place of our most intense discussions and debates, and the complement to all this interaction was a fair amount of beer and booze, creating a drunken roost of maudlin expression, as foretold by Steinbeck.

Financing the beer was a community affair that was not always equitable, but it was cheap enough that it didn't matter. Fetching the beer required two people on either end of a nine-liter case of empties to exchange for a full case. Without the empties, you couldn't get your beer because the bottles were being reused in real-time by the distributors. The closest *maquis* was only two blocks away, and if their beer wasn't cold, the next *maquis* was only a block further. The most common method to encourage two people to make a beer run was to wait until they got up from their chair and simply say, "While you're up…," which mobilized more people than you'd think. Even more effective was the, "I buy, you fly" method. Or the last two people to put their forefinger on the tip of their nose. It generally came down to who wanted it more.

I probably made this beer run a handful of times during my service. On one occasion, a volunteer named Christian and I drew the short straws. I didn't know Christian very well. He was trained as a Health volunteer and posted in a village outside of Mankano near Séguéla. Christian was always in a good mood, engaging, and quite the artist, frequently spotted with sketchbook in hand.

While on the beer run, we came upon a movie set, with floodlights, cameras, cables, and people everywhere. As novel as this was for Africa, we remained focused on the mission at hand. On the way back, with our full case of Bock Solibra, we were intercepted by the film director. They were filming a commercial and asked if we'd like to be extras. We were all for it. All we had to do was to walk down the street with our case of beer.

The scene begins with a young Ivorian couple in the back seat of a taxicab. They're kissing passionately. The bright lights from the movie set reveal every nuance and detail. The director motions for us to start walking. As we pass, we imagine the viewers at home see the couple look back through the rear window. The man holds up an unopened Prudence condom while flashing a wide confident smile. The camera zooms in to the condom wrapper while a strong, booming, manly voiceover commands *"Prudence d'abord"* to the viewers. But no African condom commercial would be complete without two drunken *toubabs* passing in the background, associating a popular beverage with their relatively unknown, un-used product. It was a wrap. Christian and I never did see that commercial, though we suspect it may have been our fifteen minutes of fame.

In Abidjan we had three brands of beer to choose from: Flag, Mamba, and Bock Solibra. Flag and Mamba were half the size, twice as expensive, and not much better than Bock, so the Bière de l'Homme Fort was our choice by default. There was also another feature of the one-liter beverage that kept us entertained for hours: Grab the neck of the bottle with the left hand, then grab a solid object such as a book or a spoon or a long flat rock with the right hand in such a way that when pressed firmly against the top knuckle of the left hand, and wedged under the cap, it would act as a lever. A quick but controlled downward movement of the solid object usually sent the cap reeling. If done properly, the cap would soar through the air some five to ten meters, marked by a thunderous boom from the rapid release of pressurized air within the bottle.

It took skill to pop the cap off a Bock Solibra in this manner, especially when challenged by the group to use a non-solid or cumbersome object such as a rolled-up magazine or a lawn chair or the wooden Santa Claus that some parent sent as a gift. Success was not always guaranteed. If done improperly, the cap could fall feebly to the ground, eliciting a chorus of boos, or a knuckle could end up bloodied, mashed between object and glass; or, worst of all, worse than any wound or laceration, the one-liter bottle could slip from one's hand, spilling its content on the porch. At the hostel, amongst our group, this was a scar that would not heal.

Once the caps were off, there was no telling what kind of bacchanalia would ensue. There was your typical binge drinking until the wee hours, various drinking games, and dancing on the lawn for those so inclined. On one occasion, someone put a case of lukewarm beer in the freezer to chill more quickly, but they crammed them in there wet and laying down so the bottles ended up freezing into one big block. When this was discovered, the volunteers did not frantically chip away at the ice and risk broken bottles. They did not unplug the freezer and wait patiently for the ice to thaw. They did not sequester two willing harpies to get more beer. Instead, they grabbed the fridge and leaned it forward until the bottles faced down, then pried the caps off one by one while someone collected the icy cold beer in a plastic basin. Yankee ingenuity at its finest.

Drinking was definitely the activity of choice at the hostel, and volunteers sometimes got out of hand, prompting the occasional late night confrontation between the sleepers and the drinkers. The porch had a way of bringing out one's inner Hyde. Never mind *serious and concentrated conversation,* when you drink at a sailor's pace you're bound to move right into *a song of death or longing* or something far more embarrassing. Despite the antics, our Dr. Jekyll never strayed too far. Most of us spent only one week each quarter in Abidjan, so any unruly behavior was short-lived. If we were not living in a remote village or a Muslim area where alcohol was forbidden or scarce, you couldn't afford to drink all the time. We enjoyed ourselves when we got together, but overall our group was a responsible and conscientious bunch of engineers and health care workers. So says me.

Before entering the Peace Corps, I resigned myself to a two-year stretch of celibacy. I imagined being alone in an isolated village with few, if any, opportunities for intimacy. I even had this ridiculous notion that if I fell for a local African girl, her father would most certainly be the village chief and I would have to defeat the strongest warrior to win her attention. When I arrived in Philadelphia, I realized this might not be the case (neither the celibacy nor the mortal combat). Our group was made up of about sixty percent women, so the odds were in my favor. As we got to know each other, our personal situations came to light. Two trainees entered the Peace Corps married to spouses who did not accompany them to Africa. A number of trainees split from their significant others just before departure, grieving the loss but ready for a new chapter. And others were seemingly in relationships, unsure if they'd go through with the Peace Corps or with the relationship, still looking for answers. The remainder was undoubtedly single. I suppose I fell in between two categories. I was single and open to possibilities, but I had no idea how to operate after eight years of being off the market. I just knew I wasn't fighting any warriors for love and affection.

The Peace Corps medical staff certainly didn't figure we'd be celibate for two years. Their lesson plan was full of statistics on the by-products of a healthy sex life in Africa. They covered the important stuff like HIV/AIDS, STDs, and pregnancy. They also had semi-serious pie charts and graphs showing the percentage of volunteers having sex, and with what demographic. The charts and graphs were telling. Not all of our predecessors were getting busy, but there was more action than I would have guessed, including fully-fledged relationships between volunteers and host country nationals. Hooking up became an objective for many, with success amusingly known as "making the pie chart."

While in Senegal, there was ample opportunity to flirt, hang out, or make advances with someone of your liking. Living in such close quarters also meant that everyone was privy to your business, and our group loved to gossip, so any extracurricular activity was weighed against protecting one's reputation. It wasn't long before relationships began to take shape. Then training came to an end and we were given our assignments all over Côte d'Ivoire. I requested to be near Man so I could be in the mountains and be close to the road system, and I was fortunate to get Bangolo, but there were a lot of trainees who were disappointed with their site assignments, having been sent to places where the population was low, access was difficult, and opportunity was limited. Making the pie chart in these remote areas would take far more effort, more bus fare, or a more localized approach.

It didn't take long to appraise my own situation in Bangolo. As previously noted, Megan was off limits, as were the local African women. By process of elimination, my dating pool consisted of volunteers in-country, travelers from other countries, or ex-pats. I rarely comingled with the ex-pats. They had nice houses, cars, maids, air-conditioning, food, and would make for extravagant partners, but most of them also had husbands. Volunteers from other countries could usually be found at the hostel for medical or dental needs. We called these volunteers: *medevacs* or *dentavacs*. Occasionally, there were attractive medevacs in Abidjan, but unless it was obvious why they were there, we always assumed the worst, that some kind of jungle rot or desert crud had festered in the crevices of their body, requiring immediate attention. As for our volunteers, they had potential, which is another way of saying they were my only option.

Being so resigned, I often questioned the standards I set for myself. I wondered if it were possible for a guy like me to develop any kind of relationship with someone from a vastly different culture, who spoke a different language and valued different things. While I spoke a bit of French and picked up a few African customs, I couldn't really communicate with the Ivoirian women. The cultural gap was too large, or my capacity was too limited. It would be many years, a lifetime even, before I understood an African woman's quirks and subtleties, her cadence and desires, her yearnings and anxieties. And if the relationship got serious, whose country would we live in? Whose goals would be deferred? Whose family would be forsaken?

Someone or something was going to be compromised. Couples all over the globe have this kind of arrangement, and they make it work, but I struggled to envision how it would work for me, even with the most captivating and nubile of African women.

Dating wasn't a common occurrence; at least not in the way one might imagine going out on a date to a restaurant, the movies, clubs, parties, concerts, etc. During the limited time that our group had together, strong social bonds had formed, but there were no phones, no texting, and the Internet hadn't been rolled out, so there was no direct way to contact someone or maintain real-time communication. In order for those bonds to survive a hiatus, we wrote letters, lots of letters, announcing future travel plans to Abidjan or another area of the country. If that special someone was a good distance away, and you could afford it, you might travel to his or her village or town, make up an excuse why you had to go there. This was as good as announcing your intentions, a prelude to something more. It was all we had. In my two years, various hookups and pairings were born and forlorn in this most unconventional way. And I eventually made the pie chart.

With every trip to Abidjan, there was always a moment when you knew it was time to go, time to catch the next bus back to your site. This moment didn't always coincide with meetings or obligations at either location. Depending on the group dynamics, you might stay up to a week or more to get your fill of social interaction and modern conveniences. No stint usually lasted more than two weeks unless you were violently ill. I started chomping at the bit after one week in Abidjan. There was only so much I could handle of drinking and carrying on. I'd get to a point where I longed for the quiet and community feel of Bangolo, even if certain frustrations awaited me there. Another two or three months would pass at site and I'd grow restless to visit the big city again. It was a peculiar cycle I shared with a core group of friends, whether we were in contact or not, whether we were introverts or extroverts, we just sensed when it was time to get out of Dodge.

This back and forth between sanctuary and fraternity, solitude and society, stayed with me for many years after leaving Africa. In fact, it was one of the more significant readjustments I had to make. In Bangolo I was able to think, breathe, focus, relax, or withdraw into my house if necessary, and the Guéré generally didn't bother me. When I did interact with people, I felt like they were engaging, whether it was with a stranger or a friend, a volunteer or a host country national. There was a definite focus on the present moment.

Back in the States, I never feel alone and I rarely have someone's full attention. If I manage to get away, there's a widespread expectation that I should be accessible and responsive by phone, Internet, or the latest device. There's no escape. It makes people nervous when you want to be alone. It makes them wonder what you have against them or what you're conspiring to do, and it can make your neighbors think you're an oddball, an agoraphobic, or a social deviant.

Then there's the fast pace of life in the States. While progress can improve the quality of life, it can also degrade it under a weight of distractions and competing interests, of obligations that sometimes don't add up to much. Don't get me wrong, I enjoy most of what America has to offer: my job, my things, and my relative freedom, but I pay for it with a degree of stress not suited to good health and well-being. It's a real challenge to stay focused on any one thing or person or activity because I live in a place that thrives on multitasking and rewards quantitative results at almost any cost to the individual.

I don't know about the other volunteers, but I felt the most alive migrating between the two relative extremes of solitude and society, between Bangolo and Abidjan. Who knows whether it was good for my psyche to live this way, or whether it's considered a lifestyle of balance or imbalance? I'm sure there's a psychological explanation for all the anxiety and uneasiness I felt when I left Africa and moved back to the States—an ISTJ *Meyer's-Briggs* personality type thrust into a different environment, or some other condition or syndrome. Time (and counseling) will tell. The good news is: I still experience brief moments of solace like I had in my Peace Corps heyday, even as a culture of Attention Deficit Disorder pervades my world.

CHAPTER ELEVEN

VOCATION

Megan and I received word one morning that our Associate Peace Corps Director was on her way to Bangolo. Her name was Julie and it was her last *tourneé* before the standard five-year hitch with the Peace Corps was over and she'd have to find employment elsewhere. Julie was a decent, supportive boss—professional yet stoic, hard to read. I didn't know her well, but the second-year volunteers had vouched for her.

That day, Konan thought to take us to lunch at a friend's house for a home-cooked meal, which was no different than what I normally ate, just served indoors on a plate instead of outdoors in a plastic bowl. Assis decided to join us. As the five of us were cramming into Konan's little red Toyota, one of the THIMO workers approached Assis with a problem. The worker had cut himself with a machete, his left hand holding a bloody rag against his face, his right hand still grasping the well-worn tool. Charles and Dao were probably into their second beer by now, clear across town. Assis was the next best thing to a supervisor, so he instructed the worker to go to the hospital.

We drove to Konan's friend's house and spent the next hour waiting for lunch while engaging in small talk. When the goat gristle in sauce made its way around the table, Assis gave Megan a hard time about her small portion, making her discretion the focal point of wisecracks for the rest of lunch. I could stomach the food just fine; it was the company that was harder to digest.

We drove back to the office at the end of *sieste*. Our plan was to mull about until Julie arrived. To our surprise, the injured THIMO worker was still there holding the same bloody rag to his face. Assis immediately reprimanded him for not going to the hospital. The worker responded that he *did* go to the hospital, that officials there told him the mayor's credit was no good. He handed Assis an invoice for 6,095 CFA to be paid in cash or treatment would not be rendered. Assis went on a rant about the high price of medical care. *"Vraiment, c'est trop!"* he bellowed as he thrust the invoice back into the worker's hand and walked away. In the process, the worker momentarily pulled the rag away from his face, revealing the extent of the wound.

I'm a resilient guy when it comes to seeing blood or another person's injury, but I just about fainted when I saw the damage. The laceration extended from the worker's ear lobe along the jaw line to the middle of his chin, about an inch wide, and right down to the bone. I hadn't seen anything like that since I was into campy horror movies as a kid. I decided to weigh in, telling Assis that the worker had probably lost a lot of blood and needed medical attention before the wound became infected. Once again, Assis was not moved by my logic. Finances were his bread and butter.

The worker's name was Lucien. He was taller than most Guéré, but he was unmistakably Guéré by the roundness of his facial features and his garbled French accent. I'd often see him working with THIMO, though I rarely heard him talk and I never saw him smile. The story goes that Lucien was cutting grass near the *gare*, logging in his half day of work. As his machete was on the downswing, it got caught up in an overhanging tree branch, changed direction, and let loose right into his face.

At the beginning of my term, I vowed not to give money away or pay for someone's purchases or debts, less a beer between friends. My take was that it was unsustainable, and it might give the locals the wrong impression about Peace Corps volunteers. Lucien's case was different. One look at him holding the blood-soaked rag to his face in near shock was enough to make an exception.

I escorted Lucien to the hospital, grabbing him food and water from a street vendor along the way. The hospital was sketchy. There were minimal furnishings and no modern medical equipment. Aside from a clerk and a doctor, the place was virtually empty. I would not want treatment there, even for something as standard as sutures for a cut. Hospital officials had no problem extending me credit after I explained I could pay in cash later that day. The doctor had a difficult time fixing Lucien, with three hours elapsing since he was cut, but he eventually got him stitched, bandaged, and on his way.

I then decided to confront Assis. I knew it was futile from the start, but I was all worked up. I told Lucien to go home and rest but he was adamant about joining me. When we entered the office, there were already a number of THIMO workers arguing with Assis. Apparently, he had told Lucien's team that they weren't getting paid for the day because they stopped work around 11:30 at the time of the incident and they did not work their full shift until noon. To add insult to injury, Assis accused Lucien of being careless with his machete. Careless? Most of these guys were using machetes before they were old enough to go to school. It's not like they were having drunken machete fights on unicycles. They were working a monotonous, backbreaking, physical job in service of the mayor.

This set me off. I told Assis it was wrong not to pay the workers and I asked him facetiously if he thought Lucien wanted to cut his face wide open at great expense to him and others. More THIMO workers joined the fracas, pleading their case one after the other until the room was a crescendo of anger and frustration. I handed Assis the invoice and told him that he owed me the 6,095 CFA. As I turned to leave, I noticed the room was a sea of blue coats. And by the doorway I saw Megan with our boss Julie. Shit!

I have no idea how much of the confrontation Julie witnessed. I certainly was not proud of my behavior, nor did I endeavor to talk to government officials in such a manner, whether I respected them or not. But when you immerse yourself in a culture, there are risks and rewards. You develop friendships and animosities. You form ideas and opinions. You hope to participate and contribute. And you make choices. I can understand how volunteers become emotionally attached to a family, a community, a cause or a conflict, and take action in their defense. Only the most disciplined can resist. Later, Julie expressed support for our approach, though she cautioned us against intervening too much in local politics. Fair enough. Megan and I had experienced enough turmoil already; we didn't need to make it the theme of our service. So I pledged to cool it with Assis, and Julie was on her way.

One of the rewards for helping out Lucien was greater recognition and support from the THIMO workers. I had no idea what they thought of me before the incident (or after, for that matter), but I now felt like I had their attention. It was August, six months since my arrival, and I was ready to start a real project, to get outside and work. I approached Dago about supervising one of the THIMO groups to do erosion control work. Each rainy season, surface water runoff cut deep channels in the dirt roads leading to the lowland *bafon*. This was especially true for the roads surrounding the mayor's office. Dago refused. He needed all the workers for cutting grass. Who could blame him? He was just carrying out the mayor's directive. If the grass grew tall in Bangolo *ville* and it started looking unkempt, or worse, if the green mamba showed up, it could cost the mayor votes and it would be Dago's ass on the line.

It was clear the onus was on me to make a stronger case for erosion control. I started small, telling Dago that the channels would grow deeper and wider over time if they weren't filled. I'm not sure he cared. Then I told him the work might re-energize THIMO, mix it up once a week, let them do something different, maybe keep them from cutting their faces with machetes. Dago didn't care whether THIMO's work was diversified or not. I cited public health reasons, reminding him that the deep holes were where people tossed their trash, or where standing water served as a breeding ground for mosquitoes. His ears perked up slightly; he was responsible for trash collection, and he knew the *palud* was a problem for many Africans. Still, no indication I could manage a team. Finally, I presented the political benefits: that we could fix the roads, make the area look clean and maintained, ensure the ride to the office was smoother for those who owned vehicles including the mayor and Dago's garbage truck (when it was working), which could translate into votes. I could tell he was seriously considering it. Politics were the impetus for many of their decisions. Even so, he resisted. Maybe he knew something I didn't. Maybe cutting grass was *that* important in Bangolo. Maybe he was stubborn by nature and couldn't bear to take advice from a young punk from America. I'm sure it all played a role.

Not long after I came to Bangolo, I had a discussion with Dago. The topic was *poubelles*, which means trash cans or garbage bins. In urban Côte d'Ivoire, a *poubelle* refers to a three-sided concrete block structure built by the side of the road where residents bring their household garbage for regular collection and disposal to a community landfill. I suggested to Dago that we should construct *poubelles* in Bangolo. His response was, "*Poubelles* don't work; I see them everywhere and they're always full of garbage." So the Chief of

Technical Services wasn't the sharpest tool in the shed, but I held out that someday he would see the wisdom in letting me do erosion control with THIMO.

Then it happened. My big break. My counterpart Charles allegedly stole the mayor's bicycle. I didn't know the mayor had a bicycle, but that was the accusation, and Charles got fired. Then, just days later, my other counterpart Dao groped the wrong woman and he was also relieved of his duties. People weren't fired very often in Bangolo, especially for such commonplace offenses as these. Dao had it coming, but I was surprised and saddened to hear about Charles. I liked Charles. He was a good man with a good family. For the remainder of my time, I would see them both in town, a bit downtrodden, reminiscing on the glory days we never really shared as they asked to borrow money.

Dago would now have to supervise THIMO by himself. Out of desperation, he asked if I could supervise a team to do erosion control. I was thrilled. I knew we wouldn't make any lasting repairs to the road—not without heavy equipment, culverts, and pavement—but it was a great opportunity to be seen out in the community and participate in the process. To kick off the project, Dago was photographed with shovel in hand taking a halfhearted ceremonial whack at the damaged road. Now we were in business.

Each week I worked with a different THIMO group. Five of the ten members would work while the other five would rest, then they'd switch roles after an hour. We started by digging shallow canals along both sides of the road to redirect surface water flow, and we placed large rocks at the bottom of the canals to absorb the energy, to prevent water from flowing too fast and carving out deeper channels. In instances where a road sloped downhill and met a crossroad, we dug pits at the ends of the canals and filled them with large rocks so the water could infiltrate the pores or disperse slowly over the crossroad. The dirt from digging new canals went to filling in the problematic channels that cut across the roads. We even had enough dirt to put a nice crown in the road.

The work continued from late August until early November at the tail-end of the wet season. On days with heavy rains, I'd go out to the jobsite in my raincoat and observe how the water behaved in the saturated soil, or how it moved along the landscape, then we'd make corrections the next day. A random person running for cover from a downpour yelled out, "Americans are crazy!" Had I known I was the torchbearer for my country's sanity, I might've stood under an eave or a tree instead. Even so, it might not have mattered.

The THIMO workers appeared to enjoy themselves, and we got a lot of work done. Lucien proved to be one of THIMO's best crew leaders, and over time his facial wound healed up nicely. The residents of Bangolo also took notice, especially *le grand types* with automobiles, stopping to talk or to shake my hand. You'd think I was running for public office. So like any good politician, I purposely failed to mention an important detail: that our work would not last through the next rainy season without another investment in labor, but it would last until May, which would give me time to build a nice constituency.

Biogas in Bondoukou! To most people, this might sound like news headline announcing an unfortunate catastrophe or a terrorist plot. For first-year UEM volunteers, it was an invitation for more training, to learn how to convert animal waste into fuel gas and fertilizer. Bondoukou is a small city, slightly larger than Bangolo, located clear across the country on the east side, twenty kilometers from the Ghanaian border. Bondoukou is also the southern gateway to the Parc National de la Comoé—the country's largest national park and one of the last remaining places in the so-called Coast of Ivory to find wild elephants. With no direct east-west route, it would take me two days to get to Bondoukou, requiring that I travel down to Abidjan, stay overnight, then get up early and head northeast another six to eight hours by bus.

The gang was all there. We stayed in the nicest hotel in town called the Marhaba, two-and-a-half-star accommodation by AAA standards, with a bathroom in each room, an outdoor pool, even a restaurant that served edible *toubab* food. It was like the Rec. Center with beds. Most of our training would be held at a local pig farm, with supplemental classroom sessions back at the hotel pool. The owner of the farm had obtained a grant through USAID to build a methane (biogas) digester, and we were there to learn about it.

I understand not everyone cares to know how to convert pig shit into cooking fuel, but for those who do, here is a short summary: The natural decay of organic material from animal and vegetable waste breaks down through processes that are either aerobic (with oxygen) or anaerobic (without oxygen). Both can yield useful by-products. An open-aired compost pile is an example of aerobic decay, yielding mature compost or humus that contributes to nutrient-rich planting soil. In nature, a layer of organic material covered by a warm lake or pond may result in anaerobic decay, where the methane bacteria decompose the material, forcing gas bubbles to rise to the surface. This natural process of anaerobic decay can be emulated in insulated air-tight containers called digesters. These digesters can be batch-load, filled at once with animal and vegetable waste, then sealed to prevent oxygen from entering and emptied when the raw material stops producing gas. Or they can be continuous-load, fed over time, producing a steady stream of gas and fertilizer with proper care and attention.

The digester in Bondoukou was made of reinforced concrete and resembled a big propane tank half-buried in the ground. The farmers fed the unit with a wet slurry mixture of water and pig waste each day, but one could also feed it with a manure mixture from horse, cow, even chicken droppings. Each load becomes food for microbes from the previous load, progressing through the digester to the far end where the methane bacteria are most active and the biogas accumulates. Once the gas is stored, it's similar to natural gas and can be used to light stoves or lanterns.

During the week, we learned about the biology of digestion, reviewed schematic drawings, and talked to pig farmers about how they hoped to benefit from biogas. While the training was informative, most of us didn't have large pig farms at our sites, and the science and technology would likely be too complex for our local counterparts. Besides, if Africans thought Americans were crazy for standing in the rain, what would they think if I asked them to gather up fresh cow patties and chicken turds so we could feed our magical fuel and fertilizer machine? I'd be run out of town for sure. Somewhere in the world, a town or village is ready to embrace the biogas digester and all of its by-products, but it sure as hell wasn't the town of Bangolo in the year 1995.

The most surreal part of the trip was not biogas in Bondoukou, however. While relaxing by the pool one evening, I met two middle-aged Caucasian gentlemen from Kentucky who were under contract to sandblast and repaint 800-foot-high radio towers—a high-risk ordeal that calls for men of courage or madness. It was an odd place to see *toubabs*, never mind two heavy-set Americans with strong southern accents. Although I had only lived in Kentucky for three months, their dialect was unmistakable. They were taken aback when I guessed what county they were from, surprised that a Yankee with a French-Bostonian accent would even know what a county was.

I proceeded to tell them about my time at Mammoth Cave, how three buddies and I had canoed 160 miles of the Green River from Munfordville to Livermore in less than four days during heavy spring rains, and how I planned to return to paddle the Green to its end where it meets the Ohio River near Henderson. One guy just about jumped out of his poolside lounger when he heard me speak so fondly of Kentucky. His name was Rick, bright red-hair, muscular build, a riverboat captain on the Ohio River when he was not making money in Africa.

Rick hustled off to his hotel room and returned with a pad of paper, a box of Crayola crayons, and a full bottle of Knob Creek Bourbon. Volunteers looked on like I was privy to some bizarre redneck drinking game. I had no idea what he had in store with the crayons until he started sketching what appeared to be the confluence of two rivers. An hour and a few drinks later, I had a color-coded map of the last ten miles of the Green River, complete with topography, river hazards, mile markers, property owners, camping recommendations, even local terminology for spots along the way. I was much obliged, and I promised that if I made it out there I'd look for him at his camp three miles from the confluence, known locally as Smokey-Joint Point.

In the summer of 1997, I made it back to Kentucky and canoed from Livermore to Henderson as promised. The river wasn't booming like it was in 1994, it was more of a relaxed 80-mile float through flat farm country under the hot Kentucky sun. That is until we reached the Ohio River and we had to paddle furiously to avoid the large tugs, barges, and riverboats that move up and down this vast powerful interstate watercourse. There was no sign of Rick or his camp, but his map was spot-on. It would have been nice to thank Rick in person for his hospitality in Bondoukou, swap tales of Africa, share a drink or two. Hell, with all the horse and cow shit along the river, we could've built him his very own biogas digester.

In October, national elections were finally held in Côte d'Ivoire. Henri Konan Bédié of the PDCI party, who took over in December 1993 when Papa Boigny died, won in a landside. The incumbent Bédié claimed that the opposition was not eligible to run for office under the country's guidelines, that they were not true Ivoirians, so the candidates from the *Front Populaire Ivoirien* (FPI) and *Le Rassemblement des Républicains de Côte d'Ivoire* (RDR) parties formally boycotted the election. The race for Mayor of Bangolo (and other cities) was delayed until February, which was bad news for progress. It looked like I'd be stuck with these rubes for at least another five months. Monsieur le mayor left his campaign signs up, but they were soon dismantled by children to better serve their needs as goal posts, ramps, and miscellaneous props.

About this time, Julie's position as APCD of the UEM program was filled by an African American woman from Los Angeles named Margaret. On the return trip from Bondoukou, we got to meet our new boss. She was relatively short, with hair trimmed close to the scalp. She had good sense of humor, was supportive, and didn't take herself too seriously. Most of all, she knew not to impose sweeping changes to a group of professional malcontents. She was the perfect choice and we took notice. Without conspiring to do so, my buddies and I took Margaret under our wing, showing her the ropes, and doing our part to set her up for success. And she responded in kind.

With elections on the minds of everyone in Bangolo, my colleagues were preoccupied, so I got permission from Margaret to go on a *tourneé* to view Peace Corps projects at sites long since established. As an unwritten rule, our group rarely expended vacation time when traveling in-country unless there was a chance we'd be gone from our sites for a lengthy period of time. For instance, I would not use vacation time if, by chance, a weekend shopping spree to Man lasted into Monday or began on a Friday, nor would I consider taking vacation time to visit my buddies in Biankouma, Soubré, or Séguéla, as these trips were spent viewing infrastructure and sharing work-related experiences. However, as a practice, I regularly informed my host country colleagues when, where, and for how long I expected to be gone. If I failed to provide this information, news of my departure or arrival spread quickly from the *gare* through town to the municipality, and my whereabouts was always known, no matter how stealthy or elusive I thought I was.

I had no qualms about sitting down with Margaret and discussing, with complete candor, recent or anticipated trips to sites in Côte d'Ivoire. As new as she was to the position, she quickly surmised the need for volunteers to get away from time to time, as long as we never compromised our work or the program's reputation. She understood that we were always on the clock, day and night, as Peace Corps volunteers and quasi-ambassadors, and she realized this level of commitment deserved some liberties.

My first trip was to visit Tim in Soubré. For a change of scenery, I loaded my bike on the bus, got off in Issia, and peddled south one hundred kilometers to Tim's place. Sitting on a bicycle seat all day with the hot sun beating down isn't the most pleasurable activity, but by forsaking the bus I experienced new villages, unique wildlife, strange sounds, and fresh air all lodged in my subconscious for later.

Tim and I grabbed dinner and a beer and talked about our favorite book quotes, our journal entries, our philosophies, and our prospects. I was bothered to learn that Soubré had superior peanut sauce. What kind of crap were they serving me in Bangolo? Tim was working on a latrine project at the school, so we spent the next day between the jobsite and his office, culminating in a short bike ride at sunset to Soubré's main tourist attraction—the turbulent falls of the Sassandra River. Before leaving, Tim and I resolved to travel somewhere around the holidays. I could hardly wait.

Next up was Stephanie's village of Gotongouiné II. She was hosting an event called the *Concour du Plus Beau Bébé* or Most Beautiful Baby Contest. This was not a beauty pageant for cute little African girls with painted faces in frilly gowns, parading around with fixed smiles and vacant expressions. In this case, the most beautiful baby meant the most *inoculated* baby. So I traveled to her village to lend my support (and to deliver a puppy from our Lebanese friends in Man). I was impressed. I don't know how they handled immunizations in Gotongouiné II before Stephanie arrived, but she and her local health aide had generated a big turnout. And what Inoculation Party would be complete without festive dancing and a big feast? It was quite a day. Mothers with offspring were sure to come back year after year.

A month after the event, I received a letter from Stephanie stateside. I was saddened to learn that she would not be returning to Africa for personal reasons. To make matters worse, on the day she was traveling from her village to Abidjan to discuss her departure with her APCD, her dog was hit by a car in Man. Our western region was losing a good friend and colleague, and the Most Beautiful Baby Contest would never be the same.

Last stop on the *tourneé* was Russ' town of Biankouma, which is a lot like Bangolo in size and services. Russ was a community development volunteer and an educator. USAID had recently constructed a new market and a slaughterhouse in Biankouma. The new market was right across the street from the old one, with covered pavilions, new pavement, drainage canals, even fresh paint delineating each stall and pathway. As African markets go, this was deluxe, but none of the *marchandes* had moved there yet. The reason, Russ explained, was that these *marchandes* had occupied their family's sacred plot for decades, if not centuries, passed down from generation to generation. USAID could have built an air-conditioned convention center; it was unlikely the *marchandes* would abandon their traditional stalls. Had they built a small port or hatch in the asphalt to place a *gree gree* (amulets that protect them against evil and bad fortune), they might have moved in mass. The devil is in the details.

As for the slaughterhouse, it had yet to see any slaughter for reasons unbeknownst to us. Tall grass had taken over the area. Cows on their daily saunter would feed on the grass, almost mocking the facility. Somewhere in Washington D.C., a well-meaning bureaucrat reported the completion of a new market and a slaughterhouse, maybe received an award, but the project's true value had yet to be determined.

When I returned to Bangolo, I found a letter from my mother with a copy of my grandfather's obituary. Raymond Henry Henrickson, my father's father, had died at home at age 80 after an illness. I was not surprised. Pa was ailing when I left for Africa, and the family was not optimistic that his health would improve. I got the sense that even Pa knew that it was his time by the way he said goodbye, the way he looked at me—thorough, sullen, resigned. The letter indicated that he had died three weeks previous. While the Peace Corps would have made every effort to reach me, my mom knew I could not make it back for his funeral, so she mailed the obituary instead.

I wasn't close to my father's side of the family after my parents' divorce when I was seven. I probably saw this set of grandparents a few times a year, usually on major holidays when my siblings and I had to attend festivities at four households in one hectic day. Up until that point in my life, Pa was the closest person I knew to pass away, and I was saddened by the loss.

The obituary had a nice photo of Pa taken not long before his death, his head full of gray hair parted neatly to one side, dressed in a shirt and tie, with a big smile that permeated through his cheeks, his eyes, and his big rummy nose. The first paragraph of the write-up listed the relatives he left behind and the place of his birth. The obituary goes on to say:

> *Mr. Henrickson was a machinist at Heald Machine Division of Cincinnati Milacron Inc. for many years, retiring in 1975. He was a member of St. Peter's Church and a former member of Webster Square Post 13, American Legion. He was an avid hunter, fisherman. He was an Army veteran of World War II.*

That's it? Four sentences revealing his vocation, where he prayed, where he drank, his hobbies and an enlistment? This didn't begin to describe the man I knew, the man in the Santa Claus hat at the far end of the kitchen table, smoking unfiltered Camel cigarettes and drinking Narragansett tall boys; the man who'd take his teeth out and chase us around the room with arms raised and gums flapping; or the man who'd take me to Breen's Café for an afternoon of skee ball, kiddie cocktails, and all-you-can-eat bar room peanuts.

The more I thought about Pa's obituary, the more unsettling it was. A man had lived on this earth for 80 years and the public announcement of his death reduced him to four impersonal sentences. The most disconcerting thing was not the short narrative or the absence of detail; it was the realization that I didn't know my grandfather aside from a few parlor tricks and tendencies. Who was this man? Did Raymond H. Henrickson enjoy working as a machinist? Did he hope to be something different? Did he believe in God or heaven? What did he think about when he was up early hunting and fishing, or up late at night walking home from the bars? Did he kill anyone in the war? Did he have any regrets? Where did he stand on the issues? I couldn't answer any of these questions.

It's possible that even if I'd visited Pa more frequently, I would not have known him any better. He may not have shared this information, or I may not have inquired, and it would just be more skee ball and maraschino cherries for us. But these details are a treasure for those who are curious, not only to get to know our loved ones better but to understand a man's perspective, his nature.

What if we wrote our own obituaries? What would we say? What clues would we leave the next generation? What wisdom would we impart about the human condition? We'd all write something different, but I imagine it would be far more lively and memorable than a stale paragraph written by a dreary stranger about our vocations and associations. We may all die in vain, but Pa's death—or rather, his death notice—inspired me to document a short span of my life, to tell a story about a young man in Africa and where he stood.

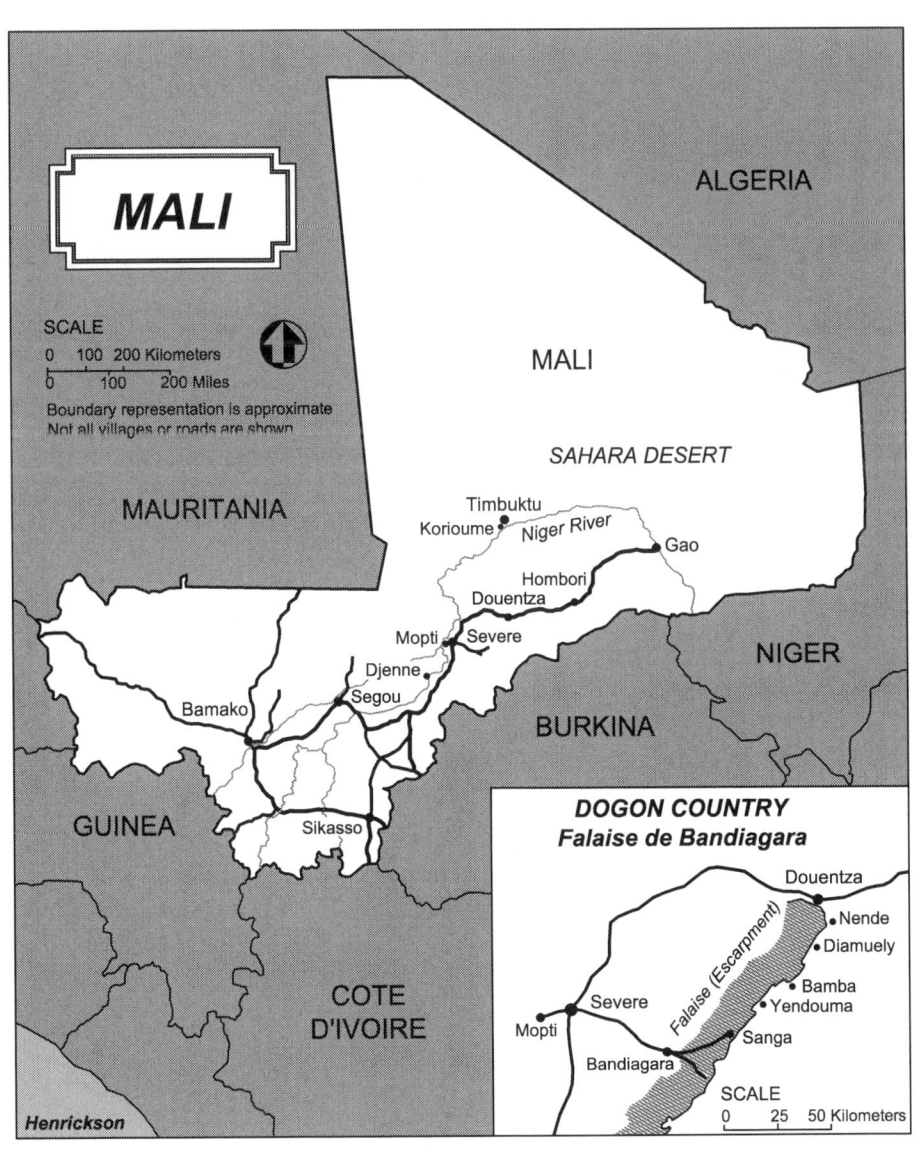

CHAPTER TWELVE

VACATION

As a benefit for toiling in the Peace Corps, each volunteer accrues forty-eight vacation days to use over a two-year period at their supervisor's discretion. That's forty-eight vacation days! Almost five weeks off per year. That's a healthy amount of time by most working-class standards, and about twice as much as the average blue collar American receives. Volunteers used this time to explore the diversity of West Africa via overland travel, while others traveled back to the States to attend weddings, funerals, or family gatherings, and a fettered few reunited with their stateside partner somewhere in the world, extending or resolving the agony of a long-distance relationship. While not all volunteers needed this kind of time off to recuperate, it was granted as a way to practice the agency's second and third goals: in a nutshell, to promote a better understanding between Americans and non-Americans. Ironically, one of those understandings might be that all Americans get a lot of vacation time, which isn't necessarily the case.

While I missed my family and friends back in Massachusetts, I could not afford a flight back home without dipping into my stateside savings, so my travel choices were dictated by my disposable income. In nine months, I had saved $300; not bad considering the high cost of beer, the occasional splurge on food, bus fare, and police bribes. But $300 wasn't enough to fly anywhere. My mode of conveyance would most definitely be cheap, uncomfortable, mechanically questionable buses and vans, complete with dust clouds and goat urine cascading through the windows from the rooftop.

I suppose I could've charged a flight on my credit card, but an impromptu getaway from Africa was hardly an emergency. And I really didn't want to leave. I was adamant that I complete this Peace Corps gig without going home and without help from others, which included financial assistance from my co-signer from afar. I felt it would be cheating the Peace Corps experience. Plus I'd be saddling my poor mother with the credit card payments. She was already mailing me spendy care packages every month; no need to rack up the bills and risk having my mom Early Terminate from her own volunteer assignment.

With Christmas and New Year's approaching, I decided to use three weeks of my vacation time to travel within West Africa with Tim, as both of us were ready to get out of Côte d'Ivoire. For me, life in Bangolo had become routine. Each day I'd sleep until 0800, make the rounds at the office, attempt to inspire, search for quality food, write letters, read books, and wait for more opportunities. It was starting to get a bit stale. By all accounts, it was the same for Tim. We needed an adventure, something grandiose to mark the beginning of our second year, a journey to chronicle the chapters of our life.

We had many destinations to choose from. We considered traveling by train from Abidjan north into Mali then west into Senegal. Once there, we'd be eating decent food, visiting old friends, reliving those glorious carefree days of Peace Corps training under bright blue African skies. After some deliberation, we figured we'd be sitting on our asses the majority of the time, visiting a country we had already seen, and we were no longer allowed to enter the training facility as volunteers. So we nixed that idea.

We considered a route northwest through Liberia and Guinea to view what remained of the jungles of sub-Saharan Africa. But there was an influx of refugees fleeing Liberia into western Côte d'Ivoire to escape war, poverty, and difficult conditions, which failed to instill the vacation spirit in either of us.

We also mapped out a route east along the coast of Ghana, Togo, and Benin to see the infamous slave fortresses, but our predecessors reported that the scenery wasn't much different along the coast of Côte d'Ivoire, but with many more *gendarme* stops. Unless you're a historian or an anthropologist, once you've seen one slave fortress you've probably seen enough.

Eventually we decided on Mali, the big foreboding desert country to the north. Vacationing in Mali was a chance to experience a climate and culture much different than that of Côte d'Ivoire. It would also be a chance to test our resolve, as Mali is one of the poorest countries in the world with about half of its population below the international poverty line of about $1.25 U.S. per day. We learned about the country's attractions and hazards from Mali volunteers while they were on medical evacuation or vacation at the hostel. Mali volunteers were a strange lot, proud of their isolation, their toe rot, and their poor hygiene, even more than us. By their standards, Côte d'Ivoire volunteers were privileged and pampered. No argument there. Life was good in the IC. But it made me realize that what a Mali volunteer might describe as an "attraction" or "hazard" might differ greatly from what I had in mind.

In the weeks leading up to our trip, Tim and I sent letters back and forth between Bangolo and Soubré, illustrated with cartoon caricatures hiking along rock escarpments in Dogon country, narrowly escaping Tuareg bandits in the desert, forging our way via camel or steamship to the remote and enigmatic city of Timbuktu, all the while living like Spartans with basic provisions and minimal rations. Though we both knew such an adventure was a bit garnished, we also knew there'd be plenty of attractions and hazards by any measure.

Day 1 - Abidjan to Bouaké (353 km by bus)

On the afternoon of December 18th, we departed for Mali after three days in Abidjan arranging for our visas and finishing our quarterly reports. Our packs were light, as intended, containing only toiletries, a first-aid kit, water bottles, iodine purification tablets, and a mess of old T-shirts and gaudy pants so as not to ruin our wardrobe in the dust and grime of travel. At the Adjamé *gare*, we boarded a relatively new, full-sized bus for our first leg from Abidjan to Bouaké, which would take five hours if all went well.

Above the driver's seat was the boxed-shape metal housing for a 19-inch television set hanging from the roof. This was a novel idea. Being able to watch TV during a bus trip would make the passenger experience a lot less agonizing. But the TV itself was missing, "stolen" according to the *apprenti*. Tim and I were as entertained by the remnants, and the notion that bus company managers—thieves in their own right—would expect to maintain this progressive service without it being immediately pilfered in Adjamé. In lieu of television, the bus had a cassette deck and blared songs like "If I No Go Work;

Momma No Go Work," or the Ivoirian favorite "C'est la Dance de Chien" (It's the Dance of the Dog), which went something like: *Woof! Woof! C'est la dance de chien, da da daaa, dada da da daaa, dada da da daaa, dada ..... C'est la dance de chien, da da daaa...* So much for making the passenger experience less agonizing.

Day 2 – Bouaké to Sikasso (472 km)

We stayed in Bouaké long enough to eat a late dinner with our PCV colleague Anne before catching the 0100 bus to Sikasso, Mali. We slept through the night in the scrublands of northern Côte d'Ivoire, home of the Senoufou, and arrived at the border with the rising sun. The police barricaded the road with a wooden fence while they searched the *gbakas* on the Mali side. We watched as they targeted women trying to smuggle textiles into Côte d'Ivoire without paying the tariff. If a tax was levied, the women could still cross the border and profit from the lucrative market of their southern neighbor so long as the border guards weren't too greedy.

Our northbound bus was allowed to enter the country without much of a search. By late morning we arrived in Sikasso, the first major town and first planned stop along our route. The plan was to search for the regional Peace Corps hostel, meet the volunteers, and gather more information about central Mali. We had no idea where the hostel was located, but if Mali was anything like Côte d'Ivoire you could find the volunteers just by asking where the *toubabs* lived. Sure enough, we were escorted to the hostel in no time.

A handful of volunteers were there when we arrived, and others were in route from their sites for the holidays. The first guy we met was King. Their hostel had a pecking order, and King appeared to be the Alpha male, a role he may have assumed over the years trying to live up to his regal name. The Mali volunteers laughed at King's jokes and groveled for his attention. It was reminiscent of Jack's tribe in *The Lord of the Flies*. This kind of social posturing probably takes place at every Peace Corps hostel, but in Sikasso I got to be an observer without a lasting stake in the outcome.

The hostel itself was small compared with the mansion we enjoyed in Abidjan, but their compound had more shade trees, giving it a homier, residential feel. We had tentatively planned to stay the night and depart for Sévaré first thing in the morning, but we never felt entirely welcome in Sikasso. This was their regional house, their place to unwind from the stress and isolation of their sites, where one can go to be amongst familiar faces. Tim and I were strangers, volunteers from Côte d'Ivoire, soft and weak from all the amenities and delicacies, and we felt they resented us as a result. So that evening, after some gear adjustments and a few vacation beers, we decided to move on.

Day 3 – Sikasso to Sévaré (466 km by bus)

We played foosball with the *apprentis* before our bus finally left just after midnight. Once again we would be getting our sleep in transit, curled up in our seats in some ghastly disfigurement. We traveled throughout the night until our bus broke down not too far from Sévaré. We got out and lay down on the small jagged stones by the side of the road, using larger, less-jagged stones as pillows, salvaging rest now that we had room to stretch. But it was cold, and we were ill-prepared for nights in the desert. We rested for an hour before the glare of a fiery sun woke us up for good, illuminating the endless scrublands in various hues of orange and yellow.

After the *apprenti* hammered on engine parts for a few hours, the bus was repaired and ready to go. An elderly man from the nearby village approached with a small blind boy. The boy began playing a makeshift stringed instrument, like a junkyard violin made from an empty #10 tomato can, with a piece of wood for the neck and a couple of pieces of steel wire for the strings. The elderly man stood next to him, one hand on the boy's head, the other hand held out to the passengers as we boarded. Despite the sharp irritating noise from the boy's instrument (like a repetitive *hee haw* from a donkey), people gave of their spare change. It was as if the worse he played, the more he was rewarded, like pop music stars in America. In Côte d'Ivoire, you wouldn't see this type of display very often; they would likely be run off, if not beaten, for their antics. But here, in one of the most impoverished countries in the world, people were tolerant and giving. Tim and I had no excuse but to give as well.

Later we learned why our fellow passengers were so charitable. Like the Senegalese, most Malians are Muslim and must abide by the Qur'an and its five pillars of faith. The fourth pillar is a purifying tax, or *Zaket*, which is the annual levy of 2.5 percent of a Muslim's valuables and savings, accrued over a period of a full year. Each

Muslim calculates his own Zaket and distributes it directly amongst the poor or chosen beneficiaries, as long as they are also Muslim. In addition to government-assessed taxes, the Zaket is required of Muslims to foster the qualities of sacrifice and attempt to rid society of selfishness and greed. Unfortunately for Malians, 2.5 percent of an individual's valuables and savings doesn't add up to much.

In western society there is a similar ritual of giving to those in need. Alms of the capitalistic West can be funneled through a government agency, a religious group, or a charitable organization to enhance the vetting and equity of the distribution. But most of these middle-men don't work for free. Sometimes the percent for business overhead is greater than the percent distributed to the poor and destitute. While I understand these groups need financial backing to be self-sustaining or prosperous, there's a point where these expenditures conflict with the intent of the donor, where the rate of return does not favor the cause. As a donor, that would be disconcerting, especially if the government, the religious group, or the organization were the primary benefactors.

A practice similar to the Zaket persists in most U.S. cities where the beggar relies directly on the judgment of a donor, which can be quite the art, business, or performance. My favorites are the men who cover themselves in silver or gold paint and stand motionless on a chair or milk crate until someone ponies up sufficient dough. At which point, they'll do a brief robotic movement before resuming their original pose. There's the "I'm not going to lie; I need money for beers or drugs" approach, which seems resonate with college frat boys. On the streets of San Francisco and Seattle, there's a legion of trust-fund kids sporting Gortex boots and REI raingear, rebelling against the establishment, choosing sloth over gumption. However, the encounter that soured me on handouts occurred in a shopping plaza in Worcester. Day after day I noticed a downtrodden man with long ratty hair sitting behind a big sign that read, "Will work for food." So I bought him a sandwich. When I rolled down my window to hand it to him, he said to me gruffly, "Beat it, kid." Way to endear me to your plight, Mister!

Tim and I arrived in Sévaré just before noon. The further north we traveled, the sandier it got. This was particularly noticeable in Sévaré, where most of the roads were nothing but sand, and the tire tracks disappeared under thick drifts. We spent the better part of the afternoon gearing up for a five-day hike through Dogon country. Evenings in the desert were frigid, so we each purchased an itchy, flea-infested, camel-hair blanket from a street vendor to supplement our clothing. We also purchased two one-gallon *bidons* for our drinking water, used at one point to contain fuel or antifreeze. No matter how well we tried to clean them, we couldn't get rid of the odor. These jugs were wrapped in a type of burlap that kept the water relatively cool through natural evaporative cooling in the dry air, which was a huge plus when your drinking water tastes like fuel and iodine tablets.

Again, we located the regional Peace Corps hostel by asking for the *toubabs*, though not everyone understood our French. Not only was it getting sandier and colder, but the people of Sévaré relied more on the local languages of Bambara or Arabic. For the first time since the start of Peace Corps training, we faced the possibility of not being able to communicate with the locals, and it wouldn't get any easier the further north we went.

The Sévaré hostel had 24-hour security, and it looked more like an army barracks than a home. The Peace Corps volunteer leader responsible for managing the hostel told us that the bunks were reserved for Mali volunteers, though we were welcome to stay in the compound if we didn't mind sleeping outside on the sandy ground. This may sound like roughing it, but after sleeping in cramped chairs on crappy buses for two nights, his invitation made us feel like honored guests.

For dinner we walked to the Mankan Té *maquis* and filled up on spaghetti and beer. By the time we made it back to the hostel, there was a crowd drinking outside on picnic tables lit by fluorescent lights. Unlike Sikasso, these volunteers were more accepting, friendlier, less likely to begrudge us for having roads and toilet paper. In fact, the volunteers at the Sévaré hostel did all they could to prepare us for Dogon. They drew us maps. They provided contact information for guides. They made sure we were plenty hydrated with Castel beer for the long trek ahead. They even offered up a place to sleep at our next stop in Douentza, as the volunteer posted there was away on leave. This was the hospitality we expected amongst our Peace Corps brethren, and it would become the measure of hospitality Tim and I would use to treat visitors to Côte d'Ivoire.

Day 4 – Sévaré to Douentza (167 km by bashé)

I slept the entire night in a horizontal position and woke up refreshed, despite the mosquitoes and the desert cold. A female volunteer from Mali and her younger sister were also heading to Douentza and offered to escort us to the vacant house. Transportation from Sévaré to Douentza was in a covered pickup truck with wooden bench seats over the wheel-wells called a *bashé*. This was the first time we traveled during the heat of the day. Bad idea, though we didn't have much of a choice as the only other vehicles traveling beyond Sévaré were the NGOs or commercial trucks. With temperatures near 100°F, the ride was sweltering and uncomfortable, resulting in a new appreciation for nighttime travel.

Douentza is an impressive little outpost on the north end of the Falaise de Bandiagara—a sandstone escarpment rising 500 meters high and stretching 150 kilometers to the southwest, home to the Dogon people. Our plan was to hike about 100 kilometers along this escarpment from Douentza to Sanga in five days, a feat commonly referred to in guidebooks as the "Dogon Death March." Twenty kilometers is a good distance to walk in one day. We'd have to finish before the sun reached its apex and the heat became unbearable.

We wasted no time settling into the house. With the help of the house caretaker Barké, we arranged for a guide. The fee for the guide included meals, but Barké advised we should probably pick up supplemental food, not only for us but as *cadeaux* for the children and village chiefs. The chiefs were easy to buy for, as they favored tea and sugar, otherwise, all we could find in the market were nuts, dried prunes, and hard candy. Unless the Dogon children relished nuts and prunes, they'd be getting the candy and Tim and I would be stuck with the ill-sorted trail mix.

Barké made us dinner while we drank in lawn chairs on the roof of the mud house, and we watched the sun set over the high cliffs in the distance. Douentza had the feel of Senegal with a more dramatic topography. It was a perfect evening, temps around 70°F, good company and conversation, the body and mind as close to homeostasis as the dead. Barké sold produce on the street during the day, so our first course was a big salad with tomato, lettuce, and beans. It was odd to see an adult African man cooking and attending to the home. In Côte d'Ivoire, this was the business of women and children. I don't think Barké cared what they did in Côte d'Ivoire, strutting around in his fancy outfit of lime green pants, a purple jacket, and an undersized black cowboy hat, happy to serve.

Barké wasn't the first PCV caretaker I'd come across. Volunteers paid Ivoirians to wash their clothes, do their shopping, cook their meals, and whatever else one might pay someone to do. By all accounts, these caretakers were receiving a fair wage. I personally chose to do household chores myself, simply because I was capable. I cleaned my clothes on a washboard in the shower; I haggled for goods at the market; and I made elaborate meals on my two-burner propane stove. What else was I going to do with my time? Read more books? Drink more beer? For volunteers with caretakers, that was their choice and I take no exception; they probably spread the wealth and improved lives. I could live with that, and it looked like Barké could too.

After Dogon, we would need to come back through Douentza to reach points north, so we had some decisions to make on how we'd get to Timbuktu. We could travel due north by camel in five days for about $55 each, or we could make our way up to Gao and take a steamship on the Niger River in less time for less money. Neither of us had been on a camel before. What an adventure it would be to ride roughshod on a camel through the Sahara Desert to a place like Timbuktu. A trip for the ages. Stuff of legend. But after one look at the ornery beasts of burden, there was no way. It would be torture. Perhaps another time when the stakes weren't so high. Maybe a spin around a maypole at a desert carnival. So we planned to get there by steamer and hoped to arrive by New Year's Eve.

Day 5 – Douentza to Nendé (20 km on foot)

Early in the morning, while it was still dark, we met our guide Aboubakar for the march of death. Our guide had a common name in these parts, so we made sure he was *the* Aboubakar. He was short and thin, fair-skinned, with nappy bed-ridden hair, a pencil-thin mustache, and a purple suit that resembled pajamas. He seemed like a nice guy, all business, setting a quick pace from the start without much talking. To get around the escarpment, we set off towards the southeast from Douentza along a series of sandy trails. As the sun was on the rise, some ten kilometers into the walk, Aboubakar had us scramble up the escarpment for our first stop along the tour. The view was amazing—an extensive stretch of desert plains marked by another escarpment in the far distance, with tall trees that looked like miniscule blades of grass from above.

In the highlands, there was a small village named Ébari, where the children had sideways Mohawks that ran from ear to ear instead of front to back. I'd never seen anything like it. I was used to kids pointing at me, running after me, demanding *cadeaux*, but these kids huddled up against each other and stared while a few ran crying to their mothers as if they'd seen a ghost. It wasn't as if this village hadn't ever seen white people. Aboubakar usually brought his clients up here for morning tea. Perhaps some of these youngsters were swaddled to their momma's back the last time *toubabs* paid them a visit. For all intents and purposes, we may have been ghosts to a select few.

The chief invited us to share in the tea we gave as a gift. We three travelers joined the village elders under a shelter called a *tóguna*, where men traditionally gathered to discuss important affairs. The structure was about four meters square, with a dirt floor, large rocks around the perimeter, and a thick roof made from millet stalks held up by crooked tree trunks. The *tóguna* is constructed with a low ceiling to mitigate violence when discussions get heated, so we walked hunched over until we were seated.

The tea I drank in sub-Saharan Africa was second to none, bold like coffee with fresh mint and lots of sugar, called "gunpowder tea." The tea is poured back and forth between shot glasses until foam builds on the top. It's consumed ceremoniously, with the first round being strong and bitter, the second and third rounds a bit watered down but with added sugar.

On the advice of our guide, Tim and I hiked along the escarpment to view an old pygmy village. We found the old village, but found no sign that pygmies lived there. Just rocks placed deliberately by the hands of man. More surprising was the large radio tower at the edge of the escarpment, a technology that snapped us back into the present where kids with sideways Mohawks and old pygmy villages are few and far between.

We worked our way back to Ébari, said our goodbyes, and descended back onto level sandy ground. It was getting hot, so we made haste with the remaining ten kilometers to the village of Nendé where we would spend our first night. I hadn't walked twenty kilometers in a single day in years. I was exhausted and so was Tim. We napped the requisite two hours on the shady side of a mud house and recovered as best we could. Later, after patching the blisters on our feet, we explored the village, played with the kids, refilled our water jugs, and enjoyed another desert sunset. Aboubakar brought us a dinner of chicken parts mixed with steaming hot rice in a large bowl. We were so hungry we dug right in, scalding our fingers and mouths. Despite the burns, it would be the best meal we'd receive on our five-day trek, as we were heading further away from Douentza, and further from commerce. When the village turned in for the night, so did I, finding a comfy patch of sand in the schoolyard just out of earshot of my cohort's snoring.

Day 6 – Nendé to Diamuely (about 20 km)

That little runt guide of ours woke us up at 0500 by kicking our feet. I suppose he was doing what we had paid him to do, which was to keep us on track, but I was sore and my body was not cooperating. Aboubakar was in spectacular shape, quick, nimble, with great endurance. We hoisted our heavy packs into place and continued the trek, eating a breakfast of stale bread and dried prunes along the way. The Falaise de Bandiagara loomed large to the west. Our footing was a sandy roadbed with small patches of exposed rock. We saw few people on this day; that is, until the last few kilometers of our sojourn when we came upon a group of five middle-aged French couples walking the same stretch.

We limped into Diamuely around noon and noticed the Frenchies weren't carrying any gear. Their luggage was stacked high on a wheeled cart pulled by a donkey. What? You can't have donkeys carry your gear on the Dogon Death March! What a bunch of lazy tourists. What is it with the French? Do they not know they should be marching in a near-death-like condition?

Tim and I were given straw mats and a nice shady corner in the courtyard to rest. While we ate our rice, the Frenchies were seated at a collapsible banquet table across the way, dining like kings on big chicken drumsticks and wine. At that moment, we realized we were lying in the family's compost pile ... at their direction. Sure, we were smelly and our clothes were ragged and dirty, but did we deserve the compost heap? At least the children weren't bothering us for gifts.

Not to be outdone, we received a random visit from a village elder later in the afternoon. He must have been eighty or ninety years old, his thin frame held up by a crooked stick, course brown skin, teeth encrusted with a rot that looked like the remnants of chewed-up cheese doodles. He wanted us to fix the zipper on his gym bag. Tim snatched the bag and realigned the slider with the zipper's teeth in no time. The old man nodded in appreciation, flashing his big cheese-doodle smile. He handed Tim a ripe mango, considered gold in these parts. As a consolation gift, I got a handful of charred minnows, great for African soups and sauces, I hear. Damn Frenchies!

In Diamuely, we were seeing more houses built into the rocky hillside, interspersed amongst small round granaries, with pointed black roofs that stored their harvest. After a nap we explored the village, gave out candy to the kids, and enjoyed the view. The story goes that the Dogon people, believers in the animist religion like the Guéré in Bangolo, refused to convert to Islam one thousand years ago and took up defensible positions along the *falaise* to repel attacks and avoid the slave trade. The Dogon remain there today, surviving in all likelihood by the collective decision to live so far removed from society, eventually integrating with their Muslim neighbors during less threatening times. Later that evening, Tim and I took up defensible positions on the rooftop of a mud house where we ate dinner, spotted constellations, and crashed for the evening.

Day 7 – Diamuely to Bamba, Christmas Eve (25 km on foot)

We awoke at daybreak and had to search for Aboubakar, who was still sleeping at a friend's house. The French and their donkey cart were gone, departing about an hour earlier, we were told. No way were we going to let them beat us to Bamba, so we put our heads down and kept a frantic pace, resting infrequently. This pleased Aboubakar and brought him out of his shell, but we were in no mood for talking. We had a goal in mind, a fixation. We caught the Frenchies about five kilometers shy of Bamba and blew by them with a *petit bonjour* and a tip of the cap, arriving in the village before noon. It was our longest stretch thus far on the DDM, logging in twenty-five kilometers.

In the afternoon I took my first bucket bath of the trip, fetching water from the village well by using one of those diaphragm pumps you manually yank up and down by a handle. What a relief it was to clean up. The well was also where we got our drinking water. While the insulated *bidons* did a fantastic job of keeping our water cool in the desert heat, the quality of our water was suspect since we didn't have a filter and we had given up adding iodine tablets due to the lousy taste.

There was another need for water on our trip. In sub-Saharan Africa, you didn't use toilet paper to wipe your bum. The method for cleaning up involved pouring water from a plastic kettle down the crack of your ass with your right hand while the left hand did all the swabbing. After a few runs you got the hang of it, but in the desert it was important to be efficient as there wasn't a lot of water to spare. This is why it's rude in West Africa to eat with or offer the left hand in salutation, as the left hand is the poop hand, no matter how well you clean it. So no need to pack toilet paper on this trip; that operation was covered.

With a bit of daylight remaining, Tim and I climbed the ladder to our new rooftop and caught up on journal writing and blister patching. Sleeping on a family's rooftop made me think of a book I'd come across before leaving the States called *Material World, A Global Family Portrait*. In it, the author presents a visual portrait of average families from around the globe. He has them place all of their possessions in front of their house. Each photograph is composed of the family, their possessions, and their house in the background. A family from Texas was depicted as the average American family. Their photo contained appliances, furniture, electronics, and vehicles, with a ranch-style home at the back end of a cul-de-sac. In contrast, there was another photo of a family from sub-Saharan African, possibly Mali. Since they had no front yard, they gathered on their rooftop with their bowls and baskets. Both families smiled for the camera all the same.

Our French friends were on the adjacent rooftop a few meters away, preparing for holiday festivities. Aboubakar promised he'd drum up a special dinner for the occasion. What he delivered was a desert bush rat in a grainy sauce. Now this might sound less than appetizing to some, but when you're eating rice and prunes and burning thousands of calories per day, bush rat is a welcome feast.

While gnawing at the last of the gristle, the French called us over to join them. We descended one ladder and climbed another. They were friendly and patient with our French, and we conversed about our worlds. They even shared their bounty of fine cheeses and red wine. The more we drank, the more we diluted our general contempt for the French. We sang Christmas carols in each other's language until midnight, and we genuinely had a good time. They were good people who took pity on two grubs alone on Christmas Eve, eating animals like animals and wiping our asses with our hands. Next time I embark on a march of death, I'm hiring a donkey cart to carry some creature comforts.

Day 8 –Bamba to Yenndouma, Christmas Day (20 km on foot)

Another day, another morning stroll in the desert. We were no longer competing with the French for bragging rights, so we paced ourselves, moving at five kilometers per hour. In Yenndouma we began to sense a change. The village looked similar to previous Dogon villages, with mud houses and granaries built into the escarpment and larger community buildings constructed at its base. But the people were different. The kids were unrelenting in their requests for gifts. Some wanted candy but most asked for *"le Bic"*, the men asked for money, and the women asked for medicine. Aboubakar ran interference for us the best he could, but there was no satisfying this crowd.

At some point in time, the people of Yenndouma had become conditioned to associate *toubabs* with gifts. It made sense. We were only a day's hike from Sanga where westerners can experience life in a Dogon village, buy Dogon trinkets, and pay to see Dogon rituals. Mali volunteers advised us to steer clear of the touristy villages near the road system, and we'd succeeded until now. As we were arranging our rooftop accommodations, we spotted the French giving out gifts from their donkey-powered sleigh. Santa had found his way to Yenndouma after all.

Day 9 –Yenndouma to Sanga to Sévaré (20 km on foot; 107 km by bashé)

We were up early to complete the last leg of our walk with hopes of reaching Sévaré by the end of the day. From the rooftop I watched a Muslim man below with his young child, standing, kneeling, prostrating, and praying. The child was barely old enough to form his own thoughts, yet he was praying to a god he likely did not know. He performs this ritual five times a day, more frequently than he eats, gets dressed, or performs any household chore. When I was a young lad in Worcester, I attended a Catholic church and followed along with the crowd, standing, kneeling, sitting, hand-shaking, reading, and singing. I remember how boring and uncomfortable it was, how I couldn't wait for church to end. It takes practice and dedication to be a good disciple. I often wondered, do the mechanics of prayer at an early age condition us to follow religious doctrine or to believe in God? I'm not sure there's a way to know, but I wonder what would've become of me if Immaculate Conception had reclining pews with comfy cushions.

The day's hike brought us onto the escarpment, over rocky outcrops, reuniting us with the ominous *baobab* tree. Plagued by cravings for meals we hadn't eaten in a long time, our conversation centered mostly around food. We arrived in Sanga before noon, commemorating our feat with handshakes all around. We checked out the tourist traps before searching for a ride. With no regularly scheduled transportation, we had to bargain with the locals. After two hours negotiating back and forth, feigning boredom and indifference, or playing hardball, we convinced a shop owner with a Mercedes to take us the forty-four kilometers to Bandiagara. From Bandiagara, we spent another three hours on a *bashé* that kept breaking down along the sixty-three-kilometer stretch to Sévaré. By nightfall we were back in the friendly confines of the Sévaré hostel. Neither one of us could believe how gaunt we looked in the mirror. We cleaned up and celebrated with more spaghetti and beer at the Mankan Té as Dave Brubeck's Take Five played from the sound system. Yet another surreal moment on the Dark Continent.

Day 10 – Sévaré to Douentza (167 km by bashé)

Aboubakar left us in Sévaré at the end of Day 9, but we would see him again on Day 11. We slept in before heading to the *gare* to catch a bashé back to Douentza. The word at the Sévaré hostel was that the Douentza volunteer was still away on leave and that it would be all right if we stayed on his roof again. We arrived in the late afternoon and put Barké to work on our laundry, then we rested until dinner. It was nice not having to get up early and march, so we embraced the downtime, enjoying a few beverages on the rooftop. We were on vacation, after all.

Day 11 – Douentza to Hombori (142 km by commercial truck)

Aboubakar stopped by to gauge our interest in camel travel to Timbuktu. The last time through Douentza, we had ruled out camels due to the higher cost and certain discomfort, but the novelty still piqued our interest. Or we could head up to Gao and take the boat as planned. Hitching a ride along the 389-kilometer stretch from Douentza to Gao wasn't guaranteed, as it required relying on the goodwill of commercial truck drivers. Timbuktu was three days' boat travel from Gao if all went well, so we'd have to get to the river early the next day if we stood a chance of being there for New Year's Eve. Either way, it promised to be a mad dash across the desert. Aboubakar left us, vowing to find us transport by day's end.

We spent the day recuperating at the house, napping in hammocks beneath fruit trees, reading books, recounting our travels, and napping some more. Our spirits were high despite the aches and pains. Tim and I had spent every waking moment together and we were still enjoying each other's company. Along the way, we had had tough decisions to make, some of which were critical to our health and welfare, but we were always in agreement. It may have helped that we both had methodical engineer brains, although that was no guarantee we'd agree on everything. Somehow, things went smoothly. Credit travel fairies or dumb luck, but we were covering all the territory from our cartoon map and we were right on schedule. The same could not be said for some of our colleagues, who later attempted to retrace our Mali route and ran into problems. To be fair, they were traveling in groups of three or more, which made it exponentially more difficult to agree on anything.

In the afternoon we began to get nervous. We dispatched Barké to find out what was going on. We were about to give up when Aboubakar rushed into the compound and told us to hurry to the paved road; the *chef du gare* believed there would be a truck heading to Gao in the evening. We squared with Barké and made it to the road in minutes, just in time for an amazing desert sunset that transformed the sky from pink to orange to deep purple. And we waited. One hour passed. Darkness set in. Two hours passed. Still no transportation aside from the occasional NGO vehicle, which were not authorized to pick up hitchhikers.

Tim and I were at our first real crossroads. We could continue to wait and take our chances, or we could go back to the rooftop, get a good night's sleep, and try again in the morning. Tim had the shits and wanted to go back. I couldn't blame him. Temperatures were dropping, the gravel road shoulder wasn't the most comfortable place to wait, and our bathroom was in the low desert brush. While I also had the shits, I did not want to spend another night on the rooftop. The theme of our vacation was go-go-go, and the rooftop felt like surrender. I remarked that the travel fairies were with us and convinced Tim to stay another hour.

While Tim was napping, a medium-sized commercial truck pulled up. Its cargo container had an open top and was full beyond the brim with hundred-pound burlap sacks of raw peanuts. The *chef* motioned for us to climb aboard. Tim and I looked at each other in disbelief, then scrambled up the metal ladder and over to the cab where we found a spot in the dips and depressions of the peanut sacks and tried in vain to get comfortable.

It was a clear night. The truck motored down the road at a good clip, which made it that much colder. My blanket did not keep me entirely warm, but the experience was unforgettable. The stretch between Gao and Hombori was lined with steep rocky escarpments on both sides of the road, illuminated by a first quarter moon. And we had a perfect viewing platform.

Day 12 – Hombori to Gao to Village (247 km by truck; 150 km by boat)

Around midnight we pulled into Hombori and stopped briefly. I peered out from beneath my blanket to confirm that Hombori was less of a town and more of an outpost or rest stop. Ten to fifteen tall, thin, brown-skinned men in long robes and turbans climbed atop the truck. At closer inspection, I saw they were armed with long swords sheathed at the waist. Oh no! These were the Tuareg Freedom Fighters, and we were surrounded on all sides. Our only escape would be to leap from the truck cab, slide down the windshield, and hightail it into the night. We probably wouldn't survive ten seconds before they caught up to us and thrust a dagger in our backs.

It's not like we hadn't been warned. Our office posted travel warnings as a result of conflicts in neighboring countries, and the skirmishes in northern Mali between the Tuaregs and the government soldiers often made news. The Tuaregs are nomadic people, Islamic people. They have thrived in the Saharan Desert for thousands of years in and around Mali, Niger, Algeria, and Libya, operating the trans-Saharan caravan between the Sahel and northern Africa's Mediterranean ports. Much of their trade has focused on food, garments, salt, and camels, but in their heyday they were known to take human captives for trade, sale, or assimilation. When the French colonists arrived during the nineteenth and early twentieth centuries, the Tuaregs put up a good fight. Since Mali's independence in 1960, the Tuaregs have engaged in various rebellions and uprisings to maintain their autonomy in hopes of forming their own nation state. At the end of 1995, they were at the tail end of a five-year rebellion in northeastern Mali, but fighting was reportedly still raging in areas.

Now they were on our peanut truck and coming at us. I looked over at Tim under his woolen blanket and grimy New York Yankees baseball cap. Tim was raised in Marblehead, MA; they should kill him first just for wearing a Yankees hat. The Tuaregs moved in a leisurely fashion, looking for their own spot to lie amongst the sacks. One found a spot right next to me near the edge, his sword placed by his side for quick retrieval. From Hombori to Gao, we snuggled for the warmth that emanated from our core. Likely, they didn't notice we were Americans. They had other business, I'm sure, or they'd sized us up and concluded that we wouldn't bring much in the way of sale or trade. Part of me likes to think that they saw two westerners in the middle of the Sarahan Desert traveling like nomads on top of a peanut truck in the frigid night, and we were all right in their books, nothing like those westerners on television. Or maybe they were just Yankees fans.

We pulled into Gao and waited until daybreak when the ferry began its first run across the Niger River—the lifeblood of Mali. Tim and I were able to get coffee and omelets from a kiosk while we waited. I noticed a big difference in Gao's architecture compared to other towns in southern Mali. Buildings were made of intricate brickwork, ascending up to three stories high. It's amazing what Africans can do with mud.

Once across the river, the Tuaregs went on their way, disappearing into the crowd. Tim and I went to speak with the *chef du gare*. We learned that the daily steamer was stuck along the river somewhere between Mopti and Kabara, three days away. He could tell we were anxious, desperate to leave. With dollar-sign eyes, he told us we could take a *pinasse*, or motorized canoe, from Gao to Kabara for 450,000 CFA, which equated to roughly $900. Nine hundred dollars? He had to be mistaken. Aside from my college education, it would be the most expensive purchase I'd make in my life; not even the automobiles I owned had cost me that much. But he was serious. Obviously, someone who resembled us had paid the *chef* a handsome sum to get out of Gao, and he must have thought it was worth another try. We were expecting to pay about 10,000 CFA (U.S. $20), so we walked away. No sense in bargaining.

There was a hotel in Gao, so Tim and I pondered the idea of waiting it out until the steamer arrived. While discussing our options, a teenage boy ran up to us, grabbing at our packs and telling us to hurry as our boat was about to leave. Sometimes you don't wait around for things to make sense in Africa; you trust your instincts, take your chances, and go through the open doors as they appear. The boy ran off and we followed, dodging and weaving around obstacles, hopping over ropes fastened to boats along the shoreline. The boy guided us to the only *pinasse* readying for launch.

The vessel was about fifteen meters in length, with a rounded thatched roof that kept the sun's rays off its passengers. Lashed to the roof were a dozen multi-colored mattresses matching the colorful artwork along the bow. The captain was not expecting us but he let us on board. About ten passengers were already seated, all white and presumably French. Apparently the teenage boy thought we were part of their tour group. Whether we were or not, young African boys are expert capitalists. If there's a commodity out there, they will find it and try to profit.

As we boarded, the *chef* and his men spotted us. They rushed over to our boat and a big commotion ensued. Tim and I were likely undermining some port authority regulation or unwritten code by circumventing the *chef*, but our captain and his crew didn't seem to care. There was nothing the *chef* could do short of hand-to-hand combat. As the men were hurling insults, we slipped the boy a few coins for his services and pushed off against the current of the Niger.

That wasn't the end of it, though. We still had to negotiate a price for the boat ride and three days' worth of food. The boat captain assumed we were wealthy French tourists. Needless to say, he wasn't thrilled when he learned we were a less affluent, less discriminate breed called Peace Corps volunteers, willing to disembark or swim in lieu of paying too much. He left the bargaining to his men, which was painful as always, but we settled on an acceptable price, about $50 each, including meals.

I've spent some time on rivers, but nothing like the Niger. Shortly into our trip, the captain pulled over so we could scramble up a large mound of sand about five stories high to take photographs. It was like something you'd see in Death Valley National Park in California. The dunes were likely deposited and shaped by Harmattan winds, which are both a nuisance and a relief to the desert people. From the top we had an extraordinary view of the Sahara Desert and a preview of what was in store down river. The terrain ahead was flat and swampy, stark and empty. If the captain said we were heading to the edge of the world, we'd be hard-pressed to refute.

As transportation goes, the *pinasse* was fairly comfortable. The group sat along the cushioned thwarts, but it wasn't against the rules to toss a mattress inside the hull and kick back. I spent my time reading under the awning or chatting with the Frenchies. Tim played chess with one of the older French men. The meals were decent, mostly rice and a grainy sauce with dried fish.

Our *pinasse* stopped sometime after dark at a small riverbank village. The captain told us we'd be shoving off at 0400. The Frenchies had a tour guide who led them and their mattresses to a nearby rooftop, much the way we slept in Dogon country. Tim slept on the sand. I would have joined him but I was paranoid that I'd oversleep or the captain might leave without us, so I slept in the hull. It didn't help that I had recently watched the movie *Apocalypse Now* at the hostel. There's a scene where one of the soldiers gets out of the boat to explore the jungle only to be attacked by a tiger. He narrowly escapes, but not without letting the others know, "Never get out of the fucking boat."

Day 13 – River Village to River Village (200 km by boat)

It was 0600 before the captain was able to wake the Frenchies and get them into the *pinasse*. I slept three more hours on my mattress in the hull before we stopped at a village to refuel. According to the crew, there was an unimproved road that ran parallel to the river from Gao to Timbuktu to supply villages, but the road was unreliable due to drifting sands.

A small group of children, thin with the distended bellies of malnutrition, approached the boat in the shallows of the river's edge. A few had injuries or lesions on their legs and arms. Two elderly women joined the children as the French were taking photographs. Neither the women nor the children spoke French. One of these women pointed at her eye, swollen and red, then stuck her hand out towards the boat. A young red-haired French girl found a bottle of contact lens saline solution in her bag and tossed it to the woman, explaining its limitations in vain as the old woman poured the contents over her face with a look of wild desperation. The Frenchies rummaged through their bags for other items. More villagers arrived, pointing at injured body parts in what looked like a frenetic version of group charades. The next item to be slung from the boat was a cheap beaded necklace, the kind you might find at Mardi Gras in New Orleans. Then, all sorts of cosmetic jewelry and toiletry products were hurled into the river, creating a stir. Some items were fought for and claimed; other items were swept up in the current and floated downstream. I'd never seen anything like it.

I looked back at the captain and his crew as if to say, "Don't lump me in with these people." The crew looked back at us as if to reply, "We see this stuff every time on these boat trips." While I'm sure the Frenchies had good intentions and gave from the heart, I felt they were causing more harm than good, that it would be better to do nothing at all. Ailments were not healed or alleviated. Nothing of real use or value was donated. Hope was not converted to lasting joy. Cultures were not bridged. If anything, the people of this faraway village became more dependent on white-skinned transients. What I witnessed was sympathetic turned pathetic in a hurry, and I hoped to carry that lesson forward in Bangolo.

Day 14 – River Village to Timbuktu (100 km by boat; 12 km on foot)

We adhered to the same routine, sleeping in different spots and getting up early. We pushed ahead against the current for another day of sun, sand, and petrol fumes from the outboard motor. We pulled into the port that led to Kabara sometime after noon. The Frenchies were continuing down the Niger River to Mopti, so we bid them farewell. It was New Year's Eve and it was looking like we would make it to Timbuktu by nightfall, right on schedule, landing on our feet once again. The cab fare was outrageous, and we'd just spent three days virtually immobile on a boat, so Tim and I decided we'd walk the twelve kilometers to the city, despite the hot sun.

At the city limits, we stopped at the *gendarmerie* depot and got our passports stamped, reaching in through a jail cell window. The stamp was recommended by Mali volunteers as a security measure as well as a coveted souvenir, proof that we had made it. When I was a child, my grandmother often threatened to banish me to Timbuktu if I didn't behave, so the Timbuktu of my youth was a mysterious, mythical place where they specialize in detention and punishment. While I definitely felt the aches and pains in the time it took to get there, I can now report back that as cities go, it's not so bad, certainly not the place my grandmother made it out to be. I don't blame her for using Timbuktu as a metaphor to help keep her grandchildren in line. What are the chances I'd go there on vacation?

Tim and I found a beer garden in town and we toasted our latest achievement. The employees at the bar gave us advice on where to stay, where to eat, and where to celebrate the festivities. While Timbuktu is primarily Muslim, word on the street was that there'd be a multinational contingent issuing in the New Year in more western fashion at the town bar. I normally don't care much for New Year's, or most American holidays for that matter, but the significance of celebrating in a place like Timbuktu was hard to deny.

The city's architecture resembled Gao's in many ways, but the brickwork in Timbuktu was even more intricate. The wooden doors and shutters bore fancy hardware and decorative artwork shaped like stars, moons, snowflakes, and imperial crosses cut out of sheet metal. Each house had something different. I learned that the city, more appropriately spelled Tombouctou, was established by the nomadic Tuaregs around the tenth century. Between the 12th and 15th centuries, in what is referred to as Tombouctou's Golden Age, the city was not only an important intersection along the trans-Saharan trade route, but also a major center of Islamic learning. Muslim scholars came to the city and established a university and a number of Quranic schools where important Arabic manuscripts were written and copied. Due to its vital trade and treasures, Tombouctou has been referred to as the "Athens of Africa" or the "Mecca of the Sahara." In modern times, civil war, desertification, and drought conditions have plagued the city, prompting aid organizations such as UNICEF, USAID, and many others to take up full-time residence.

And in the twentieth century, on the last day of 1995, two pilgrims from Côte d'Ivoire, struck by a bout of wanderlust, joined a population of about 25,000 to ring in the New Year.

We stayed at the Hôtel Bouctou, a two-story dwelling with an open courtyard and shared bathrooms located on the fringe of a wide open desert. We ran into three male Mali volunteers and a female returned volunteer from Zaire. The bar resembled an aluminum tool shed, inside and out, with two large rooms or bays. One room had a bar area and a dozen tables. The other had a dance floor (although, I'm sure it served a different function for the other 364 days of the year). It was sweltering inside, but they had lots of cold beer. After nightfall, a group of a dozen fraternity brothers from Michigan stormed the bar, having flown in from Bamako earlier that day. A few of them were walking around with unopened bottles of Jack Daniels like they were Van Halen roadies. In their midst was a lone female. Turns out, she and one of the men had recently married. The couple and their friends were on a rafting trip after the wedding when they vowed to meet in Timbuktu for New Year's Eve as an extended reception of sorts. It was an impressive turnout.

Tim and I, the quartet from Mali, and the contingent from Michigan had a blast that evening, swapping adventure stories, drinking more than we should, issuing in the New Year like never before. After midnight, the crew moved to the dance floor. Tim likes to boogie. I do not. So while Tim was in the other room, I was in the bar drinking from other people's abandoned, half empty (or half full, for the optimists) beer bottles. It was a mess. About all I remember is stumbling over tent stakes of nomadic travelers while the inhabitants stirred and their camels groaned.

Day 15 – Timbuktu to Korioume, New Years Day (18 km on foot)

It had taken us fifteen days to reach Timbuktu by a most circuitous route. It would take another eight days to get back to Abidjan. While there was plenty of country left to see, I was not looking forward to the return journey. Psychologically speaking, the trip culminated with Timbuktu. How do you top New Year's Eve in Timbuktu? There was no way. And it didn't help that I was getting sicker by the day, noticeably losing weight, so I had to balance my curiosity to see more of Mali with my desire to get back home.

We spent New Year's Day exploring the magnificent city, walking through mazes of mud walls and houses until we were lost. When the hotel staff told us we might be able to catch a *pinasse* to Mopti early the next day, we decided to walk the eighteen kilometers to Korioume that evening instead of relying on a cab in the morning. We didn't want to miss an opportunity to catch regular scheduled transportation, and we both wanted to keep moving, to walk off our hangovers. We said our farewells, threw on our packs, grabbed a bean sandwich for the road, and left before dusk.

It was a clear night, with a bright moon illuminating the way. Off the shoulder of the road, out of sight, crazed dogs barked whenever Tim and I shared a laugh, protecting their masters from harm and humor. We had no idea about the risks of walking in this part of the world at night. It certainly didn't feel safe, more like a route paved with pirates and bandits, whose voices in the shadows kept our heads on a swivel. Our vacation had long since given way to a brand of fatalism, and our fate would direct us safely beneath a fig tree on the outskirts of Korioume for a decent night's sleep.

Days 16-19 – Korioume to Sévaré (400 km by boat; 12 km by sept place)

There wasn't a single *pinasse* in port that morning, so we found a shady spot behind a small structure to wait. We were approached by a pack of seven-year-old boys trying to pimp out their teenage sisters for 150 CFA (U.S $0.30). To entertain ourselves, we haggled with them, trying to get the price as low as we could, curious to see how far we could push it before they retracted their offer. We got bored before we could find out, which tells you how well they regarded their teenage sisters.

Around noon, a cab arrived with the Mali volunteers and a cute Canadian couple who'd spent their New Year's Eve away from the crowds. Despite our haste, we did not gain the travel advantage we had hoped. Our *pinasse* arrived in the afternoon, the same size boat we took from Gao, same thatched roof, but this trip would be drastically different. This was a workboat, a freight vessel, moving goods and livestock up and down the Niger. No French tour groups on this ride. No colorful comfy mattresses. The crew was covered in grease from operating the boat's steering chains, and they spread the grease up and down the *pinasse* with their movements. Wooden pallets were placed along the bottom of the hull to keep everything above the nasty bilge water, but it was only partially effective, as cook pots and dirty rags floated back and forth on waves above the pallets. In Korioume, I unknowingly switched from color film to black and white. This couldn't have been a more fitting substitution.

We spent much of the next four days traveling atop the thatched roof, enjoying the view, tolerating the sun over the filth. During *sieste*, we'd wedge our packs and clothes by our sides so we didn't roll off the curved surface and into the drink. At night we either slept on the sand or on the rooftop, depending on the condition of the shoreline. My diet consisted of mostly oranges and butter cookies, which is all we could find in Korioume, supplemented with rice and gunpowder tea by a sympathetic boat crew. I had little choice but to drink unfiltered Niger River water to stay hydrated, and I started feeling sick, plagued with bouts of diarrhea, shitting from the gunwales. It was not a pretty sight. No wonder people get sick drinking river water in Africa.

On the fourth day we pulled into Mopti, disembarking the *pinasse* for the last time. It was good to get off the boat. After wading in the shallows, trying not to interfere with the women washing their clothes, we found the Patisserie Dogon across the street and gorged on donuts and chocolate éclairs. They were delicious, but they didn't remain in my system long. Tim and I then boarded a *sept place* (seven-seater) and rode east to Sévaré. For the third time we celebrated a travel milestone with spaghetti and beer at the Mankan Té. To our fortune, the volunteer leader allowed us to sleep in the bunks inside the hostel. Familiarity has its privileges.

Day 20 – Sévaré to Bamako (635 km by bus)

In the morning we arranged a bus that could take us to Bamako in the evening. Our original cartoon map had included a stop in Djenné to view the Great Mosque, but getting there seemed more difficult than we had originally thought. We reasoned that we'd already seen mud mosques in Dogon country, so we bypassed this side trip. In retrospect, I wish we hadn't. It was no more difficult to get there than any other place we had visited. After viewing photos of Djenné, it was clear our reasoning was affected by our weakened state. Not all mud mosques are built the same. There is one in Djenné that is built like a massive and elaborate castle that must be seen if one gets a chance.

Day 21 – Bamako (no movement)

Bamako is Mali's capital and largest city, though it was rather dormant when we arrived around 0400. We found the Peace Corps hostel near the Hôtel Tennessee, where we were welcomed warmly. The sleeping quarters looked like a World War II field hospital, with mosquito nets draped over twin-sized beds arranged in columns and rows in a big open room, which was fitting since Tim and I needed some rest and recovery. Around dusk we ventured out for street food with the volunteers, then stopped by one of *Newsweek's* Best Bars from Around the World called Le Campagnard. The place had only two beer selections and its ambiance wasn't much different than the other bars. I'm not sure it was even the best bar in Bamako; however, it was, as promised, an "Oasis in the Desert" relative to where we had been.

Day 22 – Bamako to Sikasso (374 km by Pajero SUV)

At Le Campagnard, we met one of Mali's Associate Peace Corps Directors. He was heading to Sikasso to install a volunteer and he offered to give us a ride in his air-conditioned Pajero. No fighting for seats. No piss or dust or loud music. Just four dudes talking about the Peace Corps while driving across the African Scrublands. What a difference. I could have gotten used to this kind of travel, though in other ways I am glad I did not.

Day 23 – Sikasso to Abidjan (825 km by bus)

On January 8th we caught the first bus out of town. It was the only way we'd be able to reach Abidjan by day's end, which was now our primary goal. The stretch to the border wasn't too bad, but the going was slow once we entered Côte d'Ivoire. Every ten kilometers the *gendarme* checked our driver's credentials and collected bribes from the non-nationals. It was ridiculous. Passengers were in an uproar. We attempted to lighten the mood by wagering how many kilometers it would be until the next illegal stop. When I guessed correctly at a mere five kilometers, we all shared a big laugh, but it didn't last long when travelers from Mali had to pay the officers.

North of Bouaké, we were stopped again and made to exit the bus. The *gendarme's* price was high at 10,000 CFA. The driver did not have this kind of cash so he asked the passengers to contribute. We refused and waited beneath the shade of trees. And we waited.

It was hard to imagine that Tim and I had just spent twenty-three days in the Saharan Desert; four thousand kilometers (about 2,500 miles) in or on top of a wheeled vehicle, which equates to about the distance across the U.S. from the Atlantic to the Pacific Ocean; eight hundred and fifty kilometers (about 525 miles) on a river in a motorized canoe; and one hundred and thirty-five kilometers (about 85 miles) on foot, not counting the steps we took exploring each village or town. This was no Lewis and Clark expedition, but it was something. Everything about the trip exceeded my expectations; even our cartoon map paled in comparison to the actual trip.

For me, every journey's end results in a mixed bag of sadness, joy, anxiety, satisfaction, and a slew of other emotions and dispositions. There are people who believe that life should be experienced in a continuous state of present moment awareness. That sounds both fantastic and exhausting. My untrained mind and body seems to require beginnings and ends, activity and rest, presence and absence. This trip was no exception. I was ready to get down to Abidjan and forget about life for a while.

We'd been sitting by the roadside for about an hour when one of the passengers asked what brought me to Africa. I told him I was living in Bangolo to clean up trash. The *gendarme's* roadside shack was within earshot. One of the *gendarmes* got up from his bench and walked over, hovering above me, blotting out the sun.

"Did you say you were from Bangolo?" he asked in disbelief.

"Yes. Do you know Bangolo?"

"Yes, I'm from a small Guéré village east of Bangolo. Most of my family still lives there," he said with a puffed-out chest.

"Truly, I am Guéré, one of two Guéré blanc," I said in the same dry manner that I might joke with Jerome or Clement.

The *gendarme* burst out laughing. He pulled me up to a standing position and put his arm around me as if posing for a photo, declaring, "Look, we are brothers from Bangolo," still laughing. "Your bus may go now."

I shook hands with the Guéré officer, promising that I would visit his family and pass along his greetings. As we were re-boarding, I came up from behind our bus driver, grabbed him playfully by the shoulders and said, "You owe me one, chief."

Our vacation was over. It was time to go home.

CHAPTER THIR[TY]

TRANSITION

When I left for vacation I weighed 165 lbs. When I returned twenty-three days later I weighed 148 lbs. This was no surprise. I could feel the weight coming off in Mali. Not eating much and drinking polluted water has that effect. Now, in front of a full-length mirror at the hostel, I could really see the difference. My face was gaunt. My shoulders were hunched, almost concave. I'd have to be cautious about which photos I sent back home, otherwise my mother might call Washington and demand my return.

Turns out I had amoebas, which are treated with a dozen pills each day for a couple of weeks. If left untreated, amoebas can harbor harmful bacteria that may result in inflammation, ailments, and infections. So under doctor's orders, I lounged around the hostel for another week, savoring city food and bottled water like never before.

I returned to Bangolo in mid-January after more than a month away from my site. My African friends were worried that I had left Africa for good, even though I briefed them on my vacation plans. Those who saw me for the first time assumed I was new in town and asked me for gifts and money. I was surprised that my front door was still locked and my possessions were all accounted for. In Côte d'Ivoire, a volunteer's vacant house can be a good place to find unique and valuable articles at bargain prices. I credit my neighbors for keeping watch while I was away.

When I made the rounds at the mayor's office, I learned that all seventy THIMO workers had been laid off. They retained their long blue coats, so they were easy to find, but they were no longer cutting grass or picking up trash. This wasn't good for THIMO or for Bangolo, and it wasn't good for me either. I was relying on THIMO to help me build stuff. Reportedly, one of the federal administrators in Abidjan was put in prison for extorting money from the program.

TEEN

...e tab for THIMO
... elections. To the
... coffers, no time to
...ad the election won.
...angolo to check in on
...ollection of books on
...ore like a visit from the
truck that frequented my
... ice cream truck. Also
...ssador Lannon Walker, his
...sy. The ambassador stayed
...gh to greet his local contacts
...ian woman touring with the ambassador... /, with long blond hair, well dressed—a unique ... . I bet she even shaved her legs and her armpits. We talked ... about her job and her goals, but it was hard for me to stay focused. I imagined her staying behind, being my informal counterpart, helping with vital matters or matters of vitality. Alas, moonlighting in squalor with a grubby emaciated Peace Corps volunteer was no substitute for driving around in an air-conditioned Pajero with the country's top diplomat. Not even my own entourage of streetwise children and men in blue trench coats could lure her away. And as soon as she arrived, she was gone.

On the first day of February, I received word from Dago that Eliane was heading up to Bangolo later in the day. Her mission was to replace Stephanie's vacant post in Gotongouiné II with a volunteer named Nicole who was struggling in her own village near Odiénné. I had gotten to know Nicole fairly well in Senegal. We had hung out in the compound, practicing French, processing our experiences, and I knew she wasn't thrilled about her assignment so far north. Nicole was also the girl whose favorite flannel shirt was stolen by the postal clerk in Thiés, which was no great sendoff.

Eliane arrived with Nicole in the afternoon as promised. Stephanie sent word to Abidjan that I could direct them to her house and help pack up her belongings, as she never had the chance when she left in October. Nicole and I barely had a chance to catch up before we arrived in the village. It was strange to be back in Gotongouiné II, rummaging through Stephanie's things. It felt like we were robbing the place, or worse, that she had passed away, even though I knew she was alive and well. This was part of Eliane's job, replacing wounded soldiers on the frontlines. Impersonal, but necessary. Someone had to do it. With the help of the village *petits*, it didn't take long, and Eliane and I were gone after sunset, leaving Nicole behind to carry on.

On the return ride, Eliane and I discussed the upcoming elections. Everyone in Bangolo was mobilizing for our local mayoral race and the villagers would undoubtedly be too busy for the likes of me. This was the least of my concerns, however. Elections in Africa can turn violent in a hurry, with regular occurrences of fraud, corruption, even clashes amongst tribal groups. Rather than hunkering down at *la maison bleue* reading books and hoping for a peaceful outcome, Eliane requested that I complete site surveys and resource maps for prospective village sites. I was all for it. I packed a bag and hitched a ride to Abidjan, then caught a bus up to Bondoukou. Over the course of a week, I traveled to Tanda and Sandegué in the east and Touba and Borotou when I got back west, taking stock of supplies and services, meeting with chiefs and government officials, and explaining in my best Ivoirian French what they could expect of their very own Peace Corps volunteer.

Since I had no idea when I'd be back through Abidjan, I scheduled my mid-term physical with Doctor Lomo. Christian and Forrest were editing the next issue of *Je Dis*. They knew I was generally opposed to using outside funding sources for development projects so they asked if I could write an article about the subject. I obliged by writing the following (with minor corrections):

> *When I applied to the Peace Corps in 1994, I was an idealistic engineering graduate looking to apply my technical know-how to improve the standard of living of a lesser privileged people. That's what I believed the mission of the Peace Corps and development work were all about. In the Peace Corps handbook, it outlines the mission's first goal: "To help peoples of interested countries in meeting their need for trained manpower." This is followed by the culture-sharing second and third goals, and a paragraph which begins: "These lofty goals are unique to the Peace Corps; no other organization has anyone quite like a Peace Corps Volunteer."*

A year has passed and I have yet to apply any real technical knowledge to my work. My time has been spent introducing myself and the Peace Corps to my town, gathering information about the infrastructure, establishing a rapport with the municipality and their technical team, and struggling to educate and motivate the uninspired (mostly myself) on how best to do this job.

Some of my colleagues in the Urban Environmental Management program spend their days a bit different. They've opted to use outside funding, such as Small Project Assistance (SPA) or embassy funds, to pay for manpower or obtain material resources. I've elected not to fund projects with non-Ivoirian or non-African resources for the following reasons:

- *I wouldn't be satisfying the truest intentions of the first goal.*
- *I would no longer be a catalyst for lasting change.*
- *The capability to finance projects exists from within.*

Essentially, what I wish to avoid is the "gift mentality" because it does nothing but increase the dependence on a foreign presence.

On my vacation to Mali, in a pinasse full of French tourists on the Niger River, I witnessed a most interesting sight. At a small river village, residents expressed a need for medicine to alleviate sickness, especially problems they were having with their eyes and vision. A sympathetic French woman parted with a bottle of saline solution, explaining it will only clean and not cure. This act brought more people from the village demanding more gifts. As we were shoving off, their demands were met as the Frenchies hurled everything from medicine to cosmetic jewelry into the water.

Using outside funding for development projects is not the same thing as using saline solution to correct impaired vision, but if the funding is not applied properly, it may be as worthless or as harmful as the wrong diagnosis to a medical problem.

I do not blame my colleagues for using outside funding as a development tool. We have a difficult job, one that demands our attention 24 hours a day for 730 straight days (if you are not mad enough to extend). The monotony and frustrations are sometimes severe. A SPA-funded project may be all that is needed to maintain your sanity, confidence, or resume, and not shatter the idealism that brought you to Africa.

Still, if financing projects was what the Peace Corps was about, wouldn't we be subscribing to similar development strategies as the World Bank and the various foreign government aid agencies? And we, as Peace Corps volunteers, wouldn't be so lofty.

So, instead of resorting to outside funding, what do I suggest? For the UEM program, prohibit the use of outside funding for the first generation of volunteers. Their role will be strictly information gathering. The first generation will advise their successors on which projects have the greatest chance at success using only local resources. The second generation of volunteers will conduct work using outside funding as a last resort. The last generation of volunteers will also be prohibited from spending outside funding so they may focus on education and the operation and maintenance of any new infrastructure. In short, follow a project plan tailored to local resources that stresses income-generating opportunities.

The article continued in the same prescriptive manner. To further illustrate my point, I inserted a *Far Side* comic strip showing a salesman on a boat waving goodbye to a family of Eskimos after selling them a bunch of refrigerators. Overall, my article on outside funding didn't offer anything of great value or insight, especially amongst my colleagues who were fully engaged in the art and science of development work. Months later, I'd have a change of heart on the use of outside funding. And after some additional life experiences, I'd view development work and the role of the Peace Corps volunteer a bit differently. But the *Je Dis* article, much like my journals, as well as this offering called *The Toughest Job*, all serve a purpose. They are the snapshots of a man in transition and the crossroads that he has faced. That's got to be worth something to someone, no?

By the middle of February, Bangolo had a new mayor. He was a tall heavy-set Guéré man from the same PDCI political party as the incumbent, which was a clear denunciation of the former leader by the people of the western highlands. Personally, I was glad to see the old mayor go, as his apathy permeated through the municipal staff. For local business owners and entrepreneurs (such as my pal Jerome), this change represented a great loss, as the old mayor's debts would never get paid. I suppose that's the risk you take when you accept IOUs for your soft drinks and prostitutes. For most everyone else, the mood was upbeat and the villagers were hopeful. Unless the new mayor was a tyrant, he would most certainly be an upgrade. Megan and I embraced the change and waited for the mayor-elect to return from the capital for another go at development work.

Later that month, I ran into Russ in Man while stocking up on groceries. He informed me that his dad was flying in from Massachusetts and he invited me to join them on a tour through Le Parc National de la Comoé in the northeast part of the country. It would take at least two days to get to the north entrance of the park from Abidjan. I wasn't too excited about getting back on a bus, especially after logging in so many kilometers in Mali recently. On the other hand, Russ was a knowledgeable and impassioned naturalist whose curiosity was infectious. I would likely never get the opportunity to see West Africa's native flora and fauna with such a skillful guide. Since the mayor-elect had yet to arrive, and I had no projects going on in Bangolo, I reasoned the hassles of travel were worth the trip, so I headed back down to Abidjan to meet the guys.

I've got to hand it to Russ' dad, Al. Most of the parents stayed in a nice hotel in Abidjan or a beachside hut in Grand Bassam before venturing *en brousse* to see how their children lived. Once at the volunteer's site, they were usually treated like royalty, bestowed with attention, local handcrafted gifts, and a sizable feast that decimated the village's livestock population. In contrast, as soon as Al arrived from the airport, we were running him through the squalor of the Adjamé *gare*, eating street food, and on a bus for ten hours to Ferkessédougou south of the Burkina Faso–Mali border.

There was no place to stay when we arrived into Ferke late at night, so our taxi driver offered up his living room floor. He claimed to have a cousin who regularly took people through the park in his *quatre-quatre* (4x4) Jeep. We gave the driver a small down payment for gas and arranged to meet the cousin at 0300. Russ and I slept on thin prayer mats on the hard tile floor while Al lay on a cardboard box in a separate room. But Al, sporting a walrus-style mustache and New England Patriots ballcap, took it all in stride. Maybe it was his nature, or perhaps Al had a sense that the ten-hour bus trip on paved roads through civilization was nothing compared to what was in store.

One doesn't sleep too well lying flat on a tiled floor, so we were awake and ready to go at 0300. The taxi driver took us to his cousin's house where we could hear him snoring through the louvered windows. We roused him from his slumber and introduced ourselves. Our guide's name was Kennedy, and while he was vaguely aware that he was escorting us through the park, it didn't look like that was his preference. We climbed aboard a metallic, open-top Jeep Wrangler-type vehicle with thick layers of spray paint covering years of corrosion. It was evident that this would not be a plush East African safari in a cavalcade of shiny new Land Rovers. With Al sitting up front, and Russ and I in the back grasping onto the roll bars, we headed east in pitch darkness towards the village of Kafolo at the north entrance of the park.

We pulled in at daybreak and stopped at an old resort hotel that had never lived up to its billing. We found the caretaker and inquired about the condition of the roads. Both Kennedy and the caretaker insisted the route was passable; however, in Africa you're liable to get the answer people think you want, especially when a transfer of money is involved. A map on the wall showed a *piste* running parallel to the Comoé River north-south through the park, but a *piste* is considered more of a trail than a road. Despite this, we were eager to go, raring to explore this remote and wild part of Africa.

At approximately 465,000 acres, Comoé is by far the largest national park in Côte d'Ivoire. In comparison, the Great Smoky Mountain National Park in North Carolina and Tennessee is about 520,976 acres. Côte d'Ivoire's other parks are much smaller, resigned to mountaintops and isolated patches of sacred forests. Unfortunately, the country's parklands struggle with human settlements, agricultural encroachment, cattle grazing, rampant animal poaching, and a lack of active conservation management.

If you believe the guidebook, one could expect to see over 600 plant species, over 500 bird species, eleven species of monkeys, and African mammals such as lions, leopards, antelope, warthogs, hippopotami, water buffalo, and crocodiles. There was even a chance we might see an elephant in a country whose name boasts of a time when the largest of land animals was plentiful.

At the entrance gate, men with AK-47s strapped around their shoulders checked our credentials and waved us through. Their role was to prevent the poaching of large game-type animals. I'm not sure they were up to the task though. Kennedy mentioned that two park rangers were killed by poachers a few months prior. It was a common story in these parts. Then, as if right on cue, a pickup truck full of hunters drove up behind us and were allowed to enter the park with much less scrutiny. These were the famed and initiated hunters of northern Côte d'Ivoire called the Dozo. They consist of mostly Mandé-speaking men, characterized by their long rifles, brown camouflaged clothing, and brown court jester-like hats. Once clear of the guard shack, the hunters accelerated into a clearing and out of sight as we headed down the two-track dirt road.

The first part of the trip took us through savanna with crooked, sparsely grown trees and dry grass in between, which served as cover for small mammals, vermin, and insects. Once in a while, we'd come across an enormous termite mound, two to three times the height of an average-sized man, no longer housing termites. Each mound resembled a castle or spire of mud, with sharp rivulets carved into the sides from the torrential rain. As we posed for photos in front of a mound, Russ and I recalled a time in Gouéssesso when the winged termites were swarming inside a friend's house by the overhead light, and the locals taught us how to catch, de-wing, and eat them to everyone's delight.

While Russ is an all-round nature enthusiast, he definitely favors the birds and waterfowl. Most of the time, his gaze was fixed skyward into the trees with binoculars at the ready, whereas I scanned the low brush for animals that could pounce, charge, ram, or otherwise kill tourists in a decrepit old Jeep. Mostly we saw warthog and antelope, but there was one spotting that was a mystery. About thirty yards from the road, I saw a large red-haired creature the size of a man. It jumped out of a tree, landed on its feet, and fled on two legs into the brush. I pointed it out to Russ and Al, but in the time it took for them to get orientated, it was long gone. This thing resembled an orangutan that ran upright, but orangutans are not endemic to Africa. I suppose it could have been a baboon, but it was larger than the largest species of baboon. I asked Kennedy but he didn't know. He was shaping up to be a useless guide and a marginal driver. Russ and Al assumed I misjudged the size of a monkey, or mistook a downed tree trunk for the elusive beast. Both were possible, I guess, though what I saw was so vivid and alive. To this day, I'd like to think that I discovered a rare breed of prehistoric hominid like a Yeti or Sasquatch surviving and propagating in the wilderness. Meanwhile, back at the Dozo's camp, I imagine that a young hunter is retelling the tale of how he jumped from his treestand in full camouflage and pretended to be a forest creature to mess with the Americans. For his creativity he is rewarded with a coveted spot in the Dozo hunting party. While I have no idea what I had witnessed, this was a likelier possibility than my Sasquatch theory.

For the first 80 to 100 kilometers, we moved through the park as if we were attempting to set a new speed record. It was difficult to view any wildlife, as everything was scared off by the commotion, and Russ and I were more concerned with being thrown from the vehicle. About halfway through the park, we dropped into the low-lying areas of a Comoé River floodplain and started running up against thick mud. A set of fresh tire tracks helped lead the way. At the next mud hole, the Jeep was having problems with its clutch and would no longer go into first gear without a push start.

Down the road we spotted a big blue van stuck up to its wheel-wells in mud. The van was further weighed down by a non-factory cap affixed to the roof, and a wooden bed frame strapped on top of that for outdoor sleeping above the predators. If this didn't get our attention, there was a bovine skull with horns lashed to the front grill. This big blue contraption had to be the source of the tracks. A young Caucasian couple about thirty years old emerged from the mud, both with long hair tucked under sweat-soaked bandanas. They were understandably thrilled to see us. Turns out they were German, but they spoke enough English and French for us to communicate without difficulty. They even had a German Shepherd, which was an odd sight after seeing only mutts and mongrels for a year.

Using a shovel, a rope, some branches, and all the might we could muster, we managed to push the van to safety, then got ourselves across. The Germans were good company and we needed each other's help, so we traveled together, hop-scotching mud pit after mud pit for another five kilometers. Kennedy was beginning to grow tired and he took frequent breaks while we labored. He clearly had not expected to work this much for his commission; neither had we, but there was no choice.

We were cruising along a nice patch of flat dry terrain when we came upon our biggest obstacle yet. The road crossed over a concrete bridge spanning a tributary of the Comoé River. The bridge measured about three meters wide by four meters across and it was the first manmade structure we'd seen since Kafolo. A large flood had caused the river to rise and erode the area where the bridge met the dirt road on the far side. Upon closer inspection, there was a drop off of one and a half meters from the bridge deck down to solid ground. The gap extended about three meters across to a point where the road resumed through a meadow. We stood there, gazing in disbelief. We split up and scouted the river for another place to cross, but it was fortified with thick riparian vegetation and the river channel only got deeper and wider.

A slight panic set in. This excursion was supposed to last only a day, so we had limited food, water, and supplies. We had already covered 120 kilometers of park road, pushing our way through thick mud until our faces turned red and our veins throbbed under pressure. We knew going back the way we came would be no small feat, especially with our clutchless Jeep and the German's enormous van. And it was getting pretty late in the day. Best to try again tomorrow and hope it didn't rain in the interim. We also had to consider that this was a national park in Africa where snakes, lions, and other man-eaters move about the land at night in search of prey. It was probably best we conserve our energy and stick together.

In the evening, we were sitting around the bridge debating our options when I proposed building a bridge across the gap. What did they expect from an engineer? I'd rather build something than push something through mud. Not everyone was excited about this idea, but the mood picked up when the Germans said they had an ax and five old tires in the van. Perfect. Six able bodies and all the tools we needed. With 60 to 70 kilometers of road remaining to the south boundary, we'd be feasting on chickens and lukewarm beer by nightfall. While we had no idea how good the roads were to the south, and constructing a strong-enough bridge was no certainty, we were convinced that this was our only option. When I drew it out on paper, everyone was on board, except Kennedy who continued to sigh and grumble in his usual manner.

The Germans re-apportioned their food amongst the group, which was a mishmash of macaroni and cheese, butter cookies, and dried fruit. For a moment I felt I was back in Mali, but we were thankful for every morsel, as we would need all our strength in the morning. That night, Al, Russ, and I slept directly on the concrete using whatever spare clothes we had for pillows, the Germans slept in their van, and our driver slept in his Jeep. The stars were as bright as I had seen, but we took care not to fix our gaze skyward for too long, scanning the trees for movement and listening for predators.

The night passed without incident, and the day arrived without a cloud in the sky. Time to work. We would need two long straight trees at least a foot in diameter for the beams, and a number of smaller trees for the decking. The plan was to position the top of our wooden bridge a few inches below the concrete deck; that way the vehicle would drop down onto the bridge as it crossed. We worried that if there was any kind of protruding lip, the driver might need to accelerate to get up and over, or the lateral forces generated by the vehicle could push our bridge into the hole and the vehicle would follow. Driving back to civilization via the north road was still an option; driving off a bridge was not.

To pull this off, we would need to stack the old tires in the hole against the concrete to act as supports for the beams. To get the height we desired, we would need to add additional soil before placing the tires. Fortunately, the flood deposited a large boulder right where one of our supports needed to be, which reduced the fill we needed in that area. We only needed one tire on top of that boulder and used the rest for the other support. On the far end, we would fix the ends of the beams in place by burying them in slots we dug out in the terrain. This would hopefully keep the beams from splaying outward or falling off the makeshift supports.

The first order of business was to fetch some logs. While Al, Russ, and I were out searching for candidates, the Germans were shoveling dirt, reshaping the terrain. Kennedy came with us but he wasn't excited about our project. He expressed the opinion that there was no way we could build a bridge and we should drive back the way we came. About 200 meters from the site, we found a perfect specimen for a beam. As we took turns hacking at the base, Kennedy realized we were serious about this bridge thing and he proclaimed, *"Les Américains sont fous!"* to our amusement.

Once the tree was down and stripped of its branches, it took the four of us to haul, drag, or roll it back to the bridge site. Nobody had any gloves, so blisters formed early. We found our second beam about 300 meters away. Then we started looking at trees for the decking. This was more difficult than we had imagined. Most of the trees in the park were crooked or had many branches. By the time we cut down our twelfth and final decking log, we were about a kilometer away from the bridge site. All told, I estimate we walked over ten kilometers burdened by the weight of a large unwieldy tree. It was an operation that would make even the A-Team proud.

During the harvest, it struck me that Le Parc National de la Comoé might have been designated a national park because it had relatively few lumber resources to exploit. In Bangolo, multiple 18-wheeler logging trucks passed my house daily with trunks so big they could only fit two or three on the flatbed. This taking of trees throughout West Africa has resulted in losses to the dryland ecosystems and severe encroachment of the Saharan Desert further south—an estimated fifty kilometers per year. This has had serious consequences on its inhabitants, drying up their fertile lands, eliminating their resources and opportunities, forcing them to migrate into cities where their skills as herders and farmers are of little to no value. Add desertification to the long list of troubles already facing Africans in northern Côte d'Ivoire, and it's no wonder Kennedy was so pessimistic.

With the materials on site, it was now a matter of situating the decking logs across the beams. By early afternoon, our bridge was complete. The moment of truth. We started the Jeep and advanced over the concrete bridge. The front wheels eased over the edge, dropping a few inches onto the deck. So far, so good. Slowly, the Jeep accelerated until the full weight of the vehicle was supported by our structure, and it motored across in a hurry. Kennedy was amazed. Yankee ingenuity meets German engineering. Or in this case, Yankee engineering meets German ingenuity. Then our new friends drove their monstrosity across the bridge like it was part of the route all along.

Our celebration was short-lived as we had a ways to go before we were out of the woods. Unfortunately, we had to dismantle the bridge and reclaim the spare tires. I would have preferred to leave the bridge in place, to leave our mark on this part of the world if only for a crossing or two. Fortunately, the road south was flat and compact and the ride out was uneventful. We even had daylight in which to view hippopotami in the Comoé River and a family of monkeys in a patch of old-growth forest (which would have been a better place to find beams and decking). We pulled into Kakpin under darkness, shouting and carrying on like *futbol* fans who'd just watched their team win the World Cup. We went straight to the one bar in town and ordered platters of food and many beers.

The villagers were amazed by our story, made more impressive by the disclosure that nobody had traversed Comoé Park north to south in almost two years. I could have rung Kennedy's neck for his deceptions, but we were in good spirits at this point; no need to dampen our triumphant return to civilization with a bar room brawl. While I came out of Comoé with a sense of accomplishment, I was more excited for Al. He came to Africa to see his son and to experience a bit of adventure, and Africa delivered right out of the gate. It has a way of doing that, if you're willing.

Back at the hostel porch, Al recounted the bridge story while volunteers listened intently. Each time, the gap in the earth got wider, the drop got deeper, and the predicament grew more harrowing. His excitement never waned. While I was part of Al's story, I started to enjoy it vicariously through his eyes, as if I was hearing it for the first time. Al would eventually take this tale back to his coworkers in Massachusetts where we performed acts of mythical proportion. Who's to say we didn't?

CHAPTER FOURTEEN

DOUBT

It was early March and the new mayor had yet to install himself. Most of the old municipal staff had retained their jobs. And I kept making the rounds each day, asking about the latest happenings. The staff said the new mayor was in the process of refurbishing his office into something more contemporary. They also shared that he refused to move into the space until *his* sorcerers removed the bad curse put on the office by the sorcerers of the outgoing mayor. Good thing I chose to work from home.

On occasion I'd run into my former counterparts, Charles and Dao. Dao could be found drinking at Chez Becky. Charles would usually spot me near the market across from his family's house. He'd approach slowly and greet me in the usual African manner, then he'd ask for a loan or handout. To soften his requests, he'd hold my hand and walk me down the street like we were dating, which is a gesture of friendship between men in Côte d'Ivoire. In contrast, you'd never see a man and a woman walking hand-in-hand in public.

The most polite way to say no to a request for money was to respond *prochaine*, which means "next time." Somehow, this deferral wasn't as insulting as a straight-out "no," and Ivoirians generally accepted it without further discussion. There was one time in late March when I gave Charles 1000 CFA, as he had been out of work since being fired in September. I couldn't help but think that he had blown his best opportunity for employment, and times were only going to get worse. I started feeling bad for him. I reasoned that it wasn't like he got paid extra for being my counterpart. The least I could do was "loan" him some cash once in a while. The problem was, Charles also believed that this was the least I could do.

Charles wasn't the only person in Bangolo who started asking me for handouts. About a year in, there seemed to be an increase in requests from complete strangers. At the *gare* in front of my house, I'd greet passersbys with a friendly, "Hello. How's it going?" Their response was usually: "It's going, a little. Truly, today, there are no means. Give me money!" Or they'd say: "I have a small problem. I need to buy medicine for [insert malady]." One time I was taken aback when a young man abruptly said: "Do me a service and give me a pair of your pants." I'm fairly certain he meant a pair from my wardrobe and not the actual pants I was wearing, like it was some kind of jeans heist. Most days it just felt safer to stay indoors.

People also had a tendency to show up at my doorstep; like the time a primary school teacher from a nearby village knocked on my door and asked if I could finance the construction of a wall around the school. Walls in Bangolo are useful to keep out cows and the shit they deposit, but that's about it. Every young mischievous male in Africa could jump over a wall, unless you lined it with broken glass or wire, and the value of the items in a typical school didn't add up to much, not enough to justify the cost of the wall. Hell, the number of blocks to build a perimeter wall probably exceeded the number of blocks in the actual school, but concrete walls are a cultural fixation in Côte d'Ivoire, much like the white picket fence in America. Had the teacher requested books and supplies, I probably could have arranged something. A wall is what he wanted.

Or the time an African preacher showed up to explain the merits of attending church each Sunday by telling me, "Religion is like a fire, and the sticks to start the fire are the members of the church. If you spread out the sticks, the fire will not catch. The sticks need to be together for a proper fire." I agreed with him on the architecture of a proper fire; however, I could not commit to being one of his sticks.

Another man asked me to be the president and financier of his local entertainment troupe. There were six members, all teenage boys with low-grade stringed or percussion instruments. During their audition in my front yard, they sang, *"No Woman No Cry"* by Bob Marley in English, but instead of singing "cry" they said "crime." It took all my energy to keep from laughing. When they finished I gave them a rousing applause, but later I felt bad that I didn't give them a little something for such an astute rendition of the reggae classic.

Then there was the time a man asked me if I could help him order apparel from a magazine as he handed me a copy of *Today's Christian Woman*. He pointed at the photos of the men while marveling at their shoes and formal attire. I told him it wasn't a good publication for ordering merchandise, but that I'd look amongst my things for something better. I promptly returned with a few outdated catalogs sent to me in care packages. What he really wanted was a correspondent in the U.S. for his visa application. That's what he thought the magazine subscription cards were for, to start a written exchange. Who am I to say they are not for this purpose? So I advised him that with persistence and a stack of those cards, he might someday become pen pals with Mr. Eddie Bauer or Mr. L.L. Bean.

About this time, a new character came on the scene at the Kamonda claiming to be hotel security. His name was Mesmeth and he was built like a brick shithouse. There wasn't much need for security at this rundown brothel, and probably no money to pay him, but Mesmeth's new role was never in doubt. He was a friendly guy, but when he shook my hand he'd grip with unbelievable power, mashing every bone together, even if I was ready for him. Mesmeth's request to me was simple: He dreamed of becoming an American athlete at the Summer Olympic Games, but he said he needed Jean-Claude Van Damme's home address to inquire about being his trainer. Mesmeth insisted that I take photographs of him posing in the courtyard, flexing his muscles. I tried to reason with him about the drawbacks of his plan, but that just made him squeeze harder.

Requests were not limited to the good people of Bangolo. Sometimes I'd receive letters from Africa pleading for money or information, playing the odds that a caring, vulnerable, or chronically dissatisfied soul would respond. When I returned to the States, I came across one such letter from the Director of Project Implementation for the Republic of South Africa, Division of Energy & Minerals Resources. The "Director" writes:

> *Good day,*
> *It is my great pleasure to write you this letter on behalf of my colleagues. Your information was given to me by a member of the South African Export Promotion Council (SAEPC), who was with the government delegation on a trip to your country for a bilateral conference talk to encourage foreign investors.*

I have decided to seek co-operation from you in the execution of the deal described hereunder for the benefit of all parties involved and hope you will keep it confidential because of the nature of this transaction. Within the department of Minerals and Energy Resources where I am employed as the Director of Project Management, and with the co-operation of my chairperson, we have in our possession as overdue payment bills totaling Seventeen million, five hundred thousand United States Dollars (U.S. $17,500,000.00) which we want to transfer abroad with the assistance and co-operation of a foreign company / individual to receive the said fund on our behalf into a reliable company / individual account depending on your convenience.

We are handicapped in circumstances, as we are still in active government service and more so the South African Code of Conduct does not allow us to operate off-shore accounts, hence your importance in this transaction. This amount represents the balance of the total contract value executed on behalf of my Department by a foreign contracting firm, which we, the officials over-invoiced deliberately. Though the actual contract costs have been paid to the original contractor, leaving the balance in tune of the said amount which we have in principles, got approved to remit by Telegraphic Transfer (T.T.) to any foreign Bank account you will provide by filling in the application form through the Justice Department here in South Africa for the transfer rights and privileges of the former contractor to you. I have the authority of the parties involved to discuss modalities of sharing with you should you agree to assist us.

Your share of the entire sum will be 30% (U.S. $5,250,000.00), 60% for us (U.S. $10,500,000.00), and 10% (U.S. $1,750,000.00) for taxation and miscellaneous expenses. The disbursement pattern still remains as agreed percentage if taxation in your country takes a toll of the total sum.

The business itself has no risk factor provided you treat it with utmost confidentiality. Also, your area of specialization is not a hindrance to the successful execution of this transaction. I have reposed my confidence in you and hope that you will not disappoint me. I wait in anticipation for your fullest co-operation. Please respond through the above fax or telephone numbers for any questions concerning the clarity on this transaction. Kindly notify me, your secured Telephone and Fax

Number for further details upon your acceptance of this proposal, this will enable me to call and fax all details for your understanding before we commence on this project. Thank you in anticipation for your co-operation.

What's that you say, *Monsieur Directeur*? My area of specialization is not a hindrance? There is no risk factor? We can share millions and millions in laundered money if I have a reliable bank account and the modalities to transfer? Sounds too good to pass up. Where do I send my reliable bank account number again?

What I enjoy most about this letter is that they had the wherewithal to factor in 10% taxation by our Internal Revenue Service as part of this transaction. Only ten percent? Are they mad?

Then there was the letter a friend received via email:

Dearest One,

I was compelled to write you under humanitarian ground. My name is Mrs. Hilda (Last Name). My nationality is USA. I am married to Mr. Jean (Last Name) of J.C Industries in Côte d'Ivoire, West Africa. We were married for 26 years without a child. I am a devoted Christian and I have been diagnosed of cancer a few years ago after the death of my husband. Recently my doctor told me that I would not last for the next few months due to my cancer problem. Due to my condition, I have been touched by God to donate 1.8 million dollars from what I have inherited from my late husband for the good work of God rather than allow my greedy relatives to use my husband's hard earned in an ungodly way.

Presently, this money is still in the vault of security company in Abidjan Côte d'Ivoire, West Africa. I decided to donate this fund since I know I will die soon rather than allow my greedy relatives to use my husband's hard earned in an ungodly way. I want somebody that will use this fund to help less privileged people, orphanages, widows, and propagating the word of God.

I took this decision because I don't have any child that will inherit this fund, and I don't want in a way where this money will be used by my greedy relatives in an ungodly way. This is why I am taking this decision with you. I am not afraid of death for I pray God to use my good deeds and accept my soul peaceful in His kingdom. I want you to always remember me in your daily prayers because of my upcoming cancer surgery.

Write me back as soon as possible for any delay in your reply to me will give me room in sourcing another person for this same purpose.
God bless you.
Your sister in Lord,
Mrs. Hilda (Last Name)

If any part of this letter is true, I feel for Mrs. Hilda and I hope she found peace. I also hope she was able to find a reliable outlet to spend her husband's money in a godly way, which is probably the best approach to get around the taxation issue that the Director from South Africa was having. Don't we all have greedy, ungodly relatives? I may be one myself. Who's to say the recipient(s) of this fund won't become greedy themselves once entrusted with $1.8 million? I've got news for Mrs. Hilda and her trustees: if your relatives hail from Côte d'Ivoire, there's a high probability that they *are* the less privileged. Spread the money amongst those in your husband's village. There's got to be a widow or orphan or *infirme* in the bunch who will spend their allotment wisely.

And recently, I received this offer via email:

Hello,
Please forgive me if this message comes to you as a surprise. In a brief introduction, my name is Mr. Johnson Kelly. I am a lawyer from West Africa. Can you receive the transfer of $10.5 million USD into your personal bank account for our mutual benefit? This money belongs to my deceased client Engr. M. Henriksen, a national of your country who died in an automobile accident in my country three years ago. From my numerous searches, I found out the deceased bears the same surname with you, and that is the reason why I contacted you to receive this money for our mutual benefit. If you are willing to work with me to receive this money, kindly get back to me as soon as possible so that I can give you more details about this transaction.

If you are ready for a deal, please contact me for more information via my private email address.
Best Wishes,
Mr. Johnson Kelly

I am always ready for a deal, Mr. Johnson, but I suspect more surprises await me if I contact you via your private email address, surprises that may not be mutually beneficial.

Not all requests were in monetary form. Residents of Côte d'Ivoire were prepared to trade goods and services, as evidenced from the exchange below. The scene: I am at the *gare* in Man on a wooden bench in semi-shade with my plastic bags full of produce waiting for a *gbaka* back to Bangolo. It is near the end of *sieste*, the hottest time of day, and the people are beginning to stir from their midday hibernation. Three middle-aged African men wait with me on benches arranged in a U-like fashion—one man to my left and two men to my right, one of whom is the *chef du gare* sitting on a crate on top of a bench so he's higher than everyone.

Me: (Addressing the assistant *chef*) One ticket to Bangolo please. (I pay the *chef*, take the ticket, and sit down.)
Man (R): So what are you doing in Bangolo?
Me: I am a Peace Corps volunteer. (Knowing they've never heard of the Peace Corps, but I feel it's my duty to promote the organization.) I sometimes work with the mayor's office. My job is to improve the environment. You know .... trash, latrines, better sanitation. (I get the same blank stares that I received in Bangolo when I first gave this speech.)
Man (R): How long have you been here?
Me: (Thinking of the calendar I have on my wall with the days crossed out since my arrival.) Almost twelve months in Côte d'Ivoire. My term is two years, much like the French military service.
Man (R): (With narrowed, untrusting eyes.) What country do you come from? England?
Me: No, I am an American. (I say almost regrettably, knowing what's to come.)
Man (R): (Eyes widening some.) When you go home ... Me ... You .... We leave together, OK? (He's joking, but he's not joking. I've heard this request more times than I've been asked for money.)
Me: OK, no problem. (I say with a slight smirk, hoping he

	understands that this is playful banter.)
Man (L):	I want to go to America too. (The man says with more intensity than his friend, not wanting to be left out of the conversation, or off of the flight.)
Me:	(Turning to my left.) Why do you want to go to America? We have problems there too. (Believing what I said, but knowing there's a big difference between our respective problems.)
Man (L):	But you have the dollar.
Me:	Yes, but if you stayed in your country and developed your resources, took advantage of opportunities, the CFA would be as valuable as the dollar. (Not actually believing what I said, but curious how he'd respond to the pep talk.)
Man (L):	Truly, there are no jobs, no work in Côte d'Ivoire.
Me:	(Wondering how many hours he spent each day at the *gare* talking to passengers instead of looking for work.) What kind of work can you do?
Man (L):	I am a soldier. I want to join the military. The Marines!
Me:	You want to join the Marines to defend someone else's country? (Amazed, but understanding the lure.) Why not join your own military?
Man (L):	Yes, but the Americans are strong.
Me:	But you are not American. You are Ivoirian.
Chef:	(Interrupting.) American! When you go home to the USA …. Me … You …. We leave together, OK?
Me:	(Good grief! I consider telling them how it's forbidden for me to get involved in Embassy business or I lose my job, which is an oversimplification of the truth; or how America is nothing like what you see on television; or how they'd have to pay their own way. But my explanation would be futile.)
Man (L):	Are you married?
Me:	No, I am not married.
Man (L):	Why not? You should be married by now, with lots of children.
Me:	(Suddenly understanding what American women go through.) I don't have a girlfriend, and I'm not ready for marriage. I'm only twenty-six. I'm too young.
Man (L):	How about an African woman? (He says with a big smile,

Me:	as if they hold the key to every man's needs and desires.) I don't need that kind of baggage right now. (I look at their faces, hoping the English expression translated as a lighthearted quip in French.)
Man (R):	(Rejoining the discourse.) You know, African men sometimes have three or four wives. Polygamy is common here. (Raising the stakes.)
Me:	That's three to four times more baggage than I need right now.
Man (R):	(No visible reaction.) If I give you one of my daughters (he makes a sideways pumping motion with his fist, thumb facing towards his body, as if to promote her sexual abilities), ... You .... Me .... We go to America, OK?
Me:	(Fortunately, my *gbaka* is ready to board.) Thank you but I must be going. Next time, perhaps. Goodbye.

It wasn't just the unending requests that were getting to me; I was also frustrated by the lack of progress. In the grand scheme of things, nothing ever seemed to get accomplished. Things were broken without the means to repair or replace. Small chores became major obstacles. Minor requests were mired in minutiae. Information was readily available, but the truth was always hard to find. Opportunity was put off for ceremony, and ceremony was usually delayed by circumstance. And because nothing ever happened as planned, plans were rarely made. The phrase I heard muttered the most in Côte d'Ivoire was: *C'est pas possible!* It is not possible! Decades, if not centuries, of difficulty and disappointment had resulted in an inherent pessimism, which was deeply engrained in the culture. If I didn't find a way to harness my growing cynicism, there was a chance the wheels would come off and I wouldn't last.

In the middle of March, I found myself back at the southern end of Bangolo where I first met Prince, the 92-year-old elder who claimed to have nine wives and thirty-two children. The small cluster of concrete houses and mud huts Prince called home was the village of Béoué (Bay-way), which was sponsoring the Festival of Masks that year. Masks from surrounding Guéré villages would participate in various dance competitions. The Béoué festival would not be as big of a spectacle as the well-known Festival of Masks held in Man each

November with the Dan and Yacouba tribes, but it was a chance to view traditional masks in action.

The masks were mostly made up of carved wood, straw, cloth, leather, burlap, paper, cardboard, feathers, bells, shells, paint, and a host of other items found in the local area. They can be relatively plain or wildly intricate so long as they embody the spirits, souls, or deities they intend to honor. What makes a mask unique is not the material or outward appearance, but the man behind the mask. It is said that only certain families can own a mask, and only specially trained members of that family can wear it, thus transforming the mask into something powerful, sacred, and potentially dangerous.

I had been looking forward to this event for weeks. Konan offered to take us in his Toyota. While Béoué wasn't too far down the road, it was probably wise to be chaperoned by Konan. During the hunt for bad sorcerers, Alpha from the Kamonda served as an invaluable guide and interpreter, and I trusted Konan to provide the same degree of commentary at the Festival of Masks in Béoué.

A parade of residents were jumping on *gbakas* or walking along the highway. A mask passed by my front gate as I was leaving, and it stopped and looked back at me. It was a rather simple mask—a plain wood carving with two round eyeholes, large carved lips protruding outward, and a backing made of mismatched cloth that enveloped the rest of his head. It was the first mask I'd seen, and I became unnerved as it fixed its gaze on me. Did the mask have something against tall lanky white guys with long hair? It moved toward me, slowly. I didn't know what to do, so I just froze. It got to within a meter when I heard a muffled voice from beneath the layers ask for bus fare. I guess this mask planned to complete its sacred transformation en route.

Konan picked me up in his Toyota with his friend Guero, then we found Megan and drove to the dirt soccer field for the big event. In Béoué, we ran into a female PCV from Mali who'd traveled eight hours by bus that morning in hopes of photographing the elusive masks. She sat next to us in the front row facing the field. These favorable seats were no accident. The mask handlers ask for donations, so the *toubabs* were placed right up front so we could see without obstruction and give with generosity.

The festival started late in the afternoon. There may have been thirty different masks on the field, each accompanied by a handler or two. Surrounding the masks were an untold number of Guéré spectators jostling for a view. If anyone wanted to pull off a heist in Bangolo *ville*, now would be the time. Some masks were people with painted faces. Others had extensive headgear with straw skirts draped from the neck down, such that no part of the body was visible, not even their feet. If a mask was not on its best behavior, the handler kept it in line by hitting it with a switch or a stick, yelling at it abruptly until it complied. It was like watching a lion tamer at a circus.

While masks were dancing, others lay at the edge of the crowd, silent, motionless, waiting their turn. One mask with an all white face and ragged straw mane plopped down by my feet. When I looked closely I could see an array of empty bullet casings, old batteries, and uncooked macaroni glued to paper maché. These items didn't date back very far, so it was hard to believe this was a traditional mask, unless the tradition was foraging in the landfill.

By nightfall the Festival of Masks was winding down with only a few masks performing by lantern light. The most fascinating were a set of male twins dressed as Dozo hunters. They wore dark black lipstick, garish jewelry, and acted like deranged jesters, purposefully hyper-extending their knees as they strutted around the field. They were a big hit. I donated money to the cause and got my photo taken with the effeminate twins. I relished the idea of shipping my film home to be developed into prints while my family tried to piece together a story from the images. If only I could've seen their faces when they saw the photo of the twins and me. My poor mother.

As we were leaving, a mask charged at the Mali volunteer walking ahead of us. The mask had a black painted face with round red eyes, with bells attached to the forehead so that it jingled when it moved. I remember photographing this mask when it was daylight. There was something about its red eyes in contrast with the black face that looked vacant, frightening. The handlers whipped and scolded the mask, but it had no effect and it stayed on the attack. Another handler came over to assist. Both handlers talked with the mask and managed to pacify it for a moment. They turned to the Mali volunteer and demanded she give up her camera, accusing her of taking a photo of a sacred mask.

The Mali volunteer had a nice SLR camera with telephoto lens, much better than the cheap point-and-shoot variety I was using. If an offense had been committed, she could've easily handed over the film, but the performers insisted on the camera itself. I asked Konan and Guero what was going on, but they couldn't explain. They had never seen anything like this before, and it seemed that our entire group was guilty by association. I felt like telling Konan that I see this behavior every day, but the culprits aren't usually wearing costumes. But I refrained.

The mask was impatient and decided to charge once more. I was close enough to the action that I had to consider whether I'd have to physically defend myself against a charging mask. Then I imagined the headlines in my hometown newspaper. Something like: *Worcester Native is Killed after Slugging Sacred African Mask in the Face*. Probably not a good idea. Better to flee. A group of locals advised us to leave the scene immediately; that our lives were in danger. Sage advice. No need to tell me twice.

As a Peace Corps volunteer, you are a full-time student of culture, learning the art of living in strange and eclectic places. Having been at it for over a year, I understood that the onus to adapt to any given situation was my own. For instance, if I am invited to a longstanding Guéré festival that showcases animist beliefs and customs, I need to follow their rules. If I don't, there are consequences. Likewise, when the panther-men attacked the *National Geographic* writer / photographer, he probably knew there were risks in getting a story of this magnitude. After all, these were men who'd just returned to the village after seven months in the bush, living deliberately as wild animals.

At the Festival of Masks, I felt like I was on my best behavior. By night's end, however, there was a real possibility that a man in a mask under the influence of the supernatural, backed by a growing mob, could bring harm to our group if we did not leave in a hurry. Like most mobs, they are fueled by emotion, not logic. Perhaps the mask and his people had cause to react the way they did, and the seriousness of the situation is something I'll never understand, or maybe the mask was drunk on palm wine and it just wanted the girl's SLR camera. Who knows? I really didn't care. I was more agitated than anything, struggling to endorse the Guéré mask ritual if it involved unpredictable attacks on its audience. While I knew better, I couldn't help but judge the art of living in Béoué, and I ended up with serious doubts that I belonged in Africa at all, even as an honored spectator.

CHAPTER FIFTEEN

RETURN

March was a frustrating month, and it showed in my letters back home, ranting and pontificating about all sorts of things. The cumulative effects of the mayor's hiatus, the unending requests, and the incident at the mask festival had taken its toll. Even my quarterly report to my boss was cynical, ending with a second quarter goal to master all the moves in *The Little Book of Hand Shadows*; not a very subtle remark about the perceived futility of my assignment.

My harried condition coincided with the arrival of the new crop of volunteers. Like Dennis from Issia, I offered to serve as a volunteer host. I took in two prospective volunteers—a young male and female pair assigned to Touba, north of Biankouma. Megan also hosted a young woman. They were so clean and healthy looking, so full of hope and promise, hell-bent on saving the world. My response to their questions was either, "It depends" or a blank stare with a gaping mouth. I don't remember being this oblivious in my first couple weeks. Then again, I was too sick to care.

My neighbors had recently taught me how to kill, pluck, and cook a chicken, so the Baman children chased one down for me so I could show our guests how it's done in Africa. I'm not one who enjoys killing animals, but if I'm going to eat them, and people are out there killing them for me, I have no qualms about hunting myself or being part of the process, especially if I can learn something. One can use a knife to kill a chicken by cutting off its head on a chopping block, but the preferred method in Bangolo was to grasp it tightly by the neck, raise it up above one's shoulder, and bring it straight down with a sharp quick turn of the wrist, snapping the neck. It was done this way to utilize all parts of the chicken, even the meager amount of meat in the head and neck, which the locals seemed to relish. My guests looked on in horror as a lifeless chicken dangled from my clenched fist. They must have thought I was deranged, not that they didn't have cause.

If the assassination of the chicken wasn't enough, I conspired with the Bamans earlier in the day, rigging up a system of cables and pulleys between my back door and a coconut tree inside their compound. Attached to the cables was a plastic bucket that I sent over with money inside, and they sent back however many cold beers I wanted from their *maquis*. My aim was to show that when you leave an engineer to his own devices in isolation, it could result in some creative coping skills. What made this even more ridiculous was that the distance between my back door and my neighbor's compound was about 10 meters. I could have walked to the edge of the waist-high wall in less time than it took me to wheel over the bucket. The cable and pulley idea was not something I had used before, and when my visitors left I took it down. It just goes to show that after a year in service, there's a little bit of Dennis in all of us.

While the newbies traveled to their sites for a few days before their April 8th swearing-in ceremony, I stayed in Bangolo to clean up after the party. I was in my yard, raking up freshly cut grass intermingled with plastic *sachets*, when Clement walked over from the *gare*. Megan and I were now better acquainted with Clement, having attended the christening of his daughter, whom he had named Magui, presumably after Megan and not the well-known bouillon cubes. His old scowl had long since given way to a wry but friendly smile. Clement asked if he could borrow my rake to tidy up the *gare*. I watched from my porch, astounded, as he raked up the entire lot. It was one of the only times I'd seen a grown man in Bangolo (who wasn't wearing a blue coat) do manual labor, as African men usually ordered around the *petits* to do this kind of work.

There is a Chinese proverb that goes: "Give a man a fish and he will eat for a day; teach a man to fish and he will eat for a lifetime." But what if that man can't get a hold of a fishing pole, or a net, or a spear? What then? I paid a handsome price for my rake at the Bangolo market. Not everyone in Côte d'Ivoire can afford a rake; not everyone in Côte d'Ivoire needs a rake, as residential compounds are made of dirt, swept clean with small handheld brooms. Because Clement had access to the tool he needed, and a bit of pride in his town's appearance, he took it upon himself one day to clean the *gare*.

The following is a piece I wrote for the *Je Dis*, which I've since modified for a broader audience. It tells the story of my front porch and the people that were drawn there by its utility and mystique.

For those of you who have not yet binged on my porch, or have not seen it from the not-so-distant Houphouët-Boigny National Highway, let me set the scene. This relatively small tiled porch overlooks a dirt lot that passes for the gare routière to Man. My view from this porch is only interrupted by the occasional sway of a banana leaf or the smoke from a nearby trash fire. My front yard has limited vegetation, which includes weeds, grasses, a banana tree, and some immature corn stalks. The wall surrounding my house was thoughtfully constructed at one time, but a large gap in the front allows easy entry regardless of the length of your legs, hooves, paws, or claws.

During an early-evening Mephloquine paranoia spell, I peered through the slats of my front door, and there, kneeling on plastic woven mats, were two Muslim women in mid-prayoral tilt. Apparently my imbibing platform of choice had been transformed into a launch pad to the holy netherworld. I inquired why the two women chose my porch for their vigil, like a bat chooses the underside of a bridge or a cave to roost. I was disappointed when my neighbors speculated that the noise at the gare where they sell their merchandise was probably too loud to pray, and that my porch was clean and close-by. I was secretly hoping they were honoring my Peace Corps sign, or that I had been chosen as their new chieftain or overseer, which could've helped with my mission.

Public displays of prayer in West Africa are not uncommon. Prayer is the second pillar of Islam and the ritual expression of one's humble devotion unto God Allah performed five times per day in the direction of the Kaaba Mosque in Mecca, Saudi Arabia. This ritual is usually performed in a building or structure called a mosque, but in the absence of a mosque a Muslim may pray at any location so long as he maintains purity of the body, clothes, and the surface used for prayer. I regularly witnessed prayer in places like a market, a bus station, the side of the road, an office floor, even a clearing of a plantation. Wherever you are when the time comes; that's where you pray.

The two Muslim women returned to my porch to pray on a regular basis. Sometimes I'd hear them from inside my house; sometimes I'd see them after running errands. A little girl of about three years old was usually nestled in between them. She went through the motions of prayer, but she was more interested in making funny faces with me while I waited for them to be done. Their features resembled Diallo from the kiosk where I ate breakfast, so I tried out some Pular greetings on them with success, which made them seem more relaxed around me. I even started leaving my front door open around afternoon prayer, leaving no doubt that they were welcome.

The Guinean women were not my only visitors. During the past month, I've observed an increase in my rental property's stock for a variety of spiritual and non-spiritual practices. Believing the noise one afternoon to be early arrivals to my holy terrace, I went to greet them as any good proprietor would. I was surprised to see a young family of five dressed in their Easter pastels, posing for a holiday keepsake with the lone banana tree as the backdrop. They'd even hired a photographer with his own SLR camera (maybe it was the sacred mask?), which was a rare service for Bangolo. My presence on the porch did not startle them in the least. In fact, based the impatient looks I received, I think they wanted me to move so as not to cast shadows in the frame.

Perhaps the most surprising activity that's taken place in my front yard is the occasional bowel movement. From time to time, I've caught people using my plot as an open-air latrine. It's mostly small children coming off the gbaka who can't hold it, but on occasion, the marchandes from the gare will crouch behind the compound wall to alleviate themselves. I even saw a woman letting it fly from the edge of my porch. While I've urinated off my porch late at night, I've never thought to crap off my porch. But for those in transit, it makes some sense. There's no obvious bathroom nearby, and my house looks vacant. Why not go behind the wall if emergency calls?

In a span of one month, my front porch has served as a one-stop shop for drinking, praying, posing, pissing, shitting, and who knows what else. This must be what is meant by the culture-sharing goals of the Peace Corps, which becomes all the more obvious when a random Betty saunters into your yard while you're sitting on the porch, hikes up her pagne, and squares off in the unkempt weeds to supply much needed compost to your struggling corn crop. Perhaps we should all knock down those walls that provide security and keep out the unsavories. It can only result in sweeter corn.

In the month of May, I made two decisions that would alter the course of my service. The first I made after receiving a barrage of letters from family back home. My mom's parents were celebrating their 50th wedding anniversary on June 30th of that year, and my family was planning a huge catered surprise party on the spacious lawn of my aunt Chris' suburban ranch-style home in North Brookfield. According to the letters, virtually everyone my grandparents knew would be in attendance, even my grandmother's extended clan from England. With my paltry savings account and a vow to serve my time in Africa, I did not plan to attend the anniversary. My family said they understood, figuring it would be a lot to travel all that way. But the letters kept coming, pleading for me to reconsider.

My grandparents' story is largely representative of their generation. Robert was an American soldier serving in the European theater of World War II; Doris lived in a small town near London, working odd jobs like cleaning up at a beautician's shop and grooming greyhound dogs at the race track. They met in a pub one evening and immediately hit it off. Robert was so intent on winning the approval of Doris' parents, he brought them gifts of coal, meat, and cigarettes during this time of hardship. And it worked. They married in 1946 after the war, and eventually settled in Worcester, Massachusetts. Over the years they gave birth to eight children; and those eight children gave birth to fifteen children of their own (thirteen at the time of the 50th anniversary).

Before leaving for the war, Robert was drafted by the Brooklyn Dodgers, but volunteered for combat in the Army instead. One of his childhood friends was the coach of the United States Olympic women's softball team. When it was rumored that the coach might try to attend my grandparent's party despite his busy practice schedule in Atlanta, Georgia, I better understood the magnitude of this event. This was an opportunity to celebrate an impressive milestone between two enduring souls from the Greatest Generation. This was an opportunity to honor those who gave us life. There might not be another like it. While I'm sure my grandparents would manage without me, I'd be the only grandchild not in attendance. There was no way I could let that happen. I had to go, no matter the cost or the inconvenience.

The second decision I made was *how* to spend the remaining ten to eleven months in Africa. The new mayor finally made it back to Bangolo in April, and he embraced my role as a technical consultant, forcing Dago to entertain some of my ideas. Then in May, the mayor brought in the German company, *Deutsche Gesellschaft für Technische Zusammenarbeit (GTZ)*, to hold a seminar on sustainable development. While it was too soon to size up our new leader, early indication was that he was serious, motivated, and supportive of change—a far cry from his predecessor.

It was at this seminar we made an interesting discovery. During one of the exercises, a teacher made an offhand remark about the "toilet in the grass" at the school. When Megan and I first canvassed the neighborhoods as part of the *étude*, we did not find a latrine, nor had it occurred to anyone to point it out. When the seminar concluded, I had the teacher escort me to the site. Sure enough, near the edge of the schoolyard nestled in a high patch of elephant grass, was a small building with four stalls.

The latrine was in fair condition. The wooden doors were weathered but still hinged and operational. The concrete structure was spalling in places but held its form. If you stumbled into this structure with no idea what it was used for, there was no obvious odor that gave it away; not bad considering the latrine had been buried and forgotten.

Further inquiries revealed some history about the latrine. In March 1995, just before I arrived, incumbent President Henri Konan Bédié stopped in Bangolo along the campaign trail. Ahead of his visit, the previous mayor commissioned a local entrepreneur to finance and construct the latrine to serve the military contingent accompanying the president. When asked why they didn't use the latrine after the president's visit, the teachers gave the same basic response: "The latrine was not officially donated to the school by the mayor's office, and it wasn't worth the trouble." This was not a surprise. Ivoirians take great pride in their formal ceremonies to mark an occasion or event. The fact that the mayor's office never held a *fête*, or celebration, to transfer the latrine was as good as boarding it up and prohibiting its use.

After the seminar I distributed questionnaires to the teachers about their sanitation practices and facility needs. Constructing a wall around the schoolyard was still their top priority, though they also cited a need for a bathroom for the children. Maybe they were telling me what I wanted to hear; maybe I was trying to strike while the iron was hot, to capitalize on the discussions from the seminar? Either way, there was momentum building that I could not ignore. I approached the new mayor about upgrading the latrine for school use, and he agreed.

"But where would we get funds to complete the upgrade?" he asked. "And what about the children in the adjacent courtyard? Where will they go to the bathroom?"

I hadn't thought about it, but he was right. It would take funding to do any real work. While I was still generally opposed to using outside funding, the tide was beginning to shift. In the last month, I'd observed Clement take the initiative and clean up the *gare* because he had access to the proper tool; I'd witnessed the new mayor do more in a few weeks than the previous mayor did his entire term; and I happened upon the perfect project with great potential to educate many young impressionable minds. Truth be told, I was also beginning to get a little bored walking around town every day, making observations and feeble attempts at development work. It seemed like the perfect storm for a subsidized project. I was now ready to relent and give outside funding a chance.

In early June, I traveled to Abidjan to submit a proposal to the Small Project Assistance (SPA) program in collaboration with USAID. On the return trip, I decided to visit a buddy in Séguéla to check out his ongoing trash collection project. Séguéla is only 137 kilometers northeast of Man, but getting there is a bit more difficult than traveling to, say, Biankouma or Soubré. The road to Séguéla from Man is an unimproved dirt road that crosses a number of permanent and seasonal streams. The road can become muddy, even impassable during the height of the wet season. In the dry season, it can be so dusty that it's impossible to see the car in front you. As a result, fewer *gbakas* travel this route, and those that do experience far more mechanical issues. You're almost better off going the long way around, south to Duékoué, east to Daloa, then north to Séguéla for a total of 323 kilometers, all on paved roads.

Séguéla wasn't much different than the other UEM towns in the manner that it was laid out, the available services, or the way it was managed. In other words, you could easily find your way around, stay nourished, and take a certain level of comfort knowing it was plagued by the same environmental calamities. Unlike Bangolo, Séguéla is primarily Muslim, associating itself more with the Islamic north than the Christian / animist south. This essentially meant more mosques, more clothing, and less beer. Séguéla is also a dryer climate, located beyond the northern extent of the country's dwindling forest reserves. There's something about those desert grains sweeping down from the Sahara that seems to spread the seeds of Islam, as if the Muslim people are innately one with the desert.

I walked around that afternoon with the volunteer, dissecting the contents of trash piles, talking with the *fonctionnaires* at the mayor's office, and catching up on the latest news. We capped off the day with a couple of lukewarm beers in the courtyard of his neighbor's compound. It was not like we had a choice of venues. There are few *maquis* in Séguéla, as drinking alcohol is forbidden for the majority of the population. In contrast, Bangolo had more watering holes than any other public service, more than all the schools, churches, community centers, and hospitals combined. Good to know we had our priorities straight in the Wild West.

Later that evening, some friends of the volunteers were having an impromptu birthday party. Sandor and Lyles were two white Afrikaner brothers from South Africa who'd recently moved to Séguéla to manage a diamond mining operation. Sandor was the older brother in his mid-thirties, with short dirty-blond hair. Lyles was the youngest, late-twenties, with short brown hair. I hadn't met anyone who had mined diamonds before, as there isn't much of an industry in New England, so this was a unique opportunity.

Diamonds are well known as a treasured gemstone, adored for their attractive luster, and signifying love, commitment, beauty, wealth, and extravagance. They are *a girl's best friend*, they say. They're also known for their precision cutting abilities. Approximately two-thirds of the world's diamond supply is extracted in Africa, making it a highly lucrative business. In parts of the world, it's also proven to be a very deadly business. In the last few decades, diamonds have funded insurgencies in the war-torn countries of the Democratic Republic of Congo (formally Zaire), Angola in the south, as well as Sierra Leone and Liberia. Diamonds used in this fashion are referred to as "conflict diamonds" or "blood diamonds" due to the atrocities that have been reported. Côte d'Ivoire began mining for diamonds on a small scale in the early 1990s. The country's diamonds are of a grade used primarily for cutting other diamonds. Since Côte d'Ivoire was a relatively stable country, and not suspected of exporting diamonds to war-torn areas, their diamond industry was considered legitimate.

Sandor and Lyles had a nice house, exactly what you'd expect from a couple of guys in the diamond business. Lyles welcomed us as if we were old friends from South Africa. We drank beer on couches while he talked about his mining operation. The older Sandor came into the room from the basement, clothes soiled from the workday. He grabbed a beer and made the rounds, shaking everyone's hands. When he got to me, he stopped abruptly, visibly shaken. Something was not right. Did I do something wrong? Sandor excused himself, saying he needed to clean up. While I wondered what I had done to offend our host, a slightly distracted Lyles talked about his work.

To find diamonds in Séguéla, workers used mostly shovels and small equipment, digging along the riverbed, sifting through mud and debris using pans and homemade sieves. This type of alluvial diamond mining is primitive and risky, but labor was cheap and plentiful. The biggest hazard was the presence of hippopotami in the river. These animals are large and aggressive, regarded as one of the most dangerous species in Africa, and will attack without provocation. A number of miners were said to have lost their lives to the hippo while working along the riverbank, but the workforce kept at it, unfazed by the incidents, enticed by the diamond and a steady paycheck.

After a while, Lyles went downstairs to check on Sandor; it was Sandor's birthday party, after all. Lyles returned with bad news. Sandor was not feeling well. A bit later, Lyles shared more details. When Sandor was in his late teens, he served in the South African Army during its border war with Angola. The battles took place in South West Africa (which is now Namibia) from 1966 to 1989, pitting South Africa and its allied forces against the Angolan government and troops from Cuba. Sandor was taken captive by the enemy and held in a POW camp, where prisoners were regularly tortured. He eventually made it out alive, but his best friend was not so lucky. And I, according to Lyles, was the spitting image of Sandor's friend.

So now what? What is the social etiquette for resembling your host's friend who died a horrific death at the hands of his captors? I couldn't imagine what Sandor must have been going through. I proposed to leave the party but Lyles would not allow it. Not that it mattered much. My presence had already set off a flood of emotions for Sandor, causing him to relive the trauma of a painful time, on his birthday no less. I tried to think of ways to make amends, but it was one of those situations. There wasn't much I could do except lay low. So there I sat, half-heartedly contributing to the discourse. I went from being a guest in their home to a veritable ghost.

To our surprise, Sandor rejoined the festivities. He approached the group with caution, working his way into Lyles' stories. Sandor sat next to me on the couch. I felt his gaze from the side but kept looking forward. Conversation came easier for him, though we never spoke about the war or his friend. Lyles brought out a cake and we toasted the occasion. The more Sandor engaged, the more comfortable he seemed. It even got to the point where he and I were bantering back and forth about sports and Africa, getting along as well as anyone could. Perhaps he forgot about his friend, or he repressed the memories. If I resembled him *that* much, how could he? Chances are, his friend from the war was very much on his mind. As the night went on, I was getting the vibe that Sandor was remembering him more than ever, that maybe Sandor's friend had returned for a visit, if only for one evening.

On the eve of my flight back to the States for my grandparents' anniversary, my buddies happened to be in Abidjan to see me off. There was drinking, reminiscing, speculating about what each of us would do given the opportunity to go home. It was a memorable night, dark and quiet, abnormally somber for the hostel. I got the feeling they didn't think I was going to return, that I'd be too tempted to stay and resume a life of privilege. I guess it was possible, just not likely. We began to envision a time when we'd no longer be in Africa, when we'd have jobs and families and responsibilities, and it wouldn't be so easy to get together.

My itinerary had me going from Abidjan to Dakar and on to JFK International Airport in New York. It was strange to be at an African airport of my own volition, as our previous flights had involved chaperons or handlers moving us from place to place like cattle through a complex chute of cultural peril. It was stranger to overhear English conversations in the waiting room of the Dakar airport. While I engaged in plenty of English conversations with volunteers, I was not accustomed to hearing English in public places.

The chatter was coming from a group of about twenty middle-aged African Americans returning from an African Heritage Tour to Ghana, where they'd dress in African garb; eat Ghanaian food; enjoy local music, dance, and the arts; view and purchase the work of local artisans; visit the slave fortresses and other historic sites; and generally learn about the country's history and politics. Tour companies will even research one's genealogy in an attempt to match an individual with their ancestral tribe or village. How accurate or authentic these services may be, I do not know.

As we waited for the airline to fix a mechanical problem, a male employee went around the room, passing out coupons for a free beverage at the airport store. Most of the tour group was still wearing their African garb—the men wearing *boubous* and matching *kufi* hats resembling small cloth pails, while the women wore the intricate *buba* dress with a matching head wrap and shoulder shawl. As important as it must have been for them to wear these clothes, they stood out as tourists against the backdrop of the African business traveler in their plain *fonctionnaire* suits.

I was drinking my free bottle of soda when I heard a commotion between a woman from the tour group and a male employee of the airline. Apparently, there weren't enough coupons to go around and the woman felt slighted. The employee did not speak English, but that didn't keep the woman from expressing her outrage. She claimed the airline was biased against blacks, that they gave preferential treatment to whites. I looked around the room. I was the only white person in sight. She was talking about me! As I wiped the remnants of the orange Fanta from my upper lip, I paused and thought about this woman's condemnation.

For the last eighteen months, I'd associated with either West Africans or Peace Corps volunteers. Our volunteer group was mostly Caucasian, though we were represented by other ethnicities including African American, Indian American, Chinese American, and Korean American. And while we weren't singing "Kumbayah" all the time, we got along fairly well regardless of our race, ethnicity, or gender. It helped that we were idealists with a common cause, but

I also think we were galvanized by our circumstances, living amongst some of the poorest people in the world.

Not receiving a free soda at an airport, for whatever reason, is largely a *First World* predicament, but who knows what the distressed woman at the airport had been through in her life that led her to react the way she did, or whether her claim had merit or not? In the U.S., there's an entirely different division of wealth, class, gender, race, religion, and politics. And in less than twelve hours I'd be expected to rejoin that conversation, whether I was ready or not.

When I first arrived in Africa, I immersed myself in the culture to fully understand, and possibly affect, the African plight. But if I detached from the issues that plagued my friends in Bangolo, even for a moment, I might find it difficult to continue my service when I returned. So I made a conscious decision to spend my vacation like I was on an American Heritage Tour, where I'd dress up in shorts and T-shirts, eat hot dogs and hamburgers, go hiking, enjoy a ballgame, buy a few trinkets, see the sights, and try to avoid the issues that plagued America, if it were at all possible.

A female friend from high school named Lori, and her female roommate, picked me up at the airport in New York. I was to stay with them in Staten Island for one night before they'd drive me to Worcester the next morning. As we were going through the tollbooth, I assured them that I had plenty of single dollar bills in case the attendant couldn't make change and wouldn't let us pass. They looked at me, perplexed. I heard an ice cream truck in their suburban neighborhood and felt nostalgic. We went out for dinner and I was overwhelmed by all the food and beverage choices. The crowded restaurant gave me claustrophobia, so I went outside for air. We finished dinner around 8:00 p.m. and we walked around. Why weren't these people off the street and in their homes? I tried to sleep, but there was too much stimulation from gunshots and sirens and accelerating vehicles. Where the hell was I again?

My friends brought me up to speed on recent events. I was aware that O.J. Simpson was acquitted of killing his wife and her companion, but I had no idea there was such a dramatic courtroom spectacle followed by a racial firestorm. I also learned of my good fortune to have missed the Spice Girls and the Macarena dance craze. If I were concerned about missing a slice of popular culture, I'd picked a good time to join the Peace Corps. Then again, if this is the measure, has there ever been a bad time to join? They also told me about the Internet where you can access all sorts of information from a computer. Americans were living in the future.

The only family member that I had informed of my travel plans was my sister Stacy so she could provide logistical support. I thought it would be fun to surprise everyone, especially my mom—the return of the prodigal son. I didn't want to steal my grandparents' thunder. It was their day, their moment. Though I figured there wasn't much of chance of upstaging a fifty-year marriage celebration. I was right.

I'd gained back some weight since the Mali trip, but I was still noticeably thinner than when my family saw me last. My hair was long enough to wear in a ponytail, and for some reason I shaved my beard before the flight, which accentuated the weight loss in my face. I must have resembled a captive released from a lengthy confinement. My clothes were rolled and cinched at various places, draped from me like they were borrowed from a big brother.

At one point, my sister and I got out of her car at my mom's apartment. Our neighbors Tim and Ginger were enjoying a cool drink on their screened-in porch. Believing I was Stacy's newest boyfriend, Ginger reportedly remarked to Tim that Stacy could do much better. I certainly hope so, but there was no denying their first impression of the returned volunteer.

My high school buddy Steve drove me to the party. My uncle Robs spotted me first as I was walking down the lawn towards the festivities. He looked me up and down and said, "Get a haircut, you bum." Slowly, people started recognizing me. My mom was thrilled. My grandparents were grateful. But my attendance was about as remarkable as if I had never left. Many of the party's guests had never met me. Half my cousins were too young to remember me. And the rest of my family received me in the same stoic manner they employ for all people, events, and situations.

People commented on how much weight I had lost, that I looked sickly, that the Peace Corps was not good for me. On appearances alone, they were right. Physically, I was in rough shape. Mentally, though, I'd never felt better, more attuned to the present moment as I had ever been. All in all, my return was rather humbling. After almost two years' away, I didn't feel like I missed much; it just felt like a longer hiatus between summer cookouts and birthday parties.

The highlight of the trip was a multi-day hike through the Presidential Range of central New Hampshire with Robs and some of the cousins from England. In Africa, I spent a lot of my spare time in the mountains and forests, but I was partial to the hills and hardwoods of New England. Something about a canopy of oaks and maples made me feel safe and secure. That, and the consolation that there were fewer guinea worms, deadly mambas, and men with machetes lurking in the granite state.

Returning to the U.S. was a bigger readjustment than I had expected. I had trouble with the fast pace of life. I became easily annoyed by the widespread marketing of so many unnecessary goods and services, skeptical that all this excess was for the betterment of the country and its citizens. I struggled to relate to those who hadn't given enough thought to these and other conventions. In reality, though, life isn't that simple, but at the time I felt enlightened by my experiences abroad, and I needed to share.

Returning to the U.S. was also a bit surreal. I enjoyed my time with friends, yet something was different. There was a strange vibe or feeling of detachment. I couldn't put my finger on it until a few months later, while reading *Travels with Charley, In Search of America* by John Steinbeck, I came across the following passage that provides a possible explanation:

> *My town had grown and changed and my friends along with it. Now returning, as changed to my friends as my town was to me, I distorted his picture, muddled his memory. When I went away I had died, and so became fixed and unchangeable. My return caused only confusion and uneasiness. Although they could not say it, my old friends wanted me gone so that I could take my proper place in the pattern of remembrance—and I wanted to go for the same reason. Tom Wolfe was right. You can't go home again because home has ceased to exist except in the mothballs of memory.*

CHAPTER SIXTEEN

MONUMENT

I flew back to Africa on Bastille Day. When I reported to the office, Margaret informed me that I had been granted a Small Project Assistance grant for my latrine project. The general goal of the SPA program is "to enhance a community's capability to conduct low-cost, grassroots, sustainable development activities." The SPA program distributes funds in partnership with the United States Agency for International Development. Because the program requires local contributions, the mayor offered up manual labor and equipment with an estimated monetary value of 360,000 CFA (U.S. $720). For their part, USAID doled out 675,125 CFA (U.S. $1,350). The citizens of Bangolo would be thrilled, if not for the latrines, at least for the smattering of jobs, the select markup on goods and services, and the other opportunities that come when a development worker from the western world is suddenly flush with cash.

It was good to be back in Bangolo. People generally seemed glad to see me, and the teachers, superintendents, and municipal staff were pleased to hear about our successful proposal. Dago and some of the administrative staff, who were usually apathetic to my presence, started treating me differently, friendlier, with a kind of attentiveness that suggested they now had something to gain or lose by our association.

For the rest of the month, I drew up plans of the new latrine, modeled after the one in the tall grass, with all the features of our standard Ventilated Improved Pit (VIP) latrine. I talked with vendors in town, placed material orders, and refined the cost estimate to ensure I wouldn't go over budget. While the SPA program afforded some contingency spending, there was no telling what might go wrong, though I knew the chances were high that something would go wrong and I'd need a coffer of funds to cover it.

In early August I received an unexpected visit. I was washing dishes in the kitchen when I heard a voice call out from the front gate, "*Bonjour*, Tim sent us!" I toweled off and went to the door. It was a man and a woman, both *toubabs* in their late-twenties, soiled from the road, riding bicycles so loaded down with gear you could barely make out the bikes. If I'd seen these two characters in any major city in the U.S., I'd probably think they were homeless. The man introduced himself as Steve in a thick Australian accent through a thick reddish-brown goatee; his partner's name was Emiko (Emi for short), a Japanese woman with long black hair and a vibrant smile. Earlier in the week, they'd passed through Soubré and stayed overnight with Tim, who then directed them to Bangolo.

Steve and Emi parked their chariots in my spacious living room while I fetched some beers from the *maquis*. They cleaned up and joined me on the porch where they recounted their remarkable story. In March 1989, Steve took a break from his job as an electrician to cycle around his native Australia, starting in Melbourne. Emi was a journalist for a motorcycling magazine, touring Australia alone on a Honda 600cc. In July of that year, their paths crossed at a hostel in Cairns. Emi was thinking of switching to a bicycle to get more out of the road, so Steve convinced her to join him. Emi sold her motorcycle in Sydney and met Steve around Christmas in Darwin where they set off together. To support themselves financially, Emi periodically wrote stories for a Japanese cycling magazine while Steve took photographs and did a bit of writing for English-speaking cycling enthusiasts.

When Steve and Emi pulled into Bangolo, they had been on the road for the better part of seven years. Seven years! That's three and a half Peace Corps assignments! That's the average duration of a marriage in the U.S.! That's twice the average length of a player's career in the National Football League! That's a prison term for a Class G Felony for crimes such as embezzlement, theft, and negligent homicide. Seven years on a bike! And they were still a few years from being done.

Steve pulled out a series of tattered maps that highlighted their route around the world. From Darwin, the pair cycled through Indonesia, Singapore, Malaysia, Thailand, and Japan. They flew up to Anchorage, Alaska and cycled to the northern-most point at Prudhoe Bay before turning back south. From June 1991 until August 1996, they traversed Alaska, Canada, the western United States, Mexico, Belize, Guatemala, El Salvador, Honduras, Nicaragua, Costa Rica, Panama, Columbia, Venezuela, western Brazil, Bolivia, Chile, through Argentina to the southernmost city of Urshuaia before heading north back to Brazil into Rio De Janiero. From there they flew to Cape Town, South Africa and worked their way north through the East African countries of Lesotho, Botswana, Zimbabwe, Mozambique, Malawi, Tanzania, and Kenya before turning west through Uganda, Zaire, Central African Republic, Cameroon, Nigeria, Niger, Burkina Faso, Togo, Ghana, and eventually to my *joli coin* in Côte d'Ivoire. It's hard to fathom traveling to all these countries in one's lifetime, never mind peddling a bicycle across each and every one, in succession, without returning home for a reprieve.

One can imagine all the fascinating tales that accompany such a risky venture through some of the most isolated, rugged, and treacherous parts of the world. In Africa alone, Steve and Emi had encountered poor roads; impassable terrain; extreme temperatures and weather; a near miss with a lightning strike; an oppressive sand storm; bribes and ransoms from corrupt police; warring factions and political coups; guerrillas and gorillas; extreme poverty, sickness, epidemics, and death; and refugees, smugglers, and looters. They'd also experienced the breathtaking beauty of Africa and the warmth of its people.

It takes a special kind of person to embark on such a journey, one with great physical and mental endurance. It also takes a bit of luck. And it doesn't hurt to have karma on your side by having the right intentions, as evidenced by one of Steve and Emi's credos taken from their website: "To experience the world with our five senses. To experience the world at a human pace. To meet people and to get to know their life, and preferably even share an episode of their life with them." I could write more about this dynamic couple, but that is their story to tell.

Our shared episode in Bangolo involved two recurring themes: Purpose and Time. When I met Steve and Emi, I had recently finished reading *Into the Wild* by Jon Krakauer, about a young man named Chris who hitchhiked from the Lower Forty-Eight up to Denali National Park in Alaska in the spring of 1992. Chris hiked deep into the wilderness to live off the land with little more than a .22 caliber rifle, a bag of rice, a book on edible plants, and the clothes on his back. Four months later, a hunter found his body in an abandoned bus along with his journals, which left clues about his activities and disposition.

Krakauer did an admirable job of recounting how Chris may have spent that summer, the crossroads that he faced, the likely cause of his death, and the controversy surrounding his choices. Krakauer's book was making the rounds at the hostel, and it seemed to resonate with the male volunteers. Some of us almost envied Chris, to have the courage to abandon everything familiar and live life on your own terms. His critics claimed that he was ill-prepared for the Alaska wilderness. I visited the abandoned bus (Fairbanks 142) in July of 1999 as a resident of Alaska, and it's not a place one goes to hike and camp and recreate. By all accounts, Chris was on a soul-searching quest to find meaning, and in the process, find himself. Chris attempted to live as close to a primitive, self-sufficient existence as possible without stripping down naked and behaving like a savage. His approach to life has its risks, especially in the magnificent and unforgiving country of Alaska's interior, but so does the urban workplace and a reliance on society. Unfortunately, Chris paid the ultimate price for his gamble to live differently.

I felt that Steve and Emi shared a similar sense of purpose, to live life on their own terms, contributing to the world in a less conventional way. And seven years into their quest, they were thriving at it. I'm sure there are people who cannot fathom why Steve and Emi chose to leave their homes and families to bike around the world during the prime of their lives. I'm sure they have their critics who question whether they were contributing to society or not. But I was not one of them. I could relate to their wanderlust to travel the globe, their thirst for adventure, their desire to connect with people from different walks of life in a meaningful way. The way I see it, so long as you're not a burden to others, and you don't consume more than your fair share of resources, you should be able to do whatever you want with your life. And if meeting people and having adventures is your thing, have at it.

As far as time, Steve and Emi's journey would continue through Guinea, Guinea-Bissau, Gambia, Senegal, Mauritania, and Morocco before crossing over into Gibraltar, then through Spain, Portugal, Andorra, France, Switzerland, Germany, Holland, Belgium, England, all over Eastern Europe, all over Asia, back to Australia, over to New

Zealand, then to Taiwan, finishing up in Japan in the year 2001. That's ten years total on the road, sleeping in strange places, pushing themselves to their limits, not knowing what to expect each day. What a monumental accomplishment.

In many ways, the standard two-year Peace Corps hitch is a microcosm of Steve and Emi's ten-year trip. We too had left our homes and families to live an unconventional life. We also had to come to terms with a time commitment that was daunting at the outset, and seemed as if it would last forever. To persevere, it was best to slow life down to a human pace, to experience Africa with all five senses, and to get to know the people as best we could. In the end, all that time I spent away from home felt like neither a sacrifice nor a loss. On the contrary, it felt like a lifetime within a lifetime, with vivid episodes that keep paying dividends.

The school to receive the new latrine was composed of six one-story concrete buildings—three on the west campus and three on the east, arranged in a mirror image of each other. All told, there were an estimated 1400 students enrolled in the school. That's a lot of bowel movements, even if only a small percentage of the kids attended school or had food in their systems. Between the two campuses, beneath a canopy of tall trees, were the living quarters of the four school superintendents. I made the case that the new latrine should be placed out in the open, within the children's view. "The latrine is important, but hygiene education is the ultimate goal," I'd say to the superintendents repeatedly. It was my belief that if the latrine was placed outside the school grounds, it would be swallowed up by tall grass in no time. I pointed to the derelict latrine on the east campus as an example. They agreed. It could go in a small clearing near the south access road. It was the perfect spot, not only for the children but for the superintendents' families as well.

A couple of days after Steve and Emi peddled away, we broke ground on the new latrine. We had ten weeks to meet the timetable outlined in our SPA proposal. Ten weeks was a bit optimistic to construct anything in Bangolo, but it was certainly doable. The mayor reassigned four of Dago's fourteen *manoeuvres* to dig the pit. The *manoeuvres* were mostly ex-THIMO, rehired for grass cutting and trash collection after the new mayor took office. Dago was not happy with the mayor's decision to reduce his workforce, but he agreed, with the caveat that he'd reevaluate their necessity each week.

Of the four guys reassigned to me, I knew two of them from the erosion control project. Remi was the tallest, heaviest of the four, with a face that resembled Charles Barkley of the NBA. I remembered Remi to be a bit lazy when he was with Team One, but what he lacked in work ethic he made up for in personality. Remi was always the last to arrive at the jobsite, around 0700, and each day it was the same thing, blaming his two wives and his late night frog hunts for his chronic fatigue.

Pablo was the workhorse, a picture of strength, with a chiseled jaw and ripped physique from years of manual labor. Pablo was the group leader of Team Four and the most even-keeled of the lot, so I was surprised that Dago allowed him to work on the latrine.

Gilbert was one of the newcomers, short in stature, but in good shape, with a pencil-thin mustache that suited his French-sounding name. Gilbert was always the first to arrive at the jobsite, at 06:30 sharp, but he also complained the most about the heat and the conditions, singing songs about how there was nothing in his stomach and how his waist belt was constantly falling down.

Then there was Patrice, quiet and reserved, upbeat and hard working, who complained only to mock Gilbert. Patrice laughed at my dry, self-deprecating humor. He even cracked jokes of his own, and he quickly became the go-to guy for the project.

In order to properly contain and treat the waste, the pit had to measure two meters wide by six meters long by three meters deep, which equated to thirty-six cubic meters or forty-seven cubic yards. Since we estimated two weeks to dig the pit, we'd need to dig at a rate of five yards per shift, or a dump truck's worth, every two days using nothing but picks, shovels, and wheelbarrows. That's a lot of digging in a short span, especially with hand tools that frequently broke and splintered and had to be replaced on short notice. Fortunately, the soil was mostly red clay that came off the pick in large clumps and could be tossed out of the hole by hand.

I planned on getting my hands dirty and pitching in. It was *my* project, after all. But the crew would have no part of it. "The *patron* doesn't do manual labor," they insisted. The *patron*? Is that how they viewed me? *Patron* means the employer or boss. It was difficult for me to believe I was anybody's *patron*. I probably possessed less work experience than each of these young men, and with all the joking around I felt like one of the guys. From their perspective, however, if you could acquire over one million CFA simply by filling out a form, you were most certainly the *patron*.

Each *manoeuvre* made 700 CFA (U.S. $1.40) for a half days' work, which was considered a good wage in Bangolo. That's the same wage they'd make working for Dago doing far less work, so to keep the crews energized and inspired, I bought them breakfast in the morning and a round of palm wine in the afternoon. The palm wine, known locally as *bangui*, is made from the sap of a felled palm tree that ferments almost immediately as the sap comes in contact with the air. After a few hours in the tree, the wine reaches a concentration of about 4% alcohol, though some tappers leave the sap fermenting longer for a more potent beverage. In Côte d'Ivoire, palm wine is always served at public events, ceremonies, weddings and funerals. It's customary to purposefully spill a small volume of palm wine on the ground as an offering to the ancestors before it is permissible to drink. I took part in this custom, if not out of respect for their deceased ancestors, at least out of consideration for those still in our midst.

A woman came by the jobsite each day around 1100 selling *bangui* from a large *bidon*. A half-dozen multi-colored plastic cups hung from the handle. Her brew had a sweet milky taste and a nice buzz, additionally flavored with tree bark and dead ants floating on the top from a fresh tap. One hundred CFA would buy a substantial portion of wine, which usually signaled the end of our workday. The wine also kept the *manoeuvres* coming back each day in good spirits. What more could I ask for?

The crew had the pit down to waist deep in less than one week. We were right on schedule. Gilbert was driving us nuts with his singing, but we endured. Then I suffered a personal setback. An entrepreneur had recently constructed a new *boulangerie* near my house, selling fresh baguettes of bread still warm from the oven. This was a progressive service for Bangolo, so after work I went straight from the jobsite to the grand opening. The vegetation on the lot had been cleared and grubbed to construct the building, so it was the perfect terrain for the neighborhood kids to play *futbol*. I walked out of the *boulangerie* with my notebooks tucked under one arm and a warm loaf of bread in the other. One of the kids kicked a soccer ball in my direction. It came at me fast and to my right, so I stretched my leg out to stop it. Before I knew what had happened, my foot rolled over the top of the ball and my right knee gave way with a distinct popping sound. I lay there in a cloud of dust as children huddled around me with looks of concern. Not only was I embarrassed, but I could feel the knee swell up almost immediately. When I was fourteen, I'd injured the same knee jumping over a fence, and I had had surgery to repair cartilage, so I knew this wasn't good.

I limped across the road to my house. There wasn't much ice in the freezer, but what I had I applied to the joint. I began ruminating about the cause of the injury, what I'd do about health care, whether I'd be able to finish my project or my service. The next day the knee was unstable and swollen but the pain was tolerable. To get around town, I'd coast downhill on my bike or I'd lean on it as a crutch when walking. It was back to business as usual. News travels fast in Bangolo and the crew already knew, greeting me with a good-natured ribbing about my *futbol* prowess. If I was looking for any sympathy, I wouldn't receive any here. Injury, sickness, and disease are commonplace in Bangolo, and my minor leg injury was hardly worth noting, even for a *patron* such as myself.

The day after the injury, I was sitting on the edge of our pit when I noticed a male teacher escorting a female student into a classroom across the courtyard. There was no school that day so it seemed a bit peculiar. Remi was sitting next to me, so I gave him a nudge.

"What's going on there?" I said, motioning towards the pair.

"She's hoping for a passing grade," Remi replied with a slight smirk.

The girl was in her early teens, half the height of the teacher. Remi wasn't serious, was he? I asked the other *manoeuvres* and they confirmed that it is not uncommon for young girls struggling in school to have sex with male teachers to improve their grades. I suppose this can happen anywhere in the world, and I'm sure it does, but the *manoeuvres* claimed the parents usually knew about it, even supported the act.

In Côte d'Ivoire there are far fewer opportunities for employment than in the western world, and for young Ivoirian women there are even fewer. Failure to graduate school all but ensures a life adjoined to the mortar and pestle to feed a husband, kids, and the greater village. Even the majority of young women who graduated found themselves married with kids, responsible for the domestic duties of a household. There aren't a lot of employment opportunities in places like Bangolo, except for a side job in the market or a rare job as a clerk. That doesn't mean women in Côte d'Ivoire didn't hold out hope that they might advance to university, or get a job in Abidjan, or travel to France or America and avoid the fate of generations of women before them. But sometimes, that hope comes at a high price.

After a week on the job, the mayor called me into his office. He wanted an update on the project as well as a construction schedule. An update? A schedule? I looked at him with disbelief. Nobody in Bangolo cared about schedules. For a moment I wondered if he was an imposter, a Peace Corps administrator or a SPA official masquerading as a small town mayor to keep a watchful eye on the volunteers. After the initial shock wore off, I promised him a schedule by day's end. The mayor also assigned me a liaison named Richard who would represent the municipal government and help me get things done.

Our first order of business was to hire a mason. In Bangolo, every able-bodied man was a mason or a carpenter or both, so I asked Richard to be more selective in his search. The next day he showed up at the jobsite with an older man, not quite an elder, and a younger man with no shirt and a potbelly. They didn't look like masons, though I had no idea what masons were suppose to look like. They were Richard's cousins. No surprise. Around these parts, nepotism was the rule, not the exception—one of the perks of being appointed the project liaison. And since the mayor was picking up the tab on the labor, I had to trust that they were qualified.

Concrete blocks or bricks are made to order, brick by brick, using a single metal form like the one used by kids to make ice blocks for igloos. I assumed they were made this way because business owners didn't want to tie up their capital in material, labor, and storage space for a product that might not sell when it was time to put food on the table. This was only partly true. At construction sites, I noticed that a good percentage of bricks left on the ground to cure were damaged or degraded. All it took was a good rainstorm or a bit of blunt force and the brick was useless because local masons used only the minimum amount of cement in their mixture. It was considered wasteful to do otherwise, so we set out to make twice as many bricks.

Since SPA funds were supposed to cover the cost of materials, I would have to arrange for a sand delivery and purchase cement so the masons could start making bricks. On the second Sunday after starting the project, Richard showed up at my door, quoting me a price for sand. He claimed that the municipal dump truck was out of commission, and he'd have to bring in a truck out of Man to deliver the goods. The sand itself, which could be found at a crude quarry on the north part of town, was free, but the delivery would cost me. Richard's price seemed high, so I put him off until Monday. Plus, nobody does municipal business on a Sunday. Something was up.

Sunday was the market day in Bangolo, so I coasted down the hill to pick up supplies. I was bargaining for cucumbers when a young boy walked by with a bouillon cube on his head, nestled in the middle of his short nappy hair. Africans learn to carry objects on their head at a young age (not just girls, but the boys too). As they grow, this skill is honed, so when they reach adulthood they can carry virtually anything on their noggin with ease and grace. They might start out with small items such as school textbooks and baskets, but it eventually progresses to buckets of water, suitcases, large bundles of wood, or even a sack of cement or cacao beans.

In Senegal, we tested our skills by attempting to carry buckets of water back and forth on our heads. It's a good thing there wasn't a drought in Thiés because we dumped a shameful amount of water on the ground. Collectively, we weren't very good at it, but the concept made sense. Better to carry heavy items with good posture than to hunch or amble along slaunchways. A group of volunteers decided it would be fun to have a competition to identify the largest and smallest objects being carried on someone's head. The largest object ended up being a queen-sized straw mattress. The heaviest object was a hundred-pound sack of coffee beans. I thought I'd identified the smallest object with the bouillon cube until a volunteer spotted a piece of gum the size of a Chiclet on a little girl's head. I alleged she didn't know the gum was in her hair, but I was overruled.

While at the market, I spotted *manoeuvres* with pitchforks shoveling garbage from the street into the municipal dump truck. A fully functioning dump truck! I hadn't thought to question Richard about why he thought it was out of commission, since it seemed like it was always on the fritz. He had to know the truck was scheduled for use on market day and that I might see it working. Was Richard trying to con me out of project funds? I didn't know him well enough to be sure. He wasn't part of the regular municipal staff. I'd see him on special assignments, usually when dignitaries visited the area. He seemed like a decent guy, never causing trouble, but he was a friend of Assis and that made him shady by association.

As I was walking my bike up the hill, heading for home, a man pushing a two-wheeled cart was gaining on me from behind. He was one of many *pousse-pousse* operators in Bangolo who made a living hauling a person's luggage to and from the *gare*. It was an industrious occupation that required short bursts of intense pushing, then lots of waiting around for customers. His *pousse-pousse* was like an oversized wooden wheelbarrow with two motorcycle tires connected by a single axle. Across the front panel was a *Jesus Christ* bumper sticker. When he got to within a couple of meters of me, I heard, "Pssst, I heard you might need some sand," as if he were selling drugs or stolen watches out of a trench coat.

I swung around in disbelief. A hulking figure in long ragged shorts and an unbuttoned black shirt stood there smiling. How did he know? I couldn't help but laugh. His name was David and he claimed he could deliver all the sand and gravel I needed by Monday afternoon for a fraction of what it would cost me through Richard. I had no allegiance to either of these men. While it would be risky to rebuke Richard's proposal, it would be just as risky to have a reputation as a guy who pays top dollar for sand when cheaper options exist. David and I had a deal.

As promised, David delivered all the sand and gravel I needed by Monday afternoon. Most of it was delivered to the mason's house, where he'd make the bricks away from the chaos of the schoolyard. The rest was delivered to the jobsite for the mortar and the floor slabs. David placed the sand and gravel in neat orderly piles, each encircled by a ring of hand-laid bricks to prevent migration in the event of heavy rains. As expected, Richard was not happy about my decision, but he spoke of it no further when I told him I'd contributed to the local economy rather than expend the mayor's budget on an expensive delivery out of Man, since the municipal truck appeared to be working again.

The masons began making bricks first thing Tuesday morning, and they'd finished by day's end. The bricks were left to cure in a vacant lot near the mason's house. The masons insisted on delivering the bricks to the jobsite the next day, but I pushed for more curing time. They were persistent, though. They told me that I didn't understand African bricks, which might be another way of saying that I didn't understand the limits of their frugality. Then I remembered the masons were being paid by the job, not by the shift like the *manoeuvres*, and they wanted to finish as soon as possible. They had other jobs lined up, they confessed. They couldn't afford to wait weeks or even days for the bricks to reach their ideal strength. The sooner they were done, the better. They asked me to trust them. I didn't want to prevent them from making money, so we settled on two days' curing time and hoped for the best.

On Wednesday the *manoeuvres* arrived around 0800, much later than usual. I could sense their fatigue. They petered out short of the three-meter target depth, but I didn't push it. No sense in making enemies over a few cubic yards of storage volume. While the *manoeuvres* rested in the shade, the masons climbed down into the pit to pour a footing to support the walls. Gilbert, sitting on the ground with his back against a tree, asked me for food money. I promised them breakfast, but now Gilbert wanted the money instead.

"Vraiment!" uttered Patrice, slightly embarrassed.

"Why do you want money instead of breakfast?" I replied, "I thought there was no food in your belly and your waist belt was falling down?" which got some laughs, even from Gilbert.

I arranged for the bricks to be delivered to the jobsite Thursday morning, but Richard told me the truck was out of petrol and it didn't sound like they were going to fill it anytime soon. To avoid delays I paid the driver myself, but the guys told me that he'd probably shortchange me on the fuel and pocket half of the money. An hour later, the truck arrived with the first load of bricks. The *manoeuvres* moved them from the truck bed to the flat ground near the school. Two men on mopeds showed up, asking if they could remove our soil to make bricks of their own. The clay soil would make great *banco* bricks for a village hut, but I told them we weren't done yet, and that we'd need most of it to backfill around the latrine structure once it was erected. A heated discussion ensued between Remi and the men on the mopeds. From what I gathered, Remi had promised these men soil, and they weren't happy they'd have to wait. As the men quarreled, the mason looked up at me from inside the pit and exhaled, "Ehhh, Côte d'Ivoire!"

Friday morning we learned that Remi had tried to arrange the use of the truck to deliver soil to his friends following his shift on Thursday. Richard was at the jobsite when the *manoeuvres* arrived in the morning, and he had a look of determination. Rather than reprimand Remi, he told him that the soil was dug on government time and was, therefore, government property, not his to sell. If he wanted to broker a sale with the men on mopeds, he'd have to give Richard a portion of the proceeds. Remi disagreed that it was government dirt, proclaiming that he had done all the work. Richard countered that Remi was already paid for his work. We're not talking about a lot of money here. Even in Côte d'Ivoire, dirt is dirt cheap, but it's not often that this much soil is so ripe for the taking. I chimed in with my two cents about needing it for backfill, but the two men were embroiled in debate. Meanwhile, the masons made progress on the structure, mortaring the walls up four to five block courses. At the end of the shift, Patrice dubbed the day's ordeal as the *Jour de Palabres,* which essentially means the Day of Endless Discussions or Arguments. It would not be our last.

I was fortunate to have such good neighbors at *la maison bleue*. Not only did the adults keep a watchful eye over me, but the Baman children kept me constantly entertained. The oldest was Seria, a quiet girl about ten years old, thin as a rail, with the face of a fashion model. When we talked, she'd look me in the eyes and straight through my soul, as if she knew what was in store. I always imagined that Seria's confidence and good looks might be her ticket out of the village. That's what I imagined. Chances are those same traits would bring her the type of attention that kept her in Bangolo for life, sidled to a husband and a litter of kids while her potential passed her by. Nadeje was the middle child, about seven years old, her appeal stemming from her sassiness and playful nature. Nadeje was the chattiest of the Baman children, and a handful for her parents. Not a day would go by without hearing her mother yell her name in frustration. As mischievous as Nadeje was the youngest boy Patrico, with his perfectly round face, big grin, and machine-gun giggle. Patrico was always in my yard, playing with a little rubber soccer ball until it popped and he had to wait until I bought him a new one.

It got to be that every time I heard little fists knocking on my front door, I knew it was one of the Baman children. On one particular occasion, the knock was accompanied by the shuffling of many little flip-flopped feet on my soiled porch. From my chair, I could see their shadows moving frantically against the light coming in through the door slats. Expecting an ambush, I opened the door cautiously. Nadeje had rounded up about five of her girlfriends. They stood there with great anticipation, wearing white dresses while holding improvised bouquets of pink and white flowers they'd picked from my yard. What they were really after was a photograph from my camera. How could anyone in their right mind say no?

The most humorous and eye-opening visit I received unfolded over the course of a couple of weeks. It pertained to my household trash. Since there wasn't much of a trash collection system, everyone was on their own. I disposed of my trash in a big green plastic tub I kept under the kitchen sink. When the tub was full and smelly, I'd haul it out to the back yard and dump it in an open-top concrete *poubelle*. My *poubelle* measured one meter square by a half meter high. Most people in Bangolo burned the trash in their *poubelle* or out in the open, but I felt it would send the wrong message if the environmental guy was polluting the air, so I was more conscientious about what I put in there.

I recycled as much as I could. Empty plastic containers were used to store liquids such as water or Gatorade. Cardboard boxes and manila envelopes were reused for my outgoing mail. Newspapers were donated to the women at the *gare*, who used them to wrap beignets or fried plantains. Since I purchased most of my food fresh from the market, there wasn't much in the way of packaging, less a few glass bottles, tin cans, and some plastic wrap. That left mostly peels, rinds, and seeds from fruits and vegetables, and other food refuse that would compost nicely in the bin. I was doing my part for the environment. I even had a papaya tree growing out of the middle of the *poubelle* that produced fruit my second year.

After emptying my tub one day, I could hear little voices outside yelling "*Poubelle!*" followed by some commotion. I peered through the slats and saw a half-dozen children rummaging through my bin. I couldn't make out what they salvaged, but if I were to judge by their reaction, they did quite well. A couple of hours later, I heard a knock at my door. It was Patrico and his little buddy at the bottom of the stairs, looking up at me. Patrico was holding a string attached to a toy truck made entirely out of tin cans, sticks, and plastic bottle tops.

The boys ran away in a fit of laughter, with the toy truck trailing behind them, but not before I noticed the tin cans were from food items that I'd recently consumed. Little bastards had stolen my trash!

I was glad to see the neighborhood kids make such good use out of my refuse. I couldn't have built a better tin can truck if I were given a week and all the right tools and materials. It made me think of the old adage: "One person's trash is another person's treasure." It also took me back to my own childhood. My friends and I were not so different. Most of our fun was had without toys or manufactured goods of any kind, drawing upon our imaginations and the natural surroundings for games such as hide-and-seek, war, tag, rock skipping, wrestling, swimming, hiking, running, tree climbing, observing nature, harassing animals, making snow caves, having snowball fights, and general horseplay. Add a simple accessory like a ball or an implement, and our choices of activities would increase exponentially. We were fortunate to have bicycles, modern sporting goods, and the latest technical gadgets. Seeing Patrico's toy truck took me back to a time when life was simpler, when the greatest gift I could receive was my freedom to run amok in my neighborhood. So it was no surprise that I felt slightly embarrassed about the glut of shiny expensive toys that I once owned, and expected to receive for no good reason, when I had all the luxuries a kid should need.

From that point on, I vowed not to throw away anything of value. Only true garbage. I continued to recycle and compost. I put my tin cans and glass bottles aside to give directly to the neighborhood kids. But my young neighbors were relentless. The next time I emptied the trash, I heard *"Poubelle!"* again from every direction. I peered through the slats. More commotion. More excitement. I waited anxiously to see what they found. An hour later there was a knock. Shuffling. Laughter. I opened the front door. It was Patrico and his little buddy again, both wearing sunglasses. Except these weren't sunglasses. When I sent my film home to be developed, my mom would send me a set of prints as well as the negatives. The negatives I kept, but the end strips were blank and not worth keeping. Patrico and his friend each took one of these negative strips and tied a plastic *sachet* to a hole in each end, thereby making a strap for their cool new pair of shades. I had come to Africa to train men and women, but I was being schooled in recycling by preschool children.

We made significant headway during the fourth week of the project, and things were starting to take shape. The vault was mortared to finished grade. The pit was backfilled and compacted, with enough leftover soil for Remi and Richard to both save face with a modest sale. The multiple slabs for the floor were formed and left on the ground to cure. On the east campus, all the elephant grass within a three-meter radius of the old latrine was razed to bare ground. Where chunks of concrete had spalled away from the structure since the president's visit, the masons patched the holes the best they could. The project was going so well I decided to go to Abidjan to complete some paperwork and get my swollen knee checked out.

I asked Megan if she'd oversee the project while I was gone. Megan had her own projects with a woman's group and a local Boy Scout Troop, but nothing so industrious that she couldn't spend a few hours a day at the latrine site. Megan was also working with a young entrepreneur named Celestine who took an interest in the latrine project. Celestine believed that he could profit from building latrines for schools and churches in the region. Eureka! We struck Peace Corps gold. This is about as good as you could hope for, to inspire your local counterparts to improve conditions and help them earn a living in the process. By week's end, Celestine had a copy of my drawings, cost estimate, and receipts for his business plan. And gauging by his confidence, he'd be rolling in CFA in no time.

When I arrived in Abidjan that morning, I had a phone call. I wasn't expecting a call so I was a bit unnerved. We hardly ever used the phone. Volunteers participated in a "phone chain" where parents would call the hostel to talk with their child, then call the parents of the next volunteer on the list to inform them it was their turn to call in. It would continue like this until a parent couldn't be reached or we ran out of volunteers. The phone chain usually occurred at night when it was morning in the States. I picked up the phone, readying myself for anything. Fortunately it was just Megan calling from the mayor's office in Bangolo. The mason wanted to start on the latrine walls even though I'd asked him to wait until I got back. I was concerned he might misinterpret the dimensions on the plans and the doors wouldn't fit the frame. Maybe I was being overcautious, but I wasn't interested in leaving behind a useless monument to my good intentions.

My week in Abidjan was relatively uneventful. I had hoped to see the nurse but it never happened, so I returned to Bangolo Saturday night. It was late and the residents were off the street and in their homes. Each time I'd return from a trip to Abidjan, I was surprised that my house wasn't burglarized and that I still had electrical power. Both of these misfortunes seemed inevitable. On the flipside, I was hardly alarmed by all the vermin and large insects that made themselves at home while I was away, leaving their droppings on shelves and along walls. Beneath the door was a note from Megan, documenting her week at the jobsite. It went something like this:

September 9: The manoeuvres moved the concrete floor slabs into place. It took four strong workers to move each slab. The mason is eager to start on the walls. Called Scott in Abidjan. He instructed the mason to wait until he returned. The mason says he understands.

September 10: The mason mortared the floor slabs in place. The manoeuvres dug the hole for the puit perdu on the east campus. They also cut more grass. They complained incessantly about how difficult it was to cut the elephant grass by hand and kept asking for the mayor's tractor. I grabbed a machete and chopped one stalk to death. Those things are tough as shit!

September 11: Richard says the mayor wants to see me. By the time I got there, the office was in total chaos mode. Pablo's petit frère died this morning. There's talk that there's no money to pay the workers. Dago is freaking out; he tells the mayor that we don't need the manoeuvres any longer. The mayor tells Dago to chill. Then he tells me to choose one worker, since we are done with the digging and heavy lifting. I took Patrice. The two masons and Patrice worked on a puit perdu the rest of the day. In the afternoon the mason tells me he needs more cement. I went to the hardware store, but they're out of cement. Celestine offered some of his cement at cost to keep the project moving, so I bought some from him. Receipt is attached.

September 12: Nobody showed up until mid-morning. The mason asked again if he can start on the walls. They spent an hour working on the stairs in front of the latrine on the east campus before they quit for the day.

> *September 13: There are four concrete slabs remaining. The head mason wants to move them in place but only he and Patrice showed up today. I told the mason to take the rest of the day off. Patrice cut more grass and cleaned up around both sites.*

It was no surprise that the mayor took away the bulk of our workforce. Dago had been griping about uncut grass for weeks. I was glad Megan chose Patrice as our lone *manoeuvre*. He was the most consistent, and, frankly, the nicest guy of the bunch. I was anxious to view the progress on the latrine, so I put my headlamp on and coasted down to the site. When I shined a light on the structure, I could tell something was wrong. Turns out, before they'd lifted the floor slabs into place, the mason built the vault up an additional two-brick course so that it required a three-stair riser to enter the cabins. It was bad enough that the kids didn't know how to use a shitter; now we were going to make them climb to use ours. When I looked closer, I saw that the mason used the four remaining concrete slabs across the front length of the latrine as a step, which made it look more like a Greco-Roman temple than a schoolyard latrine. The mortar was still moist, so the mason must have worked that morning, probably ordering a dozen *petits* to move the slabs into place. It was going to be another interesting week.

When I showed up Monday morning, the masons and Patrice were already sitting side by side on the long giant step.

"*Bon arrivé*," they said sheepishly, as if anticipating another Jour de Palabres.

"*Bonjour, mes amis. Comment ça va?*"

I approached the masons with my set of drawings. I pointed to the detail that showed the four slabs were supposed to be covers for the *puits perdus* at the two hand-washing stations. Without a word, he and the others began chipping away at the mortar that held the misplaced slabs into place.

Patrice then asked, "Did you hear that the mayor cut our workforce?"

They all stopped what they were doing and looked at me.

"*C'est l'Afrique*, Patrice. News travels fast."

While the guys were hard at work, an older gentleman drove up along the south entrance road and got out of his car. I'd never met this man before, but I knew if he owned a car, he was somebody. He asked who was building the latrine.

"We are!" I said, partly to be brief, partly to be obvious.

"This latrine is *mal placé!*" he said gruffly.

"What would be a more suitable location?" I replied.

He turned and pointed beyond his parked car, into the tall elephant grass bordering the *bafon*.

"That's *en brousse*," I said. "The kids will never use it over there."

He repeated his statement that it was misplaced, then revealed that he was the District Inspector of Schools for the Western Region.

Oh shit! I launched into my diatribe about the fate of the old latrine, hygiene education, and so forth, but the inspector had long since tuned me out.

I told him it was a gift for the children. He about snapped and told me, "It is necessary to come to Africa with a good gift!"

The inspector was right. As gifts go, a shithouse is a pretty lousy gift for children. I hadn't mastered the nuance of the language to elaborate further, especially in the heat of a discussion.

Two of the four school superintendents and a few teachers showed up to greet the inspector. He repeated his claim that the latrine was misplaced.

The superintendents disagreed. "The children will not use the latrine if it's *en brousse*," they said as if they were seasoned Peace Corps volunteers.

Bold move. The inspector was essentially their supervisor. We stood there looking at each other in uncomfortable silence until the inspector drove away in a fit of disgust. I don't know the purpose of the inspector's visit, but I knew he didn't get it done. While I'll always have my doubts about the true value of the latrine, for a moment I felt vindicated by the good people of Bangolo.

We started on the walls around the middle of our sixth week. Dago showed up unannounced one morning. As far as we knew, it was his first visit to the site, at least during work hours. Everyone stopped working while he fumbled around the structure, inspecting things he had never seen before. He crouched down on a floor slab and peered into one of the holes.

"There's no *caca* inside!"

"Be my guest, Dago."

He laughed like a crazy person, shaking his head back and forth wildly, then went back to his office.

In the afternoon we received another unannounced visit, this time from two green mambas. I don't know what I had expected from my first encounter with these highly venomous snakes, but I certainly didn't expect them to be so fast or such a bright green color. How did these snakes camouflage themselves in a dark green forest? I guess when you can slither at a speed of almost ten kilometers per hour (about as fast as the average man on a treadmill), you don't need camouflage.

David, the *pousse-pousse* guy, was the first to spot them, yelling "*Serpent!*" for all to hear. The announcement sent the superintendents' families into a panic. The women and children scurried in every direction. David grabbed a half brick and hurled it at one of the snakes on the sand pile. Patrice jumped in to help David. They chased the snakes around while the masons and I hung back, holding shovels in a defensive position. By the time both of the snakes were killed, there were as many bricks on the sand pile as there were in the stack.

Visitors to the jobsite were not always unwelcome inspectors and serpents. Like the latrine project in Senegal, we had our share of mascots and good company. A toddler wearing a dirty terrycloth shirt, diapers, and Jellie sandals would wander over from the superintendents' quarters to play at the site. He was a tiny little guy, no taller than my lower leg, and he'd constantly hold out his arms so I'd pick him up. The guys called him my *petit apprenti*. As *protégés* go, I could do worse.

Then there was Pigi, a young boy who'd show up with his friends to play marbles on the smooth ground right after we'd mixed cement. Pigi laughed through his toothless grin, which was great for levity during one of our *Jour de Palabres*.

Near the end of the project, a young crippled boy, with a mangled machete in one hand and a worn-down wooden crutch under the other, came hobbling over from the road. His legs were twisted and bent from a child-birth deformity. He got to within a meter or two of where I stood, looked up at me sheepishly, and said, "Good Morning, Tonton." Then he turned and hobbled back to the road and on his way.

It's difficult to express the feeling of sadness, joy, sorrow, and privilege that were balled into one powerful emotion as a result of this brief encounter with the young crippled boy. I've only been overcome like this a handful of times in my life. Here's a kid who struggled to get around, who's had more than his fair share of pain and disappointment, not to mention the general day-to-day difficulties of living in Africa, and he goes out of his way to greet me with the utmost respect. There was no other motive. I was a wreck, and I had to take the rest of the day off to process. Like others, I sometimes struggle to find meaning in this world. On days such as this, however, it descends upon you like a ton of bricks.

The masons finished the structure in the middle of the seventh week, but their work wasn't done. Buildings in Côte d'Ivoire are usually dignified with a trowel-finish of mortar to hide the seams and smooth the appearance. This final coat is commonly referred to as *crépissage*. While the masons were applying this *crépissage*, two novice carpenters installed the framing and corrugated sheet metal that would make up the roof, and they installed four new wooden doors on both latrines. And with that, we bid the masons a fond farewell with congratulatory handshakes all around. It was the end of their contract. There were bricks to be made elsewhere.

During the eighth and ninth weeks, Patrice and I installed the plastic ventilation pipes, attached the mesh bug screen over the window openings, painted both structures a dull yellow with green trim to match the color of the school, and installed the bright red barrels with spigots that would be used to contain water for hand washing.

A man on a bicycle yelled out to no one in particular, "Now you are going to shit and drink well!" It was a humorous reminder that more kids would probably drink from the spigot than wash their hands, like a garden hose to an American kid. It was going to be important for us to follow up with a hygiene education program.

While I had enjoyed laboring the last couple weeks with Patrice, it did a number on my knee. When I walked I felt sharp pain and loose parts. The formal dedication of the latrines wasn't for a couple of weeks, so I decided to phone the Peace Corps medical staff and report my condition. The nurse advised that I come down to Abidjan immediately. Two days later, Dr. Lomo accompanied me to the hospital for an appointment with an orthopedic surgeon. The surgeon told me I had laxity of the ligaments, otherwise known as an instable knee. No kidding. He doped me up on NSAIDS and acetaminophen and told me to rest for a week.

The drugs and rest seemed to help so I went back to Bangolo. Patrice and I put the finishing touches on the latrines, and I squared off my debts with the local vendors. Aside from the three stairs leading up to the latrine doors, I was proud of our work and I think the guys were too. It took eleven weeks from ground-breaking to completion—a miracle if you ask me, and I don't believe in miracles. On October 21, during a small ceremony involving Richard, the *manoeuvres*, the four superintendents, and a few of the teachers, we officially opened the latrines for business. One of the superintendents was inside a stall, standing on a set of squatter blocks. I asked if he wanted to be first to christen the facility. He replied, "Wouldn't you rather have the District Inspector of Schools do it?"

At 1800 I was on a bus heading to Abidjan for more medical appointments, and to attend our Close of Service conference in Grand Bérebi. It would, unexpectedly, be the last time I set foot in Bangolo.

CHAPTER SEVENTEEN

DEPARTURE

The Close of Service conference is a mandatory, three-day Peace Corps event held three to six months before the end of service. The purpose of the COS conference is to help the volunteer finish up at their sites, to start filling out job or graduate school applications, and to prepare for the typical readjustments to life back in the States. The conference is often held in the capital city or a quasi-resort destination to accommodate large groups of people. Symbolically, the COS marks the beginning of the end—the first formal occasion to revel in our accomplishments, if only to survive the experience.

Our conference was held in Grand Bérebi, a small coastal town near the border with Liberia, about 300 kilometers west of Abidjan as the crow flies, but the poor condition of the roads meant a full day's journey from the capital. Rather than everyone traveling separately, the Peace Corps arranged for a convoy of chartered *gbakas* to take us from Abidjan. Not since Senegal had I been in a vehicle with only *toubabs*—a preview of things to come in the U.S. where everyone is a considered a *toubab* by African standards, regardless of one's skin color or heritage, because of privilege and opportunity.

The hotel had a large pavilion near the ocean, and many small circular thatched huts with two to four beds per hut. The accommodations weren't the best that Côte d'Ivoire had to offer, but they were definitely worthy of our *grand fête*. Unfortunately, I started feeling ill soon after check-in. At first it was chills, body aches, and fatigue, which kept me from hanging out with the group; then nausea set in, preventing me from eating from the deluxe buffet; and it culminated with a massive headache, forcing me to miss most of the COS sessions.

Health volunteers remarked that I probably had malaria. I suppose it was possible. In Bangolo, the mosquitoes were relentless.

At night, the little pests would nibble at your ankles until you were itchy and swollen. I slept under a mosquito net, but it was near impossible to keep my long limbs from touching the net, which was a bloody mess from all the bloated mosquitoes that didn't escape my fury. There was no avoiding them. And I wasn't always diligent about taking my anti-malaria prophylaxis because of the wacky, adverse side effects.

When our convoy returned to Abidjan, I visited Nurse Jan about my symptoms. She prescribed pyrimethamine and sulfadoxine, otherwise known as Fansidar. In training, we were encouraged to take the three Fansidar pills in our medical kits, post-haste, if we ever felt the onset of malaria. Trouble is: how does a person with malaria symptoms make a sound judgment about their health? Do we wait until we start having visions of green-faced witches and flying monkeys? Taking Fansidar has potentially serious side effects, so taking it on top of other medicines (also with serious side effects) was not a decision to take lightly. Immediately after taking the Fansidar I felt great, like a new man, but my tests still came back positive for malaria.

That week I had x-rays taken of my knee and met with an orthopedic specialist in Abidjan. They diagnosed me with a torn anterior cruciate ligament, or ACL, which is a common sports injury. The medical team opted to send me back Washington D.C. to have surgery. On the one hand, I was relieved to be getting the knee fixed, no longer living in limbo. On the other hand, I didn't want to leave Africa yet. Though my latrine project in Bangolo was all but done, I wanted to finish with the group, even if I'd be mostly idle for the last stretch. Tim and I had planned a vacation up to Agadez in Niger, maybe as far north as Arlit, to view the mud mosques and the trans-Saharan salt caravans, reacquaint ourselves with the Tauregs, and rough it again in 100°F heat. I also wanted to take a COS trip to Morocco and France, meet people and have adventures like Cain from *Kung-Fu*. It was not to be.

The Peace Corps booked me on a redeye flight back to D.C. on November 14. That evening, there was a contingent of volunteers at the hostel to see me off. Someone rented a movie called *Night on Earth*—a collection of five vignettes taking place in a single night about the interactions between taxi drivers and their passengers in five cities: Los Angeles, New York, Paris, Rome, and Helsinki. The third vignette in Paris begins with a taxi driver from West Africa picking up two French-speaking African diplomats in business attire.

The driver stops short at a red light, jarring the passengers. The passengers become upset and declare they are important men. They look at the driver carefully, asking facetiously, "We are not from the same jungle, are we, little brother?"

The driver remains silent, glaring at them through his rear view mirror.

One of the passengers attempts to guess where he's from: "Togo? Gabon? Not Cameroon. Dakar? Benin?"

The driver responds tersely, "Le Côte d'Ivoire!"

"He's Ivoirian! That explains it," says the other passenger, jokingly. "He's *Y Voit Rien* (Can see nothing). You've run four red lights. You can't see a thing. You drive at night without your glasses. The route is over there!"

The room of volunteers erupted in laughter. It was as if the scene was written specifically for us and our near-death taxicab experiences in Abidjan.

Margaret phoned the hostel so she and her two young boys could say goodbye. I had already said my goodbyes to most of the volunteers and the staff when I learned of my fate, but hearing her children's little voices got me choked up, made me realize that this was it; I was leaving Africa for good. I would not get the chance to say goodbye to my friends in Bangolo, or seek closure on all those loose ends that predominate life in Africa.

The Peace Corps driver picked me up and took me to the airport. Surprisingly, I didn't get accosted at the lobby, check-in was uneventful, and the flight was on time. Something had to be wrong. My conditioning said so. But my flight departed without a hitch. After a short layover in Paris, the plane took off and flew over the Atlantic Ocean, Newfoundland, Canada, and New England before passing over the well-lit cities of Boston and New York. In the time it usually took for me to get from Abidjan to Bangolo by bus (including time to haggle, wait, travel, and breakdown at least once), I was back in the States.

The Peace Corps put me up at a hotel near Arlington National Cemetery, where they amassed all their medical evacuees. My roommate was a retired National Park Service superintendent named John who had been serving in Slovakia to help with the management of their national park system. Although John was forty years my senior, we had a lot in common, most notably our interest in the national parks, and our meeting was a shade of things to come.

Before surgery, I received a phone call from the parents of my roommate from training, Austin, calling from Fredericksburg, Virginia, about an hour south of D.C. Austin must have alerted them to my situation. His parents were determined to abduct me after surgery and care for me during the Thanksgiving weekend, which not only speaks to them as people, but it also speaks to the fraternity I'd come to enjoy as a returned volunteer.

On November 22, I had made my way to a hospital in Georgetown for my surgery. I checked in at the front desk and waited. I got dressed in a blue gown, climbed on a gurney, and waited some more. I was carted over to a station where they inserted an intravenous tube. An older female nurse with shaky hands inserted a needle in the back of my hand, but she missed the vein. My hand blew up like a balloon, and I began to sweat and feel faint. Three nurses from a nearby station rushed over, inserted the IV correctly, and talked me through the ordeal without my losing consciousness.

I was then carted off to the operating room. Another nurse shaved the hair off my leg and positioned me on the gurney. A man in scrubs entered the room and introduced himself as the anesthesiologist. He had a strong German accent. I could barely understand his English. Was I gone that long? He disappeared to wash his hands, still talking in his indiscernible language. I was already anxious from the IV incident, now I get a doctor who cannot communicate with his patients. What was going on? Was I supposed to entrust this man with my health and welfare? Should I get up and run? Mastering the language should have been the first thing he learned before attempting to dispense care.

The doctor's face reappeared, hovering above mine. "Count to ten," was the only thing I understood.

"One... Two..."

CHAPTER EIGHTEEN

MISSION

Not a day went by in Africa without my thinking about the Peace Corps mission or the impact of my presence on the host country people. I'd venture to say that most volunteers go through something similar, whether it's to gauge our effectiveness, or to evaluate whether we're doing more harm than good, or to wonder whether the experience is worth our time. Over two years' time, we're bound to ruminate on our circumstances, especially if we're invested in the outcome. Such a hefty preoccupation deserves to be addressed in these pages, even if it glosses over or oversimplifies some rather complex issues.

Upon reading volunteer accounts since the program's inception, it's difficult to argue that the Peace Corps was *not* used as an arm of foreign policy by the various presidential administrations. Each president takes office with a bold agenda and newly appointed staff eager to make an impression. Why not use every tool at your disposal, especially an independent agency under the executive branch, staffed by a legion of educated Americans selectively placed throughout the world?

While I never received a phone call directly from President Clinton's people, our group did receive briefings from the Washington D.C. office via our country directors. Most of these briefings were tolerated; some were thought to be unnecessary. But I had it easy, especially as a volunteer under a Democratic president during a time of relative peace. Any directive imposed on me paled in comparison to directives imposed by Republican administrations, as those generally contradicted or veered from the Peace Corps ideals, or rather, the ideals within the volunteer ranks. This is not to say that program directors appointed by Republican presidents did not make positive and lasting contributions to the Peace Corps.

They did, some more than others, but promoting world peace and friendship is hardly the battle cry of our country's right-winged bureaucrats.

Serving in the Peace Corps while the U.S. is leading a war effort overseas is another matter altogether. It can be a chaotic time sure to test one's mettle, especially if the war zone is within or in close proximity to the volunteer's country of service. It also begs the question: How can the United States spend millions of dollars each year promoting peace and friendship in select countries while simultaneously dropping bombs on their neighbors? Stateside, the response to this question would likely run the gamut, steeped in the individual ideologies of its citizens. However, in poor countries, where the government is largely a spectator to world politics, this mixed bag of peace initiatives and military missions is a bit of a paradox, made more confusing by an ever-changing political landscape, where western countries supply arms to freedom fighters in one decade only to oppose these same fighters in later decades. When I was pressed for insight on this paradox, I had no explanation. All I could do was to operate under the banner of peace and hope to clarify the issue with my conduct, either as an ambassador or an apologist, whichever was needed most.

Statesmen from the U.S. are not the only ones who have used the Peace Corps for political advantage. Host country leaders from around the world have invited, rebuffed, or expelled volunteers based on political posturing. One might even think of the Peace Corps the way one thinks of oil or textiles or any other commodity exchanged in a global market. Volunteers are an American export; albeit with a fluctuating value, so the idea of the Peace Corps being apolitical amongst foreign decision makers is a bit of a ruse.

The same could be said of the volunteers. We are installed in a place that's foreign in almost every way. We attempt to become part of a community, even though we are outsiders in every way. We learn new languages and immerse ourselves in new cultures. The level of effort we give to our village may exceed that which we've ever given to our communities back home. Being so committed, we may become emotionally attached to people or to principles. In some instances, we might involve ourselves in local politics in a direct or indirect way to obtain resources or sway decisions. In circumstances of strife or conflict, it's almost impossible not to take sides as it impacts the people we now consider to be friends and family. While volunteers may understand the benefits of remaining apolitical, it's easier said than done in the real world.

Today, the Peace Corps mission has three goals derived from the agency's founding purpose. They include:

1) *Helping people of interested countries in meeting their need for trained men and women,*
2) *Helping promote a better understanding of Americans on the part of the peoples served,*
3) *Helping promote a better understanding of other peoples on the part of the Americans.*

I lived these goals, so I know their intent, but when I recite them to the average U.S. citizen I get a lot of questions or blank stares. Through their eyes these goals are cumbersome, like they've been tinkered with far too many times by a committee of bureaucrats. So with any luck, I'm going to attempt to clarify the Peace Corps mission by delving a little deeper into my own experience. While my narrative does not speak for all parties, I still hope to shed some light on the myriad challenges facing the Peace Corps volunteer.

On March 1, 1996, about halfway through my service, the Peace Corps celebrated its 35th anniversary. At the time, there were approximately 7,000 volunteers serving in 94 developing countries around the world, also referred to as the *Third World*—a term that arose during the Cold War to define countries not aligned with either NATO (First World) or the Communist Bloc (Second World). Whereas, for me, the Third World is characterized more by its abject poverty, mangy dogs, weak concrete, windswept trash, smoldering wood fires, undrinkable water, and so on. With approximately 196 countries covering the globe, volunteers have an extensive reach, especially if you consider that most countries do not want or need the kind of assistance that the Peace Corps has to offer.

The Peace Corps is not the only organization working in economically depressed countries. Foreign government aid agencies, as well as non-governmental organizations (or NGOs), are providing assistance in the areas of public health, education, the environment, and disaster relief. In places where there's despair and uncertainty, one may find missionaries laying the foundations for infrastructure and divine providence. And everywhere in the world, one is bound to cross paths with members of the academic, scientific, military, intelligence, or diplomatic community. What these groups do on a day-to-day basis might very well be considered *development work*, which could be defined simply as: a prosperous nation providing resources to a population of a less prosperous nation during a time of need or growth. One might even look upon the Peace Corps as a development institution. I certainly did.

To have any chance at succeeding in the development arena, one must consider a host of interrelated factors. Of critical importance is the political stability of the country. If there is a risk of a government coup, civil strife, or political unrest, then garbage collection, wastewater disposal, and proper nutrition are probably not high on anyone's list of priorities. Years of progress can be unraveled in an instant if a country cannot agree on the most fundamental aspects of its government, especially if it devolves into widespread crime and violence. This is an all-too-common occurrence in developing countries, and a major source of their development woes. Similarly, if drought or natural disasters are prevalent in an area, the same precarious conditions usually exist.

Of related importance is a country's economic stability. If a country has limited resources, or it struggles in the global marketplace, or its currency has been devalued, then the economic vitality of that country and its people is sure to be impacted. Even if these conditions do not exist, there's no guarantee that all countries will prosper. Consider the tenuous state of Third World economics in the following quote from the *United Nations, Department of Social and Economic Affairs, Measures for the Economic Development of Underdeveloped Countries*, 1951:

> *There is a sense in which rapid economic progress is impossible without painful adjustments. Ancient philosophies have to be scrapped; old social institutions have to disintegrate; bonds of caste, creed and race have to burst; and a large number of persons who cannot keep up with progress have to have their expectations of a comfortable life frustrated. Very few communities are willing to pay the full price of economic progress.*

In Côte d'Ivoire, I observed these economic struggles firsthand. The Ivoirian government devalued its currency in 1994 in an attempt to facilitate the sale of African exports (namely coffee and cacao), which was the talk of the town at every *gare*, kiosk, *maquis*, and market. When I broached the subject of garbage collection in Bangolo, it was no surprise that people were less than enthused. It's not like they didn't know that garbage is dirty and unsightly, they just had different priorities. For this condition to change, garbage would need to physically get in the way of more pressing matters or detract from more lucrative pursuits. In other words, a new necessity would need to become their mother of invention (or motivation). As it was, the garage strewn about town did not hinder Bangolo's ability to fetch water, hunt, cook, labor, build shelters, make babies, play *futbol*, hold ceremonies, or otherwise make a life.

Another critical factor is the state of tribal relations in a country or region. On occasion, I'd claim to be Guéré in jest, solely for a reaction. Usually people laughed. Once a man replied that it wasn't possible because the Guéré are short and ugly. Our exchange was more akin to a couple of sports fanatics cutting up the opposing team. But not all tribal differences are as innocuous. The people of Côte d'Ivoire have strong allegiances to their tribal affiliation, which also speaks to their political leanings, the most obvious being the division between the tribes in the Muslim north and the tribes in the Christian south. While some tribes share customs and languages, others couldn't be further apart, much in the way the United States colors itself red and blue during an election year. Now condense Côte d'Ivoire's sixty tribal groups into an area the size of New Mexico, and you have high probability for discord and violence.

One cannot discuss the challenges of working in Africa without mentioning corruption. The act of redistributing, transferring, laundering, or pilfering money from citizens by those in power is all too common in Côte d'Ivoire and throughout West Africa. By all accounts, the money collected by officials is not going toward public services. Instead, there's an understanding amongst the citizenry that certain things such as operating a business or safe passage can be arbitrarily taxed by the *chefs* and *gendarmes* for their personal benefit. This is difficult for a *toubab* like me to accept, though over time you learn to comply to avoid greater repercussions. Either that or revolt, but as they say in Côte d'Ivoire: *Ce n'est pas la peine* (It is not worth the trouble*)*. Of course, corruption is not confined to just Africa, but it seems endemic to the culture, more transparent, which makes funding projects and offers of foreign aid more vulnerable.

In Bangolo and surrounding Guéré villages, there was yet another challenge that seemed insurmountable: the contradiction between commonly accepted health and hygiene practices and the tenets of the animist religion. Most people around the globe understand concepts such as microbes, germs, parasites, infections, injury and disease, but the Guéré look upon these ailments with skepticism, choosing instead to fault the deliberate work of sorcerers. Whenever I hear well-meaning politicians speak of combating AIDS in sub-Saharan Africa, I think of my brethren in Bangolo. Funding for AIDS education and condom distribution is a good start, but when a people believe with every fiber of their being that their neighbors can inflict sickness and death using spells and potions, it's going to take more than funding; it may require the transformation (or death) of a culture—a feat not easily achieved.

Not all challenges to development work are precipitated by the host country people. Outsiders can make a desperate situation worse. The sheer number of outsiders alone makes you wonder whether we're helping to create a culture of reliance. This is especially true in a country like Côte d'Ivoire, existing under colonial rule as recently as 1961, still learning to govern without guidance from its former colonial power. What we outsiders see as assistance in the form of Yankee ingenuity might very well be interference in the form of Yankee imperialism. While there's no way to know for sure, it bears mention as an issue not actively managed.

Then there's the ever-important issue of sustainability. Recall the new market and slaughterhouse in Russ' town of Biankouma. USAID did an admirable job constructing these new facilities, even though they weren't being utilized. Unfortunately, foreign governments are not always able to get to know a culture as intimately as a Peace Corps volunteer. Governments tend to arrive on short notice, shake hands, talk to officials, make assumptions, and spend money before moving on. This approach often neglects key details, which can undermine progress. Sustainability is about lasting solutions, not milestones and monuments.

So why don't volunteers step in and help out their government with projects? As stated in Section 2504(a) of the Peace Corps Act,

"Volunteers shall not be deemed officers or employees or otherwise in the service or employment of, or holding office under, the United States." This policy applies to interactions with USAID and the like. This policy does not apply to interactions with NGOs, as these groups are recognized by the United Nations as being independent, not-for-profit, and pursuant to wider social aims. Examples of NGOs include Oxfam, Save the Children, Doctors Without Borders, and UNESCO, to name a few. The Peace Corps Act Section 2513(a) allows volunteers to partner with NGOs, though this was not prevalent in Côte d'Ivoire in the mid-90s.

As bureaucratic as this may sound, I can appreciate the wisdom behind a policy to separate the volunteer from their government as much as possible. If there's any suspicion that we're involved in something other than grassroots development projects, it can lead to distrust, security, and safety concerns. More than once I was accused of being an operative for the Central Intelligence Agency because of my nationality, skin color, education level, and the disbelief that I moved to Africa to monitor trash collection. It was never a legal accusation or an indictment, but you got the sense that they fully believed the conspiracy. You hear the same CIA refrain from other volunteers, no matter what time period or host country they served. As much as I wanted to be "boots on the ground" to ensure government projects were sustainable, it was impossible to separate humanitarian motives from political ones in the eyes of the host country people, so it was best to steer clear of foreign governments altogether and learn to live with an ill-fated monument or two.

Another liability to development work is the method by which governments measure progress. Some have a tendency to report certain quantitative results, such as the number of facilities constructed or the total dollars spent, while failing to measure the appropriateness of the facility, or the impact to the community, or the satisfaction of the user, not to mention other vital measures such as sickness averted, health improved, lives saved, and so on. That's because quantitative results can be relayed to lawmakers to justify government expenditures, who relay them to constituents to justify votes. A host country will use the same quantitative results as a measure of their own contributions. This type of self-preservation is a form of sustainability, but it's not sustainable development work. While it may be more difficult to measure the subjective qualities of "appropriateness" and "impact" and "satisfaction," they are truer metrics of progress, even if they have to be estimated by the development worker in the field. Fortunately, strides are being made in this area, but it's a cautionary tale worth mentioning.

From the foreign government's perspective, sustainability might not be the most crucial outcome for large expensive development projects. At this level, there are often bigger socio-economic and political factors at play. By investing in structures such as markets, schools, hospitals, and roads, the host country population is witness to a tangible offering that can reflect positively on the donor, whether these structures are ever used or not. What results is a partnership between a foreign government and a developing country, further nurtured with trade, aid, and political support for when they need each other most, such as in wartime or in the wake of natural disasters. But this approach can backfire if the locals come to resent the offering because it failed to consider their needs.

Another nuance that development institutions must contend with is donations from third party donors to a country in need. As a participant in a USAID disaster assistance training after my Peace Corps service, our instructor relayed a story of how good intentions can go awry. During an earlier time in the agency's history, teams were deployed to a country in East Africa at a time of drought and famine. Donations came pouring in from all over the western world, arriving in large metal shipping containers. When the team opened one of the containers, it was chock-full of women's cocktail dresses, high-heeled shoes, purses, and feather boas, some with the original purchase tags attached. Somewhere along the line, the donations weren't properly screened, or someone felt the drought victims lacked a sense of fashion.

In this instance, the donation did more to serve the donor's psychological need *to give* than it did to alleviate a condition or solve a problem. Not only that, but the clothing and accessories took up valuable space in a shipping container that could've otherwise been filled with non-perishable food, clean water, and medicine. In the medical field, you might hear the comparison between "an error of omission" (not giving a patient a drug they may need) versus an "an error of commission" (giving a patient a drug that could kill them). Since every medical patient is different, it's not always clear which error is less egregious, but with development work, an error of omission is far more forgiving. The way I see it, the most valuable donation I could give is my best discretion or nothing at all.

Not to be outdone, there are factors specific to the Peace Corps that present certain challenges. In the fiscal year 1996, the annual operating budget for the Peace Corps was $234 million. On the whole, the Peace Corps budget is a tawdry 1% of the entire U.S. foreign operations budget. That's not a lot considering the program's aforementioned presence around the world. While volunteers may not demand the same level of security and technology as our State Department outposts around the world, the Peace Corps is arguably the most financially deprived program in proportion to its broad and lofty mission. I'm not talking about the salary we received; a prevailing wage of $6 U.S. per day was plenty for me to survive, and I was given benefits such as a place to live, health care, a plane ticket home, and a readjustment allowance. I'm talking about funding for tools and materials, education and training, and development opportunities that arise in the course of working in the Third World. Instead we beg, grovel, and appeal for these things, or we do without. This kind of thrift has become the trademark of the volunteer, but a small contingency of funds would go a long way if we encountered an opportunity to make a difference.

The Peace Corps is also only as good as the quality of people it sends to represent the United States. If applicants are not vetted correctly, the agency runs the risk of jeopardizing the mission as well as the country's reputation. I become skeptical when Returned Peace Corps Volunteer groups appeal to their representatives in Congress to increase the number of volunteers by waves and degrees. When this occurs, I think back to the volunteers that I've met, some teetering on the fringe of sanity, and I wonder how the Peace Corps can assure quality if it begins accepting candidates that it would've otherwise rejected. While I share the same pride in the organization as anyone who has served, there are trappings to the proliferation of volunteers if less scrutiny is applied to the selection process. As Edward Abbey said, "Growth for the sake of growth is the ideology of the cancer cell." It's important to find that *sweet spot* of volunteers for each country so we're always sending our best emissaries.

As we endeavor to achieve the Peace Corps' first goal of *helping people of interested countries in meeting their need for trained men and women,* we encounter even more challenges. For instance, what happens if the host country government requests volunteers, but the recipient community is indifferent? What if the host country people do not want training; they want money and gifts instead? What if the host country people aren't receptive to learning new ways, or they don't agree with the volunteer, or they actually know more than the volunteer in their assigned trade? These situations can be frustrating to say the least, and they can make the volunteer feel as if the assignment is futile. How volunteers handle themselves in the face of such adversity is often the toughest part of the toughest job.

One could write volumes on the challenges of development work and never cover everything. It's an enormous topic, made more complex by the subjective and fallible nature of the human race. But do not despair. There are ways to improve the human condition in a meaningful way despite the adversity. While it takes idealism to join a cause such as the Peace Corps, it takes patience and pragmatism (and a bit of masochism) to advance the cause.

As a Peace Corps volunteer, the most practical approach to the affairs of the Third World is to take the first goal at face value: "to help train men and women." This training can be delivered through classes, contests, and seminars; as part of small projects such as mud stoves and composting and erosion control; and as bigger initiatives that create environmental, social, or financial incentives. To take the first goal at face value also means engaging individuals without an expectation of saving the world, or reforming a country, or changing a culture, or even worrying about results. Success depends on the volunteer passing along knowledge through instruction or osmosis, and trusting that this information will be absorbed and diffused.

I understand that training men and women may not be fulfilling enough for volunteers who expect to improve conditions and solve problems. It wasn't enough for me. It feels too little, like a drop in a bucket that doesn't hold water. But development work is a lot like farming. While it's within a farmer's power to till the soil and plant the seeds, factors such as the growing process, the weather, insect infestations, crop yield, and market conditions are mostly out of his control. A little irrigation and fertilizer should help the crop along, but too much attention may be counterproductive, too far-reaching. Had I gone into my Peace Corps assignment with this analogy in mind, I may have planted more seeds and cultivated more crops.

If the volunteer cannot advance the first goal, for whatever reason, there are two other goals worthy of some attention. The second goal is geared towards *helping promote a better understanding of Americans on the part of the peoples served.* Or written another way: it's what the host country people learn about Americans directly from the volunteer, as opposed to what they might hear on television, or through state-sponsored media, or from public opinion. This could be anything from our local and national customs, to our habits and folklore, to our values and beliefs, to our popular culture. There is no substitute for getting to know a people firsthand. This is not to say that the host country people must like or respect Americans, but a Peace Corps presence around the world definitely promotes a better understanding of Americans, and a better understanding is key to improving relations. In some respects, the Peace Corps might be to the U.S. Armed Forces as a balanced diet and exercise are to medical care — we offer preventative steps to help ward off a more expensive and dire condition.

So how does one measure the second goal? How much understanding is passed from the volunteer to the host country people? I often think about Yague, Soleil, Sylvean, Jerome, Mathias, Alpha, Maseem, Ernest, Madam Baman, Clement, Konan, Jean-Charles, Dogbo, Diallo, Lucien, Fardi, Aboubakar, Patrice, Celestine, and a host of others I connected with on some level. What are their impressions of Americans? Did they learn anything from me? Did they understand my French? Did they think I was a harmless idiot who brought certain advantages to the village, as Nigel Barley said of the visitor to an alien race of people in his book, *The Innocent Anthropologist.* Or did they think I was just a plain old idiot?

Ultimately, there is no way to measure how my actions will influence or equip others in the span of a lifetime. It could take years before an opportunity presented itself for my African friends to follow my lead. My influence could be buried deep within their subconscious, manifesting as new behaviors. If my friends are still alive after Côte d'Ivoire's political coup in late 1999, followed by twelve years of violence and turmoil, chances are they would tell a modified version of the stories I have told, cast through their own individual realities and perspectives. As such, I can only hope that they're fond of the time we shared.

This brings us to the third goal of *helping promote a better understanding of other peoples on the part of the Americans*. This not only includes what the volunteer gets from the experience, but also what the volunteer imparts to other Americans about foreign cultures. Whether the volunteer enjoyed their membership in the Peace Corps or not, there's no denying that a better understanding of other people is reached when you live amongst them for an extended period of time. The third goal receives the most emphasis amongst volunteers and RPCVs (Returned/Recovering Peace Corps Volunteers). One reason for that is because it's happening to us personally, and we can track the impacts over time. As part of the third goal, we are obliged to share our experiences, speak to school children, volunteer in our communities, recruit new volunteers, serve in the Crisis Corps, or do a second tour. Maybe even write a book.

So what might one learn by serving in the Peace Corps? One might learn about different foods, customs, languages, and religions; one might learn about patience, resolve, and fortitude by living in the most impoverished places on earth; one might learn that you can't judge a man until you've walked a mile in his shoes. Likewise, one might learn that not everyone owns a pair of shoes, not everyone needs a pair of shoes to walk a mile, and wearing a poor man's shoes to experience what it's like may be enlightening for the individual, but it may be offensive to those who don't have a choice. One might learn that people are fundamentally the same just about anywhere you go. And one might learn more about oneself, about one's strengths and limitations, and that volunteering to promote peace and friendship isn't a bad way to serve one's country.

The three goals of the Peace Corps basically amount to spreading good will. Not every American citizen or congressional delegate supports the Peace Corps and its mission, especially those who tend to confuse nationalism for patriotism. But we all reap the benefits coming from the frontlines. Even criticisms that I may have about Peace Corps policy are tempered by the tremendous opportunity and endless possibilities of Peace Corps service. At the end of the day, support for the Peace Corps boils down to what you want your country to stand for. And as long as tens of thousands of Americans are willing to volunteer two or more years of their lives to a cause that transcends personal gain, there's still hope that a dove can emerge from a star.

ACKNOWLEDGMENTS

I'd like to thank my friends and family for their love and support despite living thousands of miles away from home for most of my adult life. I'd like to thank my Peace Corps friends and colleagues who contributed greatly to the experience, especially those mentioned in these pages. I'd like to thank the people of West Africa for tolerating this *toubab* and opening their hearts and homes. I'd like to thank those who helped me develop and edit *The Toughest Job*, especially Joe Meiman who served as a sounding board, editor, friend, and advocate from the book's inception, and Betsy Anderson who carefully reviewed my first edition and found a number of errors or opportunities for improvement. And I'd like to thank those who have purchased, read, reviewed, or recommended *The Toughest Job*.

Cheers!

Made in the USA
San Bernardino, CA
29 November 2017